MARKED WOMEN

MARKED WOMEN
*The Cultural Politics of
Cervical Cancer in Venezuela*

Rebecca G. Martínez

Stanford University Press
Stanford, California

Stanford University Press
Stanford, California

©2018 by the Board of Trustees of the Leland Stanford Junior University. All rights reserved.

No part of this book may be reproduced or transmitted in any form or by any means, electronic or mechanical, including photocopying and recording, or in any information storage or retrieval system without the prior written permission of Stanford University Press.

Printed in the United States of America on acid-free, archival-quality paper

Library of Congress Cataloging-in-Publication Data

Names: Martínez, Rebecca G. (Rebecca Gilda), 1967– author.
Title: Marked women : the cultural politics of cervical cancer in Venezuela / Rebecca G. Martínez.
Description: Stanford, California : Stanford University Press, 2018. | Includes bibliographical references and index.
Identifiers: LCCN 2017044372 | ISBN 9781503605114 (cloth : alk. paper) | ISBN 9781503606432 (pbk. : alk. paper) | ISBN 9781503606449 (epub)
Subjects: LCSH: Cervix uteri—Cancer—Social aspects—Venezuela. | Cervix uteri—Cancer—Political aspects—Venezuela. | Women's health services—Venezuela. | Poor women—Medical care—Venezuela. | Cancer—Patients—Venezuela—Social conditions. | Medical anthropology—Venezuela.
Classification: LCC RC280.U8 M249 2018 | DDC 362.196/9946600987—dc23
LC record available at https://lccn.loc.gov/2017044372

Typeset by Newgen in 10/14 Minion

To my parents Antonio and María Martínez.
Dad's matter-of-fact declaration of "I ain't no scab,"
as he joined the picket line, greatly influenced my worldview.
I miss him every day. Mom's strength as an immigrant
woman making a life in a new land inspires me every day.

Contents

	Acknowledgments	ix
	Introduction: Caracas, Venezuela: On Arrival	1
1	Hospitals, Patients, and Doctors	23
2	The Ambiguities of Risk: Morality, Hygiene, and the "Other"	56
3	Targeting Women: Bodies out of "Control," Public Health, and the Body Politic	86
4	The Hospital Encounter: Bodies Marked, Mended, and Manipulated	132
5	Women's Agency and Resilience: "The Way I Want to Be Treated"	185
	Epilogue: From Neoliberalism to Chávez	212
	Appendix	237
	Notes	241
	Bibliography	245
	Index	267

Acknowledgments

I HAVE MUCH GRATITUDE for the many people in my life who in some way supported me during the researching and writing of this book. Most of all I am indebted to the women who told me their stories and allowed me to share in such personal and vulnerable moments as their treatment process for cervical cancer. As I wrote this book, their experiences and stories kept me going page by page. The doctors and public health administrators I interviewed also gave me their time and energy, and I am appreciative of their patience with me, the anthropologist who was always asking them questions.

The Fulbright Program and Ford Foundation provided the funding for the initial fieldwork and writing of this book. My mentors at the University of California, Irvine, were invaluable to the process. I was fortunate to have had the wisdom and pedagogy of Art Rubel, Liisa Malkki, and Leo R. Chavez guiding my work. And, although I was never a student of his, without the generous help of Venezuela and Venezuelan scholar Fernando Coronil, setting up my fieldwork would have been much more difficult, if not nearly impossible. The anthropology world has lost brilliant scholars and humanitarians with the passing of Art and Fernando.

I owe my largest debt of gratitude to Leo R. Chavez, my mentor who continues to provide me with professional and personal advice. From the moment I took his undergraduate course on Mexican migration, I knew I wanted to do this thing called anthropology. He mentored me from that moment, involving me in his research projects and preparing me for academic life. As a first-generation college student, whose parents never attended high school, I didn't know what graduate school was, much less the preparation that it took to enter a PhD program. I can quite literally say that without the considerable guidance and support of Leo I would have never earned a PhD. Even before entering the graduate program in social relations with him as my adviser, he allowed me to use his office and computer to do my schoolwork. I would sometimes work until midnight, and he'd see the light on in his office on occasion and call me to tell me to be careful getting to my car and driving home. That was the type of mentorship that a first-generation Chicana college student like myself needed, and he provided it. Not only did he offer the intellectual guidance of mentorship; he went beyond that and treated me like a part of his family. For that I am especially grateful.

My friends and colleagues at the University of Missouri (MU) provided tremendous encouragement when I was feeling stuck or unsure. Just to give you an idea of the support network that has surrounded me during the book writing process, the Women's and Gender Studies Department at MU is the type of department where we will all be on a group text and send one another hearts and smiley faces. How many academics can say they have colleagues like this? I am also thankful for another MU friend and colleague, Donna Strickland, who worked with me as a writing coach and introduced me to mindfulness in writing. At times I would also mention my book writing to my students who were also struggling with writing their papers. It was a point of connection to let them know that their professors share in similar experiences. I have notes from some of my students providing me with encouragement for this book. I can't express how important these MU students have been in the process of my writing.

And now for the family part of the acknowledgments . . . this is the most difficult because, though cliché, words truly cannot express the gratitude for the everyday weight that a family takes on in living with a mother and wife who is writing an academic book. My partner and best friend, Jeff Rouder, has shared in my struggles and triumphs during the process and has always been there for me to lean on. Our children, Ben, Tomás, and Emily also provided hugs and enthusiasm when needed but also smartly knew when to stay away. My mom and brothers and sisters, Elva, Tony, Eddie, and Mary, were also always a phone call away when I needed support.

I am also grateful to the wonderful people at Stanford University Press for supporting this work, and most especially to my editor, Michelle Lipinski.

Her insights, patience (over years), kindness, and unwavering support have made this process much easier and a lot less anxiety ridden than it could have been. Editorial assistant Nora Spiegel has also worked diligently to help put together the finalized version of the book. The anonymous reviewers provided by the Press provided insights and recommendations that improved the manuscript. I am grateful to them for their thoroughness, and any shortcomings are solely mine.

MARKED WOMEN

Introduction
Caracas, Venezuela: On Arrival

FLYING OVER THE CITY of Caracas for the first time in the mid-1990s, I looked down to see the bright lights twinkling on the hillsides surrounding the city, lighting up the earth below. I remember feeling a mixture of excitement and nervousness as the plane descended. I had read about the *ranchos*, the poor neighborhoods of makeshift houses forged into the hillsides and clinging precariously to the land. They have been variously called dangerous and violent, dirty, ugly, unhygienic, and illegal and noxious, among other terms. Those descriptions were very different from what I was seeing from this altitude. Contrary to those negative images, while flying over these hills all I could think of was how majestic the lights looked encircling the valley of Caracas. I eventually came to know just how problematic those hillsides would be for many of the health professionals I met with over the years. The *ranchos*, as a metaphor for middle-class angst in the face of perceived symbolic and geographic encroachment by the poor, the "violent," the "illegals," and generally the "uncivilized," would become apparent as I settled into this bustling city. The houses perched on hillsides looking as though they might slide down at any moment, crowding one atop the other and begging for a space to exist—those were the houses where many of the women I would later meet lived.

By 1975 the urban population in Venezuela was estimated to be around 82 percent, and this trend from rural to urban continued to accelerate. Although all cities experienced this ballooning growth, by 1989 Caracas was by far the largest city, with 3.5 million residents, and Maracaibo, the second largest, had a population of 1.35 million (Haggerty and Blutstein 1993). Along with this urban growth, the *ranchos*, which at the time housed between six hundred thousand and seven hundred thousand people, quickly grew into barrios (poor neighborhoods), in the process becoming a point of contention for many middle- and upper-class Caraqueños. One Venezuelan health official whom I interviewed remarked that the barrios represent the "ruralization of the urban by the poor"—a place where immigrants, some of them undocumented, live in what are deemed to be "unhealthy" conditions. According to him, this "ruralization of the urban" occurs when people keep living in their "rural cultural ways" in the city. They are what he calls *conformistas*, or conformists, people who conform to what they have, not wanting to better themselves or their position in life. He further described the city as being two in one: "one which people know about" (the urban city) and "one which is unknown" (rural-urban barrios). Given this description, "urban" Caraqueños generally view the barrios as mysterious, backward, underdeveloped, and unruly places in which the threat of violence is great (Moreno 2016). More important, the perceived violence of the barrios is viewed as a threat to the urban (middle and elite classes) Caraqueños (Coronil and Skursky 1991). By contrast, the city center of urban Caracas represents modernity, development, progress, and a sense of order. Moreover, this same health official lamented the fact that, "unlike in other cities, which have their poor areas on the outskirts of the city, where they are not visible, ours are visible, we are surrounded." These views, which embody class, nationalism, and modernity, set up many of the themes that I encountered while conducting health-related field research in Caracas. Along with gender, social class is paramount for understanding Venezuelan configurations of cervical cancer and, in a broader sense, health and illness.

When I first arrived in 1994 to begin an ethnographic study of cervical cancer patients in two oncology hospitals, I found myself in the middle of a political climate of neoliberal austerity and uncertainty. President Carlos Andrés Pérez was under house arrest at the time, accused of corruption. Economic and political instability, along with neoliberal policies integrated into the health-care system, had largely wrought a structure that met the needs of neither the most vulnerable nor increasingly the middle class. It was clear that Venezuela's public health sector in general was at a crucial period, amid social, political, and economic turbulence; this wealthy oil-producing nation with a stable democracy on the global stage through the 1960s and 1970s produced violent episodes and political instability during the 1980s and 1990s. The timely political instability led me to one of the central questions that drew me to Venezuela: How was public health affected by austerity, and could a connection be drawn with Venezuela having some of the highest rates of cervical cancer in Latin America? As I had already developed an interest in cervical cancer through my previous work—particularly in relation to the social construction of disease and gender—Venezuela offered another dimension to study, namely neoliberalism and cancer. When I began my research and focused on the interactions of patients, doctors, and nurses during treatment—one of the components of my study—it became clear that the political landscape was critical to what I was observing in the hospitals and the public health literature I was analyzing. I began to notice a pattern: the narratives circulating about cervical cancer risk in the public health literature—as well as among administrators and physicians—fit quite well with neoliberal policies that, in a broad sense, emphasize individualism, less government involvement, and privatization of health care. Neoliberal policies that started taking root in the 1980s were shaping health care across Latin America. Since then much has been written about how these structural adjustment policies backed by the World Bank and the International Monetary Fund failed to deliver the health care benefits promised (Homedes and Ugalde 2005a, 2005b; De Vos 2006; Hartmann 2016).

The more I witnessed, the sharper my focus became on what was taking place politically and how it manifested not only in state approaches to health care, but even in the relationship among patients, doctors, and other hospital workers. What emerged is a multilayered ethnography about women's experiences with cervical cancer in Venezuela, the doctors and nurses who treat them, and the public health officials and administrators who set up intervention programs to combat the disease. At the same time, I have contextualized the experiences and interactions of patients, doctors, and health administrators historically, tracing the relationships among nationalism, modernity, and neoliberalism to show how the cultural politics of cervical cancer risk in Venezuela developed through the othering of behaviors marked by the intersections of class, race, and gender. As Virginia Dominguez asks in her work on cultural politics, it is important to understand the strategic social and political uses of culture: "When is it that one sector of society invokes a cultural argument to explain a social, political, or economic reality?" (1992, 21–22). In terms of cervical cancer in Venezuela, one of the ways in which risk was conceptualized, particularly during the time I was there in the 1990s, was in regard to culture and cultural difference; specifically, physicians and health care administrators pointed to a lack of culture and a lack of hygiene among female patients. Importantly, these risks were also encoded in the public health literature distributed to educate women about the disease. Medical health personnel framed the material largely as a concern about poor women being at risk for cervical cancer because they lacked the ability to properly receive, digest, and act upon medical prescriptions for healthy citizenship. In making sense of the connections among nation, race, gender, class, and health in Venezuela, I am concerned with the political uses of culture in health discourse (Wailoo 2006, 2012) and the implications of this discourse for medical interactions and patient healing.

At one level, this work is a vehicle presenting the narrative testimonies women provide of their varied experiences—their personal suffering, pain, distress, confusion, meaning making, resilience, and strength in the face of cervical cancer. It is about their multiple concerns coping with cancer (e.g., family, work, finances, sexuality, mental and physical well-being) and the microlevel interactions between patients and their doctors. The women's personal stories reflect their grappling with the uncertainty of their health amid the everyday anxieties, for many, of conditions of poverty. One cannot, however, begin to understand women's experiences in the hospital setting as they sought explanations and underwent treatment without attention to the broader social contexts of race, class, and gender relations. I analyze what it means for the women to confront a disease they generally know little about and that, simultaneously, stigmatizes them as social marginals, burdens on society, and ultimately as threats to the health of the modern nation. In doing so, we understand the problem of cervical cancer in Venezuela and the experiences of women who are afflicted within this broader framework.

At another, macro level, this project is also about the social and cultural configurations of a disease that emerge within a nexus of class, race, and gender relations. In particular, I examine the medical discourses surrounding cervical cancer that characterize women who are diagnosed with it (or who are "at risk" for it) as backward, uncultured, unhygienic, and promiscuous. The cultural politics of cervical cancer in Venezuela during the 1990s, therefore, is largely about how women are constructed as social dichotomies that either contribute to the nation or detract from it: clean or dirty, sexually appropriate or promiscuous, cultured or uncultured, civilized or uncivilized, to name just a few. By conducting interviews with public health administrators and health-care providers and analyzing the content of newspapers and public health documents and education materials, I argue that ordinary and mundane social and medical welfare projects are significant sites for understanding some public health intervention programs as instruments through which modernization practices are scientifically legitimized and where nationalist cultural politics intersect. Just as important, the microlevel patient-doctor interactions I observed were mediated by the scientific discourses surrounding cervical cancer. Indeed, these interactions cannot be fully understood without this multilayered approach.

When I returned to Venezuela in 2008, the political climate had changed dramatically following the election of Hugo Chávez nearly a decade earlier. As I write these words, remembering those early days compiled from field notes and persistent memories, I am struck at how so much changed since the narrative of "problematic" barrios during the neoliberal 1980s and 1990s became the epicenter of a Chávez Bolivarian revolution and rallying cry for social justice for the poor and disenfranchised. My return marked a contrast to an ethnographic project grounded in a neoliberal time and place. That same geographic space of sparkling lights that first caught my attention is at the center of this work in many ways. The lights below, as I once again flew over the city, seemed to take on new meaning, representing the margins coming to the center and challenging social, political, and economic invisibility with their bright glow. David Smilde and Daniel Hellinger (2011, 9) note:

> The largest segment of the Chávez coalition has come from within the masses of impoverished Venezuelans existing on the margins of formal citizenship (Roberts, 2003). These supporters are not strongly ideological. Rather, their support is based upon a perception, and in most cases a lived experience, that for the first time they have a government that prioritizes their plight and fights for their interests.

Returning to Venezuela, I wanted to account for a political climate that had changed substantially and to see whether this had also resulted in a shift in the cultural politics of health and disease. It was a unique opportunity to examine the state of cervical cancer representations, discourse, and care in light of the change in the social and political circumstances since I had completed my original fieldwork. Much to my delight, I was able to talk with some of the same physicians and administrators whom I had interviewed over a decade earlier, and I also met new health-care providers and administrators who were working in the two oncology hospitals that I had known so well, as they were once a part of my daily routine.

A Brief Reflection on History, Class, and Venezuelan Society

In Venezuela, class difference—and the regulation of the lower classes in particular—has historically been tightly linked to the national goals of modernity, progress, and development (Coronil 1997). Many affluent Venezuelans saw the need to regulate the poor, whom they perceive as a threat to social and economic progress. This sentiment targeting the poor had been particularly pronounced since the 1980s, because of the social, political, and economic problems that brought about instability in the county (Levine and Crisp 1995). During the Caracazo, for example, in February 1989, when hyperinflation and economic insecurity brought protest and looting throughout Caracas, "the middle-classes thought the poor were about to come hurtling down upon them from the surrounding hills to loot and pillage their homes" (Mac Gregor and Rubio Correa 1993, 105). The poor as threat is a persistent theme in Venezuelan society and one that will come up repeatedly throughout this work as I explore the configurations of a disease among women.

To contextualize, it is necessary to briefly trace how Venezuela, a wealthy oil-producing nation, struggled to locate itself within the realm of modernity while at the same time experiencing economic and political instability, which in the past decade and a half has pushed the nation more toward third-world "underdevelopment" than first-world "development." After 1958, with the end of Marcos Pérez Jiménez's presidency, Venezuela enjoyed a relatively stable political system with democratically elected presidents. For a brief time the petroleum boom of the 1970s also helped fuel economic prosperity for some. In 1977, the per capita income of Venezuelans was boosted to an all-time high, and the ranks of the middle class swelled. As Mahmood and Mutaner (2013, 63) note:

> This was the result of a political pact between the major political parties in 1958, known as the Punto fijo. While the country was experiencing this stability in the political realm, the system was exclusionary for the majority of the population. The sidelining of this majority sentiment started becoming obvious in the

1970s and 1980s. Venezuela is predominantly an oil-based economy. A small, elite group had tightened its grip on this major source of economic power with close ties to political power. Exclusionary policies started creating profound social inequities which, along with other macro-economic crises, brought the level of people living in extreme poverty to 54% by the end of the 1980s.

Moreover, in the mid-1980s, during the presidential terms of Jaime Lusinchi (1984–1989) and Carlos Andrés Pérez (1989–1994), serious economic crisis and political scandals implicated the presidents and several of their ministers, setting the stage for civil unrest and violent protests (Ellner 1994). Pérez, though speaking a populist discourse and promising a return to the economic stability of the 1970s, instead implemented a plan known as El Paquete, which rested on recommendations from the World Bank and the International Monetary Fund (IMF). This plan included "privatization of public enterprises, reduction of public expenditure, liberalization, and deregulation . . . as well as providing a greater opportunity for foreign oil companies to exploit Venezuelan oil" (Mahmood and Mutaner 2013, 63). As Hartmann (2016, 2146) documents:

> The Latin American debt crisis of the early 1980s, coupled with US-supported dictatorships and democracies, resulted in a wave of neoliberal and structural adjustment policies developed by economists from the United States and Latin America alike. The International Monetary Fund (IMF) and the World Bank perceived mounting public debt to be a result of state inefficiency, bloated social spending, and economic policies that hindered the market economy. In exchange for economic loans, these 2 organizations required Latin American countries to adopt a suite of neoliberal ideological reforms that cut social spending (particularly in the health sector), reregulated the economy in favor of free and open markets, privatized state-owned corporations and services, and opened borders to foreign investment.

These policies generated popular mobilization against him, which led to his removal and to that of his successor, Rafael Caldera, who maintained the same neoliberal trajectory. The most significant of these events of public protest included the Caracazo that left hundreds dead (Burggraaff and Millett 1995) and two attempted coups: one on February 4, 1992, and a second attempt later that year, on November 27. In May 1993 the Senate voted to suspend President Pérez after he was indicted for misuse of public funds.

When Pérez was placed under house arrest on charges of corruption, the mood of the country was, among other things, that of embarrassment. When I arrived in 1993 to begin my preliminary research, the topic was of considerable chagrin to many Venezuelans I spoke with, from taxi drivers to doctors. One taxi driver told me, "I don't even want to talk about it, it's an embarrassment to the nation that such a thing could happen." Venezuela, a country that prided itself for being one of the Latin American countries with the longest history of democracy and a wealthy oil-producing state, was experiencing a great blow to its national honor. Many Venezuelans asked, "How could this happen to such a great nation?" Coronil (1997, 389) has traced this demise, noting:

> The Venezuelan state has presented itself as the miracle worker that could turn its dominion over nature into a source of historical progress. But largely because much of its power is borrowed from the powers of oil money rather than being produced through its master over nature, the state has been limited to magic performances, not miracles. By analyzing the enactments that have constituted it as a magical state, I have examined its historical transformation during this century, tracing its role in the frenetic rise of Venezuela as a financially wealthy oil nation and its no less violent fall as an indebted third-world country.

If these economic and political crisis were not enough, in early 1994 banks across Venezuela began to collapse. At the beginning of the year, monetary authorities shuttered Banco Latino, the country's second-largest bank (Goodman 1995).

Well before the political and economic upheavals of the presidencies of Luisinchi and Pérez, though, the continuing legacy of the Punto Fijo political pact, along with excess spending of Pérez's first administration (1974–1979), which was carried on by the governments of Luis Herrera Campíns (1979–1984) and then Luisinchi's administration (1984–1989), set the country up for grave economic problems. Throughout these years, Venezuela's economic system had been based on massive subsidies, extensive government controls, artificial employment, and highly distorted protectionist trade policies. As a result, the economy experienced major structural damage, rendering the distribution of income and wealth increasingly inequitable (Goodman 1995), with only the Venezuelan elite benefiting from the economic policy. From 1980 to 1992 it is estimated that average Venezuelans lost over half of their purchasing power. In addition, the late 1970s to the early 1990s saw individual daily caloric intake drop from 2,651 to 1,350 and the proportion of the population under the poverty line increase to 64 percent. The number of poor increased from 7.8 million in 1987 to 9 million in 1989. When I arrived in Caracas in late 1994 to conduct my research, I found myself in the middle of the economic, social, and political crises that had been in the making for decades.

Against this background, Chávez's social democracy represents a transformative political change from the earlier administrations' focus on privatization and austerity. The Chávez administration, which began as a social democracy and gradually shifted to what Chávez himself described as the socialist Bolivarian Revolution (Smilde and Hellinger 2011), rejected neoliberal privatization in the economy broadly and of medical practice in favor of social medicine more narrowly. The administration developed a number of new ministries meant to provide a larger role for government in areas such as health, education, and housing. One of the greatest changes in health policy was the development of the Misión Barrio Adentro program (Inside the Barrio), which put community clinics in the barrios of Venezuela—the barrios that had been virtually ignored in terms of health services during previous administrations. The shift marked an embrace of horizontal community-based health care that took up the recommendations put forth in a document known as the Declaration of Alma-Ata drafted at the 1978 International Conference on Primary Health Care in the former Kazakh Soviet Socialist Republic (Paluzzi and Arribas Garcia 2008). This document was the first of its kind calling for a global health initiative, "expressing the need for urgent action by all governments, all health and development workers, and the world community to protect and promote the health of all the people of the world" (WHO 1978).

The Inside the Barrio program included bringing approximately twenty thousand Cuban doctors to Venezuela to work in the barrios and health clinics around Caracas to serve the poor and those who had no access to private or military-based clinics. Because such striking changes had taken place, I returned to examine whether such transformations in public health were also reflected in discourses of disease, particularly that of cervical cancer, since I had last been there. In light of the cultural politics of health care that had shaped the previous period, the opportunity to consider how disease discourse could transform along with a radical shift from neoliberalism to social democracy (and eventually socialism) is important for understanding just how this political transformation can affect definitions of disease and ultimately national responses to health care.

Specifically, during the neoliberal period, risk centered largely on individual behaviors that were classed, raced, and gendered in ways that reinforced broader goals of reduced government in health care in favor of an atomized approach that would allocate fewer resources to the health-care system. After all, if the framing of risk was such that largely behavior, rather than structural inequities, put people at risk—marginalized people, in particular—it would make perfect sense to construct "at risk" populations as ultimately tasked with keeping themselves healthy and to blame them, rather than an inability to access preventative health care, if they got sick. By contrast, under the Bolivarian democratic framework established by Hugo Chávez, I found that disease risk discourse is conceptualized as a structural problem, rooted in what medical anthropologist and physician Paul Farmer (1996, 369) describes as structural violence, "a series of large-scale forces-ranging from gender inequality to racism and power—which structure unequal access to goods and social services." Although the political uses of culture still figure prominently—largely in reference to calls for a return to Bolivarian roots of the *pueblo*—the focus is not on individual responsibility but, rather, on state responsibility to health. Thus, in returning to Venezuela, I was interested in determining how risk factors for cervical cancer shift along with political changes. I argue in these pages that risk factors for cervical cancer in Venezuela are, at least in part, a product of place. In other words, the risk factors that I documented in the mid-1990s, during my initial fieldwork research in Venezuela, were cemented in the context of the Venezuelan neoliberal climate. The political orientation of the Chávez government that came into power after the political upheaval of President Pérez also corresponded to a shift in health and disease discourses, including that of the risk of cervical cancer. The implications for women's health in microlevel interactions with physicians and in the broader context of public health are contingent on configurations of not only risk but also what it means to think about health in terms of individual responsibility versus social responsibility.

The opportunity to look at another possible shift in the cultural politics of health and disease occurred after the death of President Chávez on March 5, 2013. He embodied the very definition of charismatic leader, and there was speculation in political and media circles as to whether the interim president Nicolás Maduro, who had been vice president under Chávez, would be popular enough to win the special presidential election on April 14, 2013. Maduro would run against Henrique Capriles, a Venezuelan politician and member of the right-leaning political party Justice First and a lawyer by profession. A Capriles victory could mean another change in the political landscape, having implications for the public health sector. In the end, Maduro was elected in a narrow victory. Capriles filed an electoral dispute with the Supreme Court, asking for an audit of the electoral register. In an interview he gave to *El País* on May 10, 2013, he exclaimed: "They stole the election from me. Those guys stole the elections." A ruling was given in favor of Maduro, and so, for now, the socialism of the Chávez era continues with Maduro, likely a continuation of health policy that continues to build on social medicine.

Currently, we also see growing oppositional response to the socialism of Maduro and the Bolivarian Revolution. It is not easy to define the opposition, as the intervening years since the death of Chávez and the election of a less-than-charismatic leader of the revolution—in the figure of Maduro—has coalesced disparate groups of people in a seemingly unified front. Even though we can point to former middle-class Venezuelans who were already on the edge of losing economic ground, they aren't the insurgent citizenry (Holston 2008) who have demanded inclusion and fought for equity from the periphery of poverty. What will happen with the insurgent citizenry who formed the base of the Bolivarian Revolution as the neoliberal narrative of capitalist privatization increasingly encroaches on the narrative of equity through a focus on equality? The lens of equity asks us consider policies that bring the periphery to center. The narrative of equality is to treat everyone the same, which requires those at the periphery to keep struggling with the social, cultural, and political inequities they were dealt. The current political moment in Venezuela also necessitates the next step in acknowledging the neoliberal framing and querying the future of the Bolivarian Revolution.

Why Cervical Cancer? A Woman's Disease

The study of "women's diseases," as such, has a long and at times controversial history. Much scholarly work has focused on the practices of US and European physicians and scientists in their treatment of women's bodies as objects and the development of specialized knowledge and procedures. For example, Barbara Ehrenreich and Deirdre English (1978) presented a history of medical procedures performed on women "for their own good" that have adversely affected women's lives, including women's sexuality and reproduction. Emily Martin (1987) explored the development of obstetrics and the technological tools created to deal with the "problems" of childbirth in its medicalized form. Scholars have also examined the historical circumstances of the emergence of gynecology as a medical specialty and the consequences of this development. Elizabeth Sheehan (1997), for example, looked at the influence of a Victorian doctor in the implementation of a "harmless operative procedure"—clitoridectomy—to cure hysteria, insanity, and epilepsy. Moreover, women's reproductive and sexual body parts have historically been associated with psychological disorders (and the naming of psychological problems) such as insanity, depression, and hysteria, among others.

There are many works (I have mentioned only a few here) that stand as testaments to the tenacity of medical projects that have been inscribed on women's bodies for the regulation of women and women's diseases. I emphasize the "otherness" that the category of "woman's disease" creates in marking women's bodies as somehow dangerously different from those of men, particularly those bodies of nonwhite and nonheterosexual women (Somerville 1997). To this end, scholars of colonialism have addressed the ways in which "native" female bodies, particularly in discourses of biomedicine, have been viewed as sexually, physically, morally—and ultimately *naturally*—threatening to colonial bodies (Vaughn 1991; Comaroff 1992; Whitehead 1995). "Women's diseases" raise the specter of threat, mystery, and danger that has been associated with historical understandings of women, their bodies, and their fluids (Douglas 1966). What this scholarship has in common is that medical knowledge is not taken as an a priori starting point from which to discern "truth" about bodies and disease. It is this cultural embeddedness of meanings associated with so-called women's diseases that partly drew me to the study of cervical cancer in Venezuela.

As I worked on analyzing the ethnographic interviews from my graduate student work on beliefs about cervical cancer among physicians and Latinas in the U.S., what came from the interviews with doctors set the stage for my interest in the social construction of medical knowledge. I was particularly fascinated by the perceptions surrounding cervical cancer, as they were embedded in a moral discourse that focused on women's perceived "nonnormative" hypersexual behavior. At the time, scholars were looking at the moral discourses surrounding HIV and AIDS (see Patton 1992). I was familiar with that literature but was quite surprised to see the extent to which socioculturally constructed ideas about women's sexual behavior were such a part of what some physicians were saying about the risks for cervical cancer. For example, the word *promiscuity* was presented as a medical risk factor, but it is marked with morally judgmental social meaning and is often associated with a negative notion of women's hypersexual behavior (Martínez, Chavez, and Hubbell 1997). Men's sexual behavior is not typically judged in this way—except when referring to the behavior of gay men during the early part of the AIDS epidemic, when they were often described as having a not only deviant but an out-of-control sexual lifestyle. Focusing increasingly on the moral discourse surrounding women's sexuality in relation to cervical cancer, my interest in the problem of cervical cancer grew, and I knew that I wanted to work on it. This led me to look at high rates of cervical cancer in Latin America and to my eventual fieldwork in Venezuela.

Disease and Embodiment

While anthropology has been historically geared toward the study of "folk" illnesses, there has been increasing attention paid to the study of biomedically defined diseases such as cancer, high blood pressure, hypoglycemia, and tuberculosis (Martínez, Chavez, and Hubbell 1997; Wood, Jewkes, and Abrahams 1997; Chavez et al. 1995; Balshem 1991; Hunt, Browner, and Jordan 1990; Garro 1988; Rubel and Garro 1992). These projects take as a premise that biomedical illnesses carry cultural meanings, like so-called folk illnesses, and are therefore suitable objects of anthropological study. One of the overarching goals of the literature has been to unmask the cultural assumptions inherent in biomedicine and to demonstrate how these assumptions are embedded in the creation and transmission of medical knowledge and practice (Comaroff 1982; Wright and Treacher 1982; Scheper-Hughes and Lock 1987; Martin 1987; Gordon and Lock 1988; Kuipers 1989; Lindenbaum and Lock 1993; Lupton 1994). As Gordon (1988, 19) has noted:

> While biomedicine has successfully created and hoarded a body of technical knowledge to call its own, its knowledge and practices draw upon a background of tacit understandings that extend far beyond medical boundaries.... It draws upon and projects ... understandings of *personhood, society, morality,* and *religion* (what is sacred and profane).

This emphasis on understanding medical practice as a cultural practice is necessary for problematizing the disease of cervical cancer. The research presented here takes as a basic premise that medical practice cannot and should not be divorced from cultural experience. Implicated in medical practices and representations of disease are judgments about morality, social class, gender, and race. Rosner (1989, 241) has argued this point quite succinctly:

> To assume that scientific practice today tends to lower the importance of moral and social judgments is naive. Any number of medical historians have illustrated that social class, race, sex and ethnicity are all critical factors in determining professional decisions regarding treatment and care.

When the medical field began taking this charge seriously and started to research issues such as racism in medical encounters, a number of studies corroborated the racism and potentiality of racism in medical encounters (see Smedley, Stith, and Nelson 2003; Hardeman et al. 2016). I take this argument further by adding that these judgments are made not only in regard to treatment and to care; in many cases, they represent the definition of disease, which includes its accompanying risk factors. As a scientific institution, medicine appears to generate medical evidence solely from scientific fact. In practice, however, medicine cannot extricate itself from the sociocultural milieu in which it is produced. To understand how, for example, diseases are historically configured—or even how biomedicine has come to enjoy a certain privileged position in most parts of the world—requires understanding medical discourse and practice as a social construction. The social construction of cervical cancer in the context of neoliberalism enables us to interrogate the production and circulation of disease knowledge that goes beyond the medical context. In this case, the discourse of cervical cancer risk is where the convergence of these seemingly separate localities (of scientific medicine, politics, and culture) are made visible. It is not my goal to enter into the debate of science versus culture; it is a debate with no victors and nothing to gain. My only attempt is to reveal—without, I hope, re-creating boundaries—the shared places and spaces that this division may serve to obscure.

Why Cervical Cancer in Venezuela?

The more I studied the epidemiological research on cervical cancer, the greater my awareness grew of the global scope of the problem of cervical cancer. Worldwide, cervical cancer is the second most common cancer in women. It is particularly high in those areas that are deemed low- or middle-income countries (Sahasrabuddhe et al. 2012). Rates of cervical cancer in Latin America and the Caribbean are four and a half times higher than in the United States and Canada. In Venezuela, cervical cancer is the third leading cause of death among women (behind cardiovascular disease and gastrointestinal cancers); it is also one of the most curable cancers if caught in its early stages (WHO 2013). Thus, one of the great tragedies of cervical cancer in Venezuela is the devastatingly high mortality rates for a disease that is largely preventable and curable through early detection. Poor and working-class women bear the brunt of this cancer because they are particularly likely to end up with advanced cancers that are more difficult to treat and to cure owing to lack of access to health care. Cervical cancer is also among the most preventable cancers, yet it has the highest mortality rate among women in Venezuela. At the time I started my field research, human papillomavirus (HPV) was thought to be related to this cancer, but the connection was not as well established as we know now, with particular types of HPV most likely causal agents in the development of the disease. Thus, greater interpretations for risk were available at the time of the initial fieldwork. Nevertheless, the ambiguity, at the time, does not negate that gaps were filled in with perceptions of risk that have relied on raced, gendered, and classed constructions. In fact, when I returned in 2008, a time when certain strains of HPV had been causally linked with cervical cancer, narratives were still circulating among some physicians and the Venezuelan Cancer Society that relied on those constructs.

A Comment on Emotion

The word *cancer* evokes emotion—usually fear—in most people. I would be remiss to not acknowledge emotion in fieldwork, given that my work took place in two oncology hospitals, and I was surrounded by human fear, sadness, pain, and suffering, as well as hope. The uncertainty related to diagnosis, treatment, and outcomes were part of my daily interactions with women I interviewed and even those I just chatted with in the waiting rooms. At the same time, their emotions elicited emotional reactions and empathy in me. How could they not? Many days after being at the hospital, I felt exhausted and drained. In retrospect I am sure that much of this wrenching personal experience had to do with what I was seeing and hearing and the emotions I was absorbing. Some days were at times also fraught with those in-the-moment methodological and ethical decisions that ethnographers have to make, even if we feel ill prepared to do so: Should I say something? What, exactly? Should

I help? How, exactly? If I do so, will I be stepping on someone's toes, so to speak? Even not acting in the moment is a decision. Navigating power dynamics can be especially tricky in the midst of ethical and emotional situations. One of the very definitions of ethnography is our lack of certainty in our surroundings. We aren't in the controlled environment of a lab. Instead, we are observing and interacting with the ebb and flow of daily life. We also become part of the environment that we study, and our presence can be disruptive in a range of ways, small and large, as can our integration.

During my fieldwork, I experienced many emotions that I could not have written about at the time. The perspective granted by the distance of years, however, has enabled me to analyze with a balance of retrospective clarity. No one ever discussed emotions with me as part of my ethnography training. I learned about interview techniques and methods, but the psychology of fieldwork was virtually absent. And so I naïvely began my project immersed in the world of cancer, having neither consciously thought about nor prepared myself for the emotions it would bring. Until relatively recently, the emotions of the researcher have largely been ignored and left undertheorized (Hedican 2006). Davies and Spencer (2010) bring needed attention to the subject in *Emotions in Fieldwork.* They argue that emotions can strengthen our work by providing insights in a similar way that psychological self-awareness does. Hedican (2006, 6) argues that it is integral to ethnographic research:

> Emotional work is part of the epistemology of qualitative methods. . . . It is therefore not only a state of being but also a process by which knowledge is a product of our processing of information as individuals. In the social sciences, there is a tendency to focus only on overt behavior, as if this were the only significant aspect of the research endeavor . . . an examination of our inner experiences, especially in terms of our attempts at emotional introspection, is an equally important aspect of sociological enquiry.

When we can step back and acknowledge both the emotional and intellectual aspects of fieldwork, we are able to do better work. Negating the empathy and emotions that connect us to other people at the core ignores the humanity of our interactions. Throughout this book, I reflect on the role of emotions during my fieldwork at various intense episodes: as I discuss talking with women who were dealing with the uncertainty of diagnosis, as I held the hand of a woman who I knew was likely going to die, as I sat bedside a twenty-seven-year-old-woman with advanced-stage cancer who I refused to believe would die and, more directly personal, as I navigated sexual harassment and my research thinking if I angered the well-established male doctor I could lose my research project.

As I explore in various relevant chapters, acknowledging my emotions was important for the observations and descriptions that I analyzed and reflected on in the act of writing this book. This process of introspection has provided methodological clarity as well. The psychological practice of sitting with our emotions and analyzing them before acting has important implications for our daily lives, including the way we go about our lives in "the field," as we are prone to calling it. As researchers we may not pay enough attention to the fact that we are emotionally reacting to and in concert with the people we study. These internal observations affect the external ones that we weigh so heavily. It makes sense then that we include them as integral to our research and writing. Although my fieldwork in oncology hospitals with women diagnosed (and potentially diagnosed) with cancer may be thought of as more connected to emotion and empathy than other fieldwork unrelated to health, life, or death, the desire for human connection is a part of all types of fieldwork. It is an obvious and notable gap that we do not discuss the emotional aspect of our work, given that what psychologically healthy human beings most desire from one another—and a fundamental aspect of our behavior—is social connection (Lieberman 2013). We may feel joy, pain, grief, fear, loneliness, embarrassment, and other emotions as we spend weeks, months, and years connecting with others in our ethnographic fieldwork.

Scope of This Work

This monograph promises to contribute to anthropological studies on culture and illness, and power and medicine (particularly in Latin America), and it addresses broader questions of social inequality and relationships of power, which come out of but are not reducible to the process of treating cancer among women. This study is concerned with the anthropological examination of the social, cultural, economic, and political meanings that cervical cancer takes on among women in Venezuela who may be afflicted with cervical cancer (women who have had a positive Pap smear result indicating "abnormal" cells, which may indicate cancer); physicians and other medical personnel who treat it; and public health administrators who set up programs to combat it. I focus on the interaction of patients, physicians, and other medical personnel in the first phase of treatment of cervical cancer, with a particular emphasis on the relations of power that shape those interactions.

Previous research on cervical cancer has primarily focused on causes and prevention, with minor attention paid to the experience of women who are diagnosed with this cancer. Little is known about the impact of the medical encounter and treatment process on these women and the narrative evidence they can provide about their illness (Posner and Vessey 1988). Even less is understood about how physicians and other medical personnel (e.g., nurses) who treat women with cancer interact in the treatment process. I am referring in particular to the nature of cervical cancer intervention treatments and their unseen effects in terms of the social disciplining of women's lives. An important goal of this work is to understand the different ways in which knowledge of disease and the body is invoked, manipulated, deployed, appropriated, and transformed among Venezuelan doctors, patients, and public health administrators in the configuration of cervical cancer and how this relationship influences treatment. These findings, though, reach well beyond the Venezuelan experience and can also speak to other neoliberal health-care projects and illuminate the impacts that a behavior-based construction of disease can have on even microlevel patient-doctor interactions.

This approach, which includes the patient-doctor interaction as well as the examination of public health regimes, is necessary to develop a comprehensive understanding of the ways in which cervical cancer is socially constructed with the mechanism of a cultural politics within neoliberal Venezuela and elsewhere. This refers to the processes and effects of naming cervical cancer in particular ways—as a sexually transmitted disease, as an effect of "unhygienic" practices, as a disease of the poor, in effect, as a disease of morality. The treatment, as well as public health campaigns designed to combat cervical cancer, provide the sites in which I analyze these intersectional relations among illness, power, gender, and class. An absence of this social context would risk an overly simplistic analysis of a health system consisting of "bad" doctors and "complaining" patients (Todd 1989). Observations from the Chávez administration also indicate how risk factors for cervical cancer shifted from a gendered and classed focus on behavior to a social medicine perspective on inequities of access in naming risk.

Moreover, much scholarly work on the history of gynecological medical practice has focused on the practices of US and European physicians and scientists; less is understood about the historical and contemporary practices of gynecology in other parts of the world, particularly Latin America. Additionally, there is not a great deal of work that actually situates women's personal experiences with cancer within an historical, social, and political climate and at the same time offers ethnographic analyses of patient-doctor interactions, including women's and doctors' experiences during the medical exam and office consultation and women's and doctors' perceptions of those experiences. I also contextualize these micro processes within the broader macro level of information generating and sharing outlets, such as public health administrators, private cancer associations, and print media. As such, this work not only contributes to understandings of the ways cultural politics are implicated in the social configuration of biomedically defined diseases but also problematizes how we think of taken-for-granted notions of medical risk and causes us to look carefully at the social, cultural, and political milieu in which they are produced. Although this ethnography is about the experiences of women in Venezuela seeking treatment for cervical cancer, it also speaks to gender issues in general as I explore questions of representation and women's bodies, and the sexual and reproductive disciplining of women that reach beyond the setting of Venezuela.

There are broad implications for this work outside of the geography of Venezuela and the specific problem of cervical cancer. As I trace the social configurations of this disease from the neoliberalism of the 1990s to the socialism of the Chávez and Maduro era, I map out the ways in which class, gender, and (to a lesser extent) race shape disease as a cultural politics. The very definitions of disease are formed in specific social, cultural, and historical moments. Although this work deals with the particular place of Venezuela and the specific disease of cervical cancer, scholars in the fields of anthropology, sociology, history, and gender studies who work on issues of health, illness, and disease can benefit from looking at how cultural politics figures into understandings of these categories, and the implications that this has for both state responses to health and patient-doctor interactions. Disease, in this sense is not just a product of biological discovery. It is created, transformed, inscribed, and experienced as a cultural politics.

The Structure of the Book

In the chapters that follow, I present a framework of the ethnographic study of cervical cancer in Venezuela. As I introduce the field sites where this research was carried out, when, and with whom that work was conducted—I conducted formal open-ended interviews with a total of seventeen doctors and forty-five patients, as well as public health officials and hospital administrators—I also introduce a concise, but important, economic and political history of Venezuela, focusing on dramatic changes that have occurred from the 1980s to the present and that have taken this wealthy oil-producing nation from prosperity to hyperinflation, unemployment, and alarming violence, particularly in urban areas such as the capital city of Caracas. Understanding the contemporary social, economic, and political situation in Venezuela is necessary for situating this research historically and is explicated in the coming chapters. After establishing this context, I turn my attention to the problem that this negative shift has had on public health in Venezuela in general and on cervical cancer in particular.

Already by 1995, during the time of my initial ethnographic fieldwork, Venezuela was following a decidedly neoliberal path in government policies in the area of public health. Ethnographic descriptions of the two hospitals where I worked bear out this point, namely Instituto Oncológico Luis Razetti and Hospital Oncológico Padre Machado. Through vignettes I introduce the women whose stories are a central part of this project, as well as those of the doctors who treat them. I focus on five women in particular whose voices represent a variety of experiences at every stage of the treatment process; their stories are interwoven into the broader theoretical and historical frameworks throughout the book.

I next include an epidemiological profile of cervical cancer risks found in the medical literature and compare them to those perceptions of cervical cancer risk mentioned by the doctors and patients whom I interviewed. It quickly becomes clear that risk attains meaning as a product of history and society with political, economic, and social referents and implications.

The Venezuelan doctors whom I interviewed mentioned epidemiologically supported risks for cervical cancer such as multiple sexual partners and sex at an early age, as well as risks that are not supported epidemiologically (e.g., lack of hygiene, lack of culture). I pay particular attention to the importance doctors give to social class, culture, hygiene, and morality in their profiles of cervical cancer risk.

In terms of the factors mentioned by patients to explain the development of cervical cancer, some were similar to or the same as those stated by the doctors but others were unique to the women. The women's explanations concentrated on the effect of economic disadvantage on access to medical care, though not in relation to behavior (promiscuity and uncleanliness), as can be discerned from many of the doctors' discussions of cervical cancer. Although morality did play a role in women's discussions of cervical cancer risk, unlike doctors, it was configured largely in terms of their relationships with men. Culturally appropriate norms regarding morality emphasize monogamy on the part of a woman and of her partner. In stressing the role that the partner's "immoral" behavior can play in putting her at risk for disease, women are drawing on their own personal experiences with male partners.

I next investigate the role of public health education in the prevention of cervical cancer. In particular, I analyze public health literature designed to educate women about this disease. I also include information presented in media outlets, such as newspapers, and look at the ways they present information about cervical cancer. Before presenting this analysis, I situate the literature by addressing popular ideas about the relationship among class, culture, and health, including interviews with public health officials, articles in national newspapers, and scholarly research on class and violence in Venezuela. Threats to progress, modernity, and Venezuelan culture are pervasive themes in discourses about poverty and disease. Just as important, the discourse surrounding cervical cancer in Venezuela must be understood within a social, economic, and political climate that over the past twenty years has been unstable and, at times, even volatile.

I argue that the historical circumstances in Venezuela have set the stage for a cultural politics of disease in which culture (and cultural difference) has emerged as a significant means for understanding and explaining the problem of cervical cancer by the media, the public health arena, and the medical community in general. In Caracas, in particular, much emphasis (especially in conservative newspaper accounts) is placed on the negative consequences of internal migration from rural areas and undocumented immigration from neighboring countries. The increase in violence, overcrowding, and poverty over recent decades has been characterized as a problem emanating from the city's poor, who are targeted as the carriers of not only disease but also social, moral, and cultural disintegration.

Because health education is directed at poor women—the "at risk" group for cervical cancer—negative perceptions and stereotypes about the poor, in general, their morality, cleanliness, intelligence, and living habits do not escape the literature that targets them for cervical cancer intervention. I point out the ways in which the text and images used for the goal of benefiting women's health also serve to regulate, control, and discipline (poor) women's lives in subtle ways.

I then shift focus to the medical examination itself, with emphasis on relationships of power in this very physical—bodily—manifestation of the patient-doctor interaction. It becomes clear that the body is an important site for understanding how distinctions—of class, in particular—are produced, inscribed, and represented in the bodies of women (e.g., the state of her cervix, cleanliness). Special attention is paid to the ways in which the patients are treated as objects of medical knowledge and manipulation: the ways they are positioned, inspected, and talked to (or not). In doing so, I underscore the structural problems that contribute to a lack of resources at the public hospital including little space, improper equipment, and insufficient time to interact adequately with patients and better inform them of their medical conditions. I also offer narratives of the women's perspectives on their medical treatment, which are, at times, acted on to contest and circumvent some disciplinary forms. Women's stories and observations give voice to patients' concerns, including structural problems within the hospital (e.g., lack of information, difficulty making appointments, getting timely appointments), and their strategies for dealing with these challenges.

Moving on, I introduce the ways in which women especially are disciplined and regulated in the hospital setting. This category of women includes female patients, nurses, secretaries, *doctoras* (female doctors), technicians, and the female anthropologist. I also look at negotiation and compliance in the disciplinary process and the ways women create, partake in, and contest that process. I include my own experiences of gender and identity negotiation in the hospitals.

Finally, I consider some changes that have taken place in health care under the socialism of the Chávez administration. Cultural politics of health functions very differently under the neoliberalism of the 1980s and 1990s compared to the Chávez era. As I trace the social configurations of this disease from the neoliberalism of the 1990s to the era of socialism, I map out the ways in which class, gender, and race shape disease as a product of cultural politics. In other words, I reveal how the very definitions of disease are formed within specific social, cultural, and historical moments.

1 Hospitals, Patients, and Doctors

Settling In

Before beginning my research at the Razetti and Padre Machado hospitals in October 1994, what would be the start of nearly a year of fieldwork in Caracas, I spent my first month looking for an apartment, getting to know the city and meeting with people who had assisted me during my preliminary field research. At that time, I had quickly learned the importance of meeting the friend of a friend of a friend of an initial contact person. This is the way things get done in Venezuela. Contacts I made previously helped me to set up my research at these hospitals, the only two functioning oncology hospitals in Venezuela. Originally, I had intended to live in the barrios where some of the women whom I would be interviewing would probably be living (at least those seeking medical attention at the public hospital). However, I determined that without a contact person who could help me find a place to live within the barrio, it was best to not pursue that plan. Instead, I rented for approximately US$150 (that I found listed in the newspaper) a bedroom from a widowed schoolteacher in the apartment that she shared with two grown sons and her mother in a middle-class neighborhood of Caracas. It was approximately a forty-five-minute metro and bus ride to either of the two hospitals. Living with a family in this area of Caracas ended up giving me great insight into the class dynamics that I would see throughout my fieldwork. Henriqueta, two of her sons, José and Félix, along with *la abuela*, Amalia, came to be my family in Caracas. Even Delia, the elderly, chain-smoking upstairs neighbor, who would come over just when it happened to be dinnertime, grew on me. She grated on José's nerves because he said she came from a wealthy family but always managed to eat their food. Henriqueta, nonetheless, always welcomed her—to José's chagrin—and the three of us women often ended up playing cards. All of us were in some way alone and kept one another company across generational divides. Even though Henriqueta and her family lived in a middle-class neighborhood, their financial situation was precarious, which is why she had put an ad in the paper to rent one of her rooms. She was working part-time as a teacher, but finances were always a topic of conversation. Félix was in dental school and José is an artist who was working irregularly. Henriqueta had her husband's pension from the military, but as inflation was hitting Venezuela and the cost of living was going up, she worried that they would have to move out of the apartment. Despite her difficult situation, Henriqueta was a very upbeat woman, always optimistic and only hinting at the things troubling her. One was the health of another son, who lived in another town and was a recovering drug addict, and the other was money. I would often talk with Henriqueta about my days at the hospitals, and she was a source of support when I experienced sexually harassing comments from one of the doctors at Razetti. I elaborate on this challenge in my fieldwork in a later chapter that focuses on gender and sexism in the hospital settings. As time went on, I grew close to Henriqueta, and the apartment, where we interacted daily, became home and also another sort of ethnographic site; Henriqueta, José, and—to a lesser extent—Félix, and I discussed the economy, politics, culture, religion, and health care, as well as personal things that were going on in our lives.

As part of "settling in," this chapter gives an overview of the hospitals where I conducted ethnographic fieldwork, as well as the patients and healthcare providers who I interviewed and interacted with at the hospitals. The context of place and people sets up later chapters, where I analyze perceptions of risk, medical encounters, public health, and the gendering of hospital interactions. As often happens with ethnographic research, spaces that I had not anticipated providing insights into social dynamics did, in fact, open up fissures that could not be explored as readily through formal or informal interviewing. In the following section, I reflect on one such space on my first day of fieldwork that put race in Venezuela at center stage. Because Venezuelans often deny that race is as an organizing principal of society, paying attention to the snapshots of race in quotidian spaces is important for understanding this obfuscated reality.

Café con leche in the Cafeteria

On my first day at Razetti, I learned that the cafeteria hospital in Venezuela was no different than in the United States: everyone who visits or works there will find their way to the cafeteria. And so did I, in search of coffee. A man wearing a doctor's coat and a woman in a nurse's uniform caught my eye because they were chatting excitedly, and she had what looked like a framed, 8″ × 10″ picture in her hand. Coffee mugs, plates, utensils, X-ray placards, and even mobile IV drips are things commonly found in a hospital cafeteria, but not a framed photo that could hang on a wall or sit on a table. And this photo, in particular, was oddly out of place. I could make out that it was a portrait of a woman in a long white wedding gown. This had now really piqued my interest, so I focused on them and let the clamor of voices and clanking of dishes around me fade away. She was telling him pointedly, "Look, she is white! She is white! I told you my daughter is white." Her tone was filled with a sense of urgency that conveyed her desperate attempts to convince him of this fact. His body language was saying no before the words came out of his mouth: arms crossed with a slight smile while he shook his head from side to side. The oddness of the interaction took me a moment to register and to reflect on what I was witnessing and hearing. It certainly was not the schema of a conversation I would imagine while gazing at a wedding photo. He insisted—in a declarative manner that seemed more as if he were commenting on the world being flat rather than rendering a personal opinion on a photo—that the woman in the photo was not white: "She is black," and he added, "She isn't even light." The conversation wasn't tense but instead ended with an exasperated laugh on the woman's part. She had failed to convince him of her daughter's whiteness, and she slipped the picture back into the bag that had protected it. I would later learn that the woman was indeed a nurse, and she worked in the hospital's breast cancer department, along with the unconvinced doctor, who was the head of that department.

I was left to contemplate what had just transpired. I had not heard the entire conversation, but I was still privy to enough that left me formulating some of the following questions in the immediate aftermath: Why was she interested in seeking agreement from this doctor that her daughter is white? Why did it seem that her daughter's being white was so important to her? What did it mean that she, a black nurse, was seeking this verification of whiteness from a white doctor? Why did the doctor appear so certain in commenting on her whiteness? Race, some Venezuelans had already told me, is unimportant in the sense that they see themselves as a racially blended society. In addition, according to Winthrop Wright (1993), for more than a century, Venezuelans have claimed their society to be a racial democracy, referring to themselves as a racially mixed, or mestizo, people, likening themselves to *café con leche*, or coffee with milk. This phrase refers to the "racial mixture" of Venezuela's population, which reflects a colonial legacy of slavery from Africa and the Caribbean, as well as European immigration and native indigenous populations. Venezuela's population in the 1990s was estimated at approximately twenty million people: 68 percent mestizo (mixed race), 21 percent Caucasian, 10 percent African, and 1 percent Indian (Haggerty and Blutstein 1993). Venezuelans thus pride themselves on the belief that because they are a "blended" society, they have achieved racial democracy—the popular belief of racial equality as the notion that people of all races live free from prejudice and discrimination (Wright 1993). Given the claims of harmonious racial mixture, I was struck by the cafeteria conversation I stumbled upon on my very first day, which put race at center stage. What about the *café con leche* society where everyone is blended and color doesn't matter? It's not that Venezuelans claim to not notice color in a U.S. "color-blind" sense. They have similar or the same color-conscious "nicknames" that exist in much of Latin America (e.g., *negro* to refer to a dark-skinned person).

However, it is difficult to imagine that Venezuela has achieved racial democracy given the interconnectedness of race, gender, and class. In a society where class differences are quite marked, one cannot dismiss the role of gender and race in the configuration of these distinctions. While I do not attempt to provide in-depth analysis of race in the medical encounter, there are instances that come up in my observations that I believe reflect not only attitudes about gender and class but also attitudes about race. A number of Venezuelan scholars are attempting to get at this very issue of current-day racism. Not a lot of work has been done toward understanding racism in Venezuela in a systemic and interdisciplinary way (Bolivar 2009). However, Venezuelan scholars have addressed this *café con leche* contradiction through various disciplinary lenses. Bolivar and colleagues point, in particular, to the work of psychologist Ligia Montañez (1993, 292), who notes that Venezuela is "a society that has historically boasted about valuing egalitarianism but that maintains racism in a 'hidden' way, so that prejudice and discrimination 'persist, hidden by the apparently non-racist society of current Venezuela.' . . . Consequently, behind the metaphor of the '*café con leche*' country, there seems to be a hidden desire for the 'equality' that is not necessarily practiced in everyday life."

And, in a more forceful argument that links racism and classism in Chávez-era Venezuela, Jesús María Herrera Salas (2004, 10:2, 111) states: "a profound racism exists in Venezuela, not just against Afroamerican and indigenous inhabitants, but also, particularly, among the common people in general—the ones who are continually discredited as '*tierrúos,*' '*niches,*' '*zambos,*' '*negros,*' '*indios,*' '*pata en el suelo,*' '*chusma*' by the upper classes and those opposed to the processes of change." These derogatory terms intersect with race and class, and they demarcate some of the divisions that were already present. Under Chávez, discourses around race were brought to the fore, so much so that some Venezuelans suggested that Chávez fomented divisions by openly discussing racism. For example, in a 2005 interview in *El Nacional* with journalist Milagros Socorro, Venezuelan anthropologist Michaelle Ascencio was asked, "Do you think President Chávez invented the idea that there is racism here to divide and manipulate us?" I quote Ascencio's response at length because she provides important insight into the national dynamics of racism:

> In Venezuela there has always been racism against the Indians and against the black people, fundamentally. What President Chávez has done is to uncover that and utilize it like a flag that divides and confronts us. But the thing is that Venezuelans are determined to repeat that we are a racially mixed country—we are biologically speaking—and because of that there aren't any conflicts between the races, that we are harmonious and don't have racism. And we don't see, like in all societies (more in the Caribbean ones where the rates of poverty are highest), we have a series of contradictions that we haven't resolved and that we don't want to see. We are mixed, yes, but that doesn't mean the racial mixture has been consented to by both sides, nor much less is it idyllic; racial mixture can be an indication of violence. Racism is an attitude about certain people for their physical characteristics; and in Venezuela, many times, that attitude is to reject. But since the nineteenth century there has been a discourse determined to deny the tensions between diverse groups that comprise Venezuelan society. And because our local racism isn't like that of the United States, for example, that has served as an alibi to continue denying it because in Venezuela they don't kill anyone for being black. . . . [T]hey use a barometer of extreme violence to minimize the violence that we live. In reality, the

violence is the same but it is expressed more subtly among us; its the looking you over from top to bottom; its the twisted mouth; its the delivery person, when I open the door of my house, asking me to please call the lady of the house. (Socorro 2010)

The question posed by the journalist of whether Chávez "invented" the idea of racism in Venezuela to divide the populace is provocative and speaks to the attention brought to racism under his administration. It also reflects the idea that there is no racism in Venezuela, an example of the *café con leche* ideology. The other part of the narrative, that bringing up racism is itself racist and causes division, is a way to close down any discussion of it—a trope that is also popular in the United States. Global histories of colonialism and imperialism have a collective desire to mask the realities of their legacies in the present. Chávez did not invent the idea of racism in Venezuela, but he did make it part of his critiques of inequality. As is the case in most parts of the world, one cannot speak of classism without reference to its intersection with racism. The lack of willingness to broach the subject of racism in Venezuela has contributed to its tepid acknowledgment by citizens. When I was there the first time in 1994, the absence of the subject was even more pronounced than it is today.

My own observations in hospitals before the Chávez era reflect this "hidden" racism that Montañez (1993) articulates and the intersections with class that Herrera Salas (2005) points to. When discussions of race would come up in my conversations with hospital personnel, the emphasis would often be on the lack of racism in Venezuelan society. Not surprisingly, the well-blended society of *cafe con leche* was invoked in these descriptions. In fact, when I questioned one of the social workers at Razetti about the use of the category "skin color" on the interview schedule for the department of social services, she went to great lengths to explain that it was a useless category. She said that there was really no reason for its inclusion on the form, and it was probably there because the form had been modeled after American forms, which contain categories of race and ethnicity. She went on to explain, as if to persuade me of the inappropriateness of this category for Venezuela, that it would not appear on the new interview schedule that was being developed. Any suggestion that racial categories have relevance in Venezuela was quickly disavowed. The implication is that there was no basis for racism to exist there. As will become clear in later chapters, class distinctions, in contrast, were widely invoked to explain difference—bodily, psychological, and behavioral. Race, however, was always beneath the surface, intersecting with class and gender, framing many of the interactions that I observed in the hospital settings, if not at the individual level, then at a structural one. The myth of racial harmony that is part of historical and contemporary (re)constructions of *café con leche* society was not overtly betrayed in these conversations but rather insistently maintained and defended.

This silence around racism in public health in Venezuela, in particular, would later be shattered by Charles Briggs and Clara Mantini-Briggs (2004) in their seminal work on the topic, *Stories in the Time of Cholera: Racial Profiling During a Medical Nightmare*. The authors trace the roots and aftermath of a cholera epidemic in the Orinoco Delta region in the Venezuelan state of Delta Amacuro, located in the northeastern part of the country. The epidemic killed nearly five hundred people between 1992 and 1993. Briggs and Mantini-Briggs document the structural racism in various government public health agencies at local and national levels that both led to the outbreak of cholera and allowed it to reach epidemic status. Their work was instrumental in bringing the issue of racism in medicine and public health painfully to the fore in the country.

One of the most forceful contemporary arguments about the broad and enduring role of racism in Venezuela can be found in Jesús María Herrera Salas's 2005 book, *The Political Economy of Racism in Venezuela*. In this work, Herrera Salas, a Venezuelan anthropologist, argues: "Racism has been a fundamental element of the ideology, practices and hegemonic politics in Venezuela from the Conquest to the present day. One of the principal ideological functions has been precisely to legitimize the economic and political privileges of the dominant classes" (13). While he takes seriously a complex understanding of racism that does not underestimate the many matrices that shape it, he argues that a political economy approach is of great value not only for analyzing racism but also for increasing the necessary political consciousness to effectively combat racial discrimination in Venezuela. His approach centers the actions, strategies, policies, and organizational forms that government adopts that privilege the economic and political interests of the dominant classes and, in doing so, either enact racist policies and/or effectively function as such, given the relationship between racism and classism. The result is that generally speaking it is the indigenous and Afro-Venezuelan populations that also experience the greatest poverty and economic inequities.

In thinking about the silence around racism that I encountered, Herrera Salas's work helps to illuminate the political economy of racism that existed in the public health-care system at the time of my initial fieldwork, and that Briggs and Mantini-Briggs (2004) later documented in the cholera epidemic. As a result, the neoliberal austerity projects of the 1980s and 1990s can then also be understood as political economies of racism. Moving from the political economy of racism to the political economy of health care, the following section provides an overview of Latin American Social Medicine and the works of those researchers who have critically examined the relationship between societal conditions of marginalization and the health of populations.

Latin American Social Medicine and the Political Economy of Health Care in Latin America

The problem of health cannot be reduced to the phenomena of disease, nor does it merely comprise the individual dimension. Health is a complex, multidimensional process that requires focusing on the social processes that generate or determine health conditions.

Jaime Breilh (2010a, 3)

The origins of Latin American Social Medicine (LASM) can be traced to Rudolph Virchow, a nineteenth-century physician and social scientist. Virchow insisted on understanding health and disease in their social context and sought to prevent disease, rather than simply focus on treatment after the fact. He also advocated for state-sponsored health-related initiatives that would help workers and women. Later, Virchow would influence Salvador Allende, who became Chile's first minister of health and then president of Chile from 1970 to 1973. It was Allende who introduced national policies based on social medicine and was a catalyst for progressive health reforms across Latin America (Hartmann 2016). Across Latin America, LASM is a broadly known and well-respected field of research focused on understanding "the links between social conditions and the health of populations" (Eldredge et al. 2004). It is also embedded in the philosophy and praxis of social justice (Krieger 2003). Briggs and Mantini-Briggs (2009, 549) describe LASM scholars and practitioners as those who "endorse collective rather than individual approaches to health care, stress the importance of political-economic and social determinants of health, and promote holistic approaches to health-disease-health care processes. . . . These scholars promote practices and policies that treat health as a social and human right and extend universal and equal health care access, oppose the privatization of health and its transformation into a free-market commodity, and advocate strengthening the state's role in guaranteeing access to health services."

Public health practitioners in English-speaking parts of the world, and particularly in the United States, are less familiar with the important theories, methods, and approaches of LASM to understanding health (Waitzkin et al. 2001b). LASM as a research field takes on various health emphases in Latin America—given the diverse social, economic, and political histories throughout the region—but all seek to understand the political economy of health and the structural inequities that shape the health of populations. By this, I am referring to the political and economic conditions that shape the structure and delivery of health care; "such an approach stresses that the provision of health care is independent of health factors per se and that access to health care is not equally distributed throughout a population" (Chavez 1986, 344).

In tracing the history of LASM from the late 1960s, Howard Waitzkin and colleagues (2001a) draw upon the personal histories of physicians and other medical professionals to show just how dangerous working to bring about health-care reforms and shape health systems was during that period. LASM represented a threat to autocratic governments, like that in Argentina at the time, because the focus on social conditions required that public health reforms be tied to government reforms. Later, in the 1970s and 1980s, LASM continued to grow in popularity, but those working in social medicine still faced marginalization in academic and medical institutions throughout Latin America. Ever since it has remained the most important approach to health care in the region. This brief history helps us to contextualize the importance of social medicine and the public-sector opposition to and mobilization against neoliberal public health policies that would arise a decade later, especially in Bolivia, Ecuador, and Venezuela.

The works of Latin America scholars in social medicine such as Óscar Feo (2003, 2004, 2008), María Urbaneja (1991), Asa Cristina Laurell (1982), Asa Cristina Laurell et al. (2000), Eduardo Menéndez (1981, 1983, 1990) and Jaime Breilh (2010) are central in the field of LASM. For example, Asa Cristina Laurell is a groundbreaking thinker in the field, contributing extensively to theory and method through her work in Mexico and incorporating analyses of gender in social medicine. Jaime Breilh, an Ecuadorian epidemiologist, is recognized as pioneering a new branch of studies in public health in the 1970s known as critical epidemiology, which "articulates an innovative view of spatial health analysis that intertwines the contributions of philosophy, political economy, and social geography to rethink the social determination of urban-rural relationships and health" (2010, 83). The work of Óscar Feo critically engages the effects of neoliberal policies that negatively affect the health of already-marginalized populations. Feo was also the deputy gender coordinator of the Latin American Association of Social Medicine and is currently the national coordinator of a community health program, training physicians in Venezuela (Hartmann 2016). In rejecting individualism as a guiding principle in state health policies, Feo (2004, 65) articulates a broad goal for public health reforms in the following way: "It is essential that we understand that the first great task we have in public health is to develop, strengthen and create a culture for life and health that is expressed in the prioritization of health promotion and in the construction of networks. . . . We are also faced with the challenge of *meeting the health needs and demands of the population*, which requires moving from a dynamic that prioritizes the offering of services to one that centers, not on what the public health sector can provide, but on the health demands of the population."

Importantly, neoliberalism had profound effects on the health-care systems of Venezuela, Bolivia, and Ecuador. Adhering to mandates imposed by the World Bank and the International Monetary Fund, these countries greatly reduced their health-care budgets and decentralized health-care funding and decision-making, leading to large-scale privatization of health-care services, insurance, and delivery; this in turn resulted in structural segmentation and fragmentation. The elevated costs of private health care meant that substantial disparities in health-care spending by sector were common and that less money was being allocated to the poor (Muntaner 2006; Mahmood and Muntaner 2013; Hartmann 2016). The field of social medicine has illuminated the disparities wrought by neoliberal reforms and has developed theories, methods, and approaches to collectivist health care that stand in contrast to the individualism promoted through austerity that further marginalizes the poorest populations.

In the next sections I introduce the hospitals where I conducted my ethnographic research. As will become apparent, the lack of resources available to the hospitals exemplifies problems that the political economy of health care illuminates and is indicative of the struggles that populations face with unequal distribution of health care.

Razetti: Background

The Razetti hospital is a public oncology hospital that at the time I was there received most of its funds from the then government-run Ministry of Health and Social Assistance (MSAS). Although it is a public hospital and provides care for free, patients at that time were asked (but not required) to give a donation to help with the costs of their consultations and/or treatments. At the time of my first field research, patients were asked to give 200 bolivares (official exchange rate of 170 bolivares to US$1) for a consultation usually consisting of pelvic exam or Pap exam or biopsy or a combination of these. The hospital is located on the outskirts of a sector known as Cotiza in the northwestern part of Caracas. The hospital's neighborhood and another barrio a few blocks to the south are known colloquially as *la zona roja* (the red zone), which I was told (by physicians and nurses) meant that it was a "dangerous" area. I personally never felt unsafe there and did not experience any problems with my person or possessions. Two doctors, however, related that their cars had been broken into and a secretary warned me against wearing my gold wedding band.

The Razetti hospital was formerly a convent and retained a rather picturesque appearance on the outside, with white walls and blue trim. Once inside, however, one could see the effects of the country's economic problems on the public health system. The floors and walls were dingy and cracking, paint was chipping, and rusty bars covered the windows. During the time of my fieldwork many of the items needed to treat patients were in short supply, including gauze, bandages, latex gloves (ostensibly disposable but sterilized and reused for examinations), and anesthesia for surgery. Even electricity was sometimes absent, causing consultations and surgeries to be canceled. Additionally, the hospital's two machines for radiation treatments had not been functioning since 1990. Patients needing this treatment were sent to either the Universidad Central de Venezuela (UCV) hospital or the Hospital Oncológico Padre Machado (Padre Machado). The former was free of charge for those who could not afford to pay, but it was so crowded that appointments were unavailable for six months or longer unless one had the proper connections. Padre Machado, though associated with the private Venezuelan Cancer

Society, also received funding from the public health sector and was technically supposed to be accessible to those who could not pay, but as I witnessed, and was also told, this was not necessarily the case.

Razetti is a hospital that requires patients to have a referral from another medical institution (e.g., hospital, clinic, doctor's office) indicating that they need oncological medical care. However, in some cases (as with a few of the women I interviewed) patients could bypass this referral if they had connections through someone at the hospital (e.g., doctor, nurse, secretary) who was able to get them appointments. Such patients are called *pacientes de cortesia*, or courtesy patients. The women who I interviewed were usually referred by a clinic, hospital, or private doctor because of what the doctors commonly called "abnormal results" or "suspicious lesions" on their pathology report. The usual procedure for any patient was to be seen first by a social worker and doctor in admissions. The hospital social worker would interview the patient, asking about medical history, place and type of residence, and financial resources, and evaluating his or her psychosocial state of mind (specifically, whether the patient was aware of why she or he had been referred to the hospital). A nurse would then take the patient's medical history and a doctor would do a physical examination. The doctor in admissions then noted the patient's medical condition in the chart so he or she could be given an appointment for the proper department (e.g., gynecology, urology, head and neck).

The Servicio de Ginecología (Department of Gynecology), where most of my time at the hospital was spent, consisted of two small examination rooms, one larger examination room with an office attached, a conference room (also used as an office), a bathroom, a utility room (with a sink, refrigerator, lockers, and sterilizing oven), and a small office that was largely unoccupied where I conducted interviews. Gynecology used these rooms in the mornings until 11:00 am, at which time the Servicio de Urología (Department of Urology) took over the use of the rooms (this arrangement was at times confusing for the patients).

The department of gynecology consisted of the following staff: one female secretary in charge of getting charts and collecting appointment cards, three female nurses (each of who had worked at the hospital for ten or more years), and five male *médicos adjuntos* (attending physicians within the hospital who hold positions of seniority within the hospital ranks), one of whom served as the director of the department. There were also a number of residents and interns (female and male) from other hospitals on surgical oncology and gynecology rotations (called *pasantías* and usually lasting three months) as well as two-year residencies in surgical or gynecological oncology. Some of the doctors doing *pasantías* were obstetrics and gynecology residents at another public hospital, Maternidad Santa Ana. Because a national public health campaign around cervical cancer at the time included better training for physicians to perform Pap exams and to recognize possible cancerous lesions of the cervix, the Maternidad Santa Ana had an arrangement with both Razetti and Padre Machado to provide some oncology training to obstetrics and gynecology residents.

The gynecological consultations were held Monday through Thursday, when women with all types of gynecological disorders were seen (including those with uterine and vaginal cancers). However, Mondays and Wednesdays were usually reserved solely for women who had or may have had cervical cancer (*lesión sospechosa*, or suspicious lesion, was a phrase commonly used). The attending physicians rotated shifts, each one usually doing consultations twice weekly. At least one attending physician was required to be present to answer questions for the medical residents and to see first-time patients. I was told by the director of the gynecology department that first-time patients are seen by an attending physician, who takes a history and conducts a complete exam (including another Pap to confirm whether a lesion is present). The residents saw only patients who were returning for their *control*, a term used by the hospital personnel (e.g., doctors, nurses, secretaries, social workers) to describe follow-up treatments and exams to control the disease.

The doctors had other duties in addition to examining patients. The attending physicians engaged in *docencia* (teaching residents), and some also held administrative positions. The resident doctors in turn were required to do weekly presentations on oncological gynecology. Both also practiced surgery and attended to patients who were hospitalized. Every Friday morning the *reunión de médicos* (doctors' meeting) took place. The doctors met to discuss "difficult cases" and to suggest courses of treatment. The women whose cases would be discussed were asked to come in for their appointments that same morning. They were examined by most or all of the doctors who were present for the meeting and their cases were discussed among the doctors after the patients had left. It was also considered a good teaching day for residents, who were able to see cases that they might not ordinarily come across.

Before beginning to interview the women and doctors, I took some time to find my way around the hospital and figure out how things were run. While

I had some questions in mind to include in an interview, I was not ready to develop an interview schedule until I had some time to interact with doctors, nurses, patients, and staff in the hospital setting. In this way I would be open to identify issues and questions pertinent to the research that could be addressed in the interview. In addition, I needed some time to understand the hospital's daily routines so that I could set up the logistics for my project: who to interview, how, when, and where.

I could take the time to become familiar with my new surroundings without feeling rushed to begin interviewing since the doctors told me that the number of patients they see usually goes down in November and December because of the holidays. This is particularly true for first-time patients to the hospital, the group I would interview so as to follow their stories from beginning to end of treatment if at all possible (as fieldwork goes, this turned out to be rather difficult). The doctors explained that the women want to be at home with their families, and more important, there is no money to travel for those coming from other parts of the country, especially *el interior* (the interior of the country, which is largely rural). For women traveling long distances (anywhere from five to fifteen hours on a bus), seeing the doctor involved bus fare to and from Caracas, transportation within the city, and hotel and meals, especially if they did not have family they could stay with in the city. These costs were multiplied if the women were accompanied by relatives, spouses, and/or children. Because the Razetti and the Padre Machado hospitals were the only functioning oncology hospitals in Venezuela at the time, women seeking treatment from other parts of the country had to travel long distances for oncological medical attention.

I mainly observed from the large office located in the back of the department, partly because of available space and partly because it seemed to be the most active area, with patients, nurses, *médicos adjuntos*, and residents coming in and out. My usual space was against a wall next to a table that held a coffee maker and some medical forms for referrals and prescriptions. The large office also held a picture on the wall of what I did not recognize at first but was told by one of the doctors was a "clean and healthy cervix." This phrase sets up a contrast in which other cervixes that did not fit this description were dirty and diseased. As I develop throughout the book, this discourse of clean and hygienic cervixes was intimately linked to the moral state of the woman herself. The detached and disembodied imagery of the clean and healthy cervix hanging on the wall would later attain symbolic meaning, as women who were examined just a few feet away came to be reduced to the state of their cervixes—objects not on a wall, but on an examination table.

An examination room was next to the office, separated by a wall with an open doorway. However, from the office, the examination table was not visible, despite the open doorway. I was given a white doctor's coat lab coat and told by Minerva, the department secretary, that I would be required to wear one while working there. I wasn't too pleased about this directive, as I didn't want the coat to create a distance between myself and the women who I would be interviewing, but she was insistent, and I didn't want to make waves. She was the person to later set aside the charts of the first-time patients so I could call them to be interviewed. Minerva generally raced around the consultation area and always seemed to have a folder or chart in her hand.

On my first day observing at the hospital, Dr. José Vargas gave me a small space with a chair next to his desk and said that I could observe from there. He introduced me to his first patient of the day as she sat down in the office, explaining that I was a *doctora* there to observe for a project on women's health (however, he didn't facilitate a reciprocal introduction by telling me her name). Even though I introduced myself as a student working toward her doctorate, the doctors and staff would refer to me as *doctora*. This categorization allowed them to make meaning of my role within the hospital setting. This was the office space where he would call in patients to talk to them before examining them. Before entering the office I mentioned to Dr. Vargas that I was concerned about the issue of patient privacy and confidentiality: was it really OK that I was in the office while he talked with his patient? He gave me a bewildered look and said that my presence was perfectly fine. Later, as the day wore on, I realized why. The office door was never closed, patients who were waiting to be seen were often right up against the doorway, and nurses and other doctors came in and out as did the secretary. Because Dr. Vargas was an attending physician, the residents came in often to ask him questions regarding the patients they were examining. Also, during these first few days I noticed that when there were numerous patients and the offices and exam rooms were full, the doctors would share the desk in the larger office with each having a patient on either side of the desk. The conference room was also used in this manner, accommodating three or four doctors and their patients at a time. Medical histories were being discussed, courses of treatment, and so on. In such public settings, privacy issues seemed irrelevant, even pointless. There was, however, one place that I did not enter without permission from the patient—the actual exam room. Although the doctors would often invite me into the exam room while a patient was being examined, I would decline because I felt doing so would be extremely intrusive. They were often bewildered as to why I didn't want to view and "examine" women's cervixes along with them. This was, after all, a teaching hospital, and they insisted that it was a part of my learning experience, even though I was clear that my interest was in interviewing, not examining, the women. To them I became another type of medical student, one who asked a lot of questions and was not at all interested in viewing the women's cervixes.

After Dr. Vargas's patient and I exchanged nods and smiles, I soon realized that the office interaction would not be an exchange of patient concerns and him answering her questions. Rather, he mostly asked them their names and where they came from, to make sure that the information matched the chart. Almost immediately he asked the women to step into the adjacent examining room. He had read over the charts earlier and did not exchange any details about their health or ask whether they had any questions. As I detail in the following chapter, this brief patient-doctor scenario was normative and came up as a concern for some of the women whom I interviewed.

Moreover, the lack of communication and lack of concern for patient privacy was due in part to a paucity of resources; but it was also reflective of doctors' perceptions of the type of patients they were seeing. In my analysis of patient-doctor interactions, I argue that because most patients were of low socioeconomic status, the assumption was made that the patients would not understand what was being said (including what was said to the patient herself), thus making any concern for patient privacy (in terms of verbal communications in front of other patients) unnecessary. The issues of privacy and confidentiality that came up during my first few months of observations were central to the questions of how and where I would conduct interviews in the hospital setting.

I also had hoped to follow some of the women through their treatment process, but because of the logistics of appointments and treatment plans, there were only a handful of women who I saw more than once. The same issues were present at Padre Machado, because it was difficult to know when the women would end up returning for their follow-ups. Sometimes the women would also be referred for radiation to the UCV medical school. In those cases of out-referral it was impossible to maintain contact. As a result, I tended to look for patterns in the interactions that I observed, and when I could maintain contact with the women I interviewed, I expanded on their experiences where possible.

During the observations, I focused on a number of characteristics of the interactions of doctors, patients, and nurses, including time spent in the office before the exam; time spent examining the patient; questions asked by patients, doctors, and nurses; responses or lack thereof to questions; and generally the dialogue among these groups. In addition, I dedicated time to just "hanging out" at the hospital, talking informally with doctors in the cafeteria over coffee, with patients in the waiting area, with secretaries, and with the nurses in the department after the morning consultations were over. On Friday mornings I attended the *reunión de médicos* in the gynecology department. After these Friday meetings the doctors would occasionally go out for lunch and would invite me to come along, which I did.

As I became more familiar with the hospital, I also volunteered some time in the social services department, calling patients who had missed appointments to find out whether they were still alive. If it was determined that they were deceased, their files could be closed; if not, I was to remind them to come back to the hospital for their follow-ups. I often did not reach patients because of phone disconnections or, most often, because the phone number was that of a neighbor or family member who was entrusted to relay the message. Those who did not have phones were sent letters. It was not uncommon for some of these letters to be returned—many were *barrio* addresses. I was told that it is difficult to deliver mail to these addresses because sometimes two or more houses have the same number or no number is given at all, just a barrio name (e.g., Barrio San Ángel). Interestingly, this was given as an example of the general chaos of the barrios.

The head social worker, María, was in charge of my training. She was also the one who had told me that the category of "race" on the intake forms was outdated and meaningless, letting me know they would be updated. She was a friendly woman who worked long hours and always had patients at her desk wanting to speak with her about various problems, usually financial in nature or some missing piece of paperwork that needed a signature or stamp. She also spent much of her time trying to locate treatment at other hospitals for those patients needing radiation therapy. However, it remained unclear how patients would be helped by declaring any problems to the social workers. Resources were scarce, and it wasn't as if there were psychologists on hand to refer patients to if they disclosed any psychological difficulties with having been referred to an oncology hospital. I soon came to realize that all parties were engaging a well-known sequence of practices. Going through social services was a gatekeeping requirement for treatment. This process was similar at every public hospital. By the time they were referred to Razetti, patients knew the routine and tried to make the process as easy as possible. Saying everything was fine got you in to see a doctor more quickly than if you articulated distress of any kind. This became clear when patients who I interviewed expressed not knowing what was going on with their medical situation, yet their profile in the social services intake paperwork often indicated "Patient is aware of diagnosis." It was as if neither side wanted to acknowledge anything that would hold up the routine. The necessary steps were taken, but often little information was exchanged. No social services were really available in any case, and the paperwork would be dutifully filled out for the next steps. Patients would then be off to wait at the next line, whether it be to make photocopies, turn in paperwork to another entity, get X-rays taken, have blood drawn, or finally see a doctor.

At both Razetti and Padre Machado, patients spent a lot of time just waiting. The act of waiting is likely something they were used to. Waiting is an experience that the urban poor repeat over and over as they try to access various state services. Waiting, as Auyero (2012) argues in *Patients of the State: The Politics of Waiting in Argentina*, is a form of discipline in which the state regulates the poor, as they are made to spend time in long lines for social services, IDs, and other government needs. I elaborate on the concept of regulatory waiting in Chapter 4, where I analyze the medical encounter. Before even seeing a doctor, patients will have had to navigate a number of medical departments, requiring them to wait and wait and wait.

In late November I learned of a meeting taking place at the hospital to report the results of an evaluation of the hospital prepared by the Ministry of Health and Social Services (Ministerio de Sanidad y Asistencia Social, MSAS). The ministry put together a committee consisting of former Razetti doctors as well as doctors working within the ministry. The meeting took place on December 2, 1994, at the hospital auditorium, with approximately eighty hospital and MSAS staff (mostly doctors and administrators) present. I went to the meeting with Dr. Muñoz, an attending physician from the Servicio Oncológico Mamario (oncological mammary department). He was the doctor who I had first seen a few months earlier talking with the black nurse, telling her that her daughter was not white. Given that the oncological mammary and gynecology departments were very near each other, I got to know Dr. Muñoz as I either purposefully or haphazardly ambled the hallways in my role as participant-observer. Before the meeting started, there was a lot of chatter. The auditorium was nearly full, with people also milling around in the back. The air felt thick and stuffy. There was a sense of nervousness in the atmosphere. As we were waiting for the meeting, another doctor came up to Dr. Muñoz; her face held tension and her words poured out quickly, like water gushing from a faucet. She said she was nervous because the committee was going to "name names." I didn't know what that meant, but it soon became clear. The committee members were seated on the stage and introduced one at a time; one of the health ministry's administrators then stood up to report the results of an evaluation. I was awaiting a long-drawn-out introduction, as would have been likely in the United States, but instead he immediately began to name specific people who were found not to be doing their jobs, including such things as not renewing their license to practice medicine, not coming into work but collecting a paycheck, engaging in private practices interfering with work at the hospital, and having problems with supervising employees. Because I was still new at the hospital, I wasn't familiar with the names, but I was pretty sure they were people who either had too much power to care (i.e., were in stable positions) or were powerless anyway. Other problems mentioned included malfunctioning machines used for radiation treatment, broken air conditioning and elevators, and outdated equipment. According to the evaluation, only 30 of the 170 beds at the hospital were filled, because of the financial problems at the hospital. The director of the MSAS, Dr. Carlos Wálter, also spoke, stating that the goal of the report was to problem solve and not to persecute anyone, although the doctors who were grumbling and rolling their eyes certainly weren't convinced of that. Walter said that the people who had been named would have a chance to defend themselves and that he only wanted to see the problems resolved. He spoke of the need to look to the future and to improve the oncology hospital, to treat the sick "for the good of the nation." It was clear to me that placing the problems at the hospital on the shoulders of individual physicians was a way of deflecting the problems facing the ministry. Structural problems in health care emanating from the austerity programs of the 1980s that were then embraced again by the Carlos Andrés Pérez administration, could not be fixed by shaming doctors. The spectacle of the meeting could, however, provide a performative moment to perhaps circulate in the media showing that the ministry was "doing something."

The meeting provided insight not only into some of the problems facing the hospital but also into the relationship between hospital staff and the MSAS. After the meeting I spoke with some of the doctors in the gynecology and mammary departments who had attended. They said that the meeting presented no new information to them, that they knew of the problems in the hospital. Two of the doctors expressed that some of the committee members were hypocrites who had at one time worked with them at the hospital and had engaged in the same behaviors for which they had publicly castigated other doctors. The director of the gynecology department, who had been named in the report, stated that the report was "helpful" for the hospital but that the major problem was a lack of financial resources coming from the MSAS. It seemed that his use of the word *helpful* was for my benefit; his crossed arms and tight lips betrayed his use of that word. Later in the year, the subject of poor hospital funding from MSAS would come up again by an act that caused great animosity between hospital staff and the MSAS. The director of the MSAS donated money to the annual televised fund raiser of the Sociedad Anti-Cancerosa (Cancer Society), which oversees and finances the Padre Machado (the private hospital where I also conducted fieldwork). Many of the hospital staff at Razetti expressed disbelief, frustration, and a sense of betrayal (Razetti is run by the MSAS) that the MSAS would fund another oncology hospital while Razetti was experiencing such dire financial problems.

Immersion in the hospital setting (through observations, conversations, and attendance at meetings) provided a base from which I could then begin to interview patients and doctors. Before introducing the women and doctors who were interviewed, I provide in the next section a description of the private hospital where the comparative part of this research was conducted.

Oncological Hospital Padre Machado

After almost three months at the Razetti, I began the comparative portion of my research at the Oncological Hospital Padre Machado. I had previously visited this hospital in September 1993, during my preliminary field investigation. Like Razetti, Padre Machado is a referral hospital, but unlike Razetti, it is considered a private facility, although 12 percent of its annual US$4 million budget is allocated by the Venezuelan government. I was interested in comparing the treatment of patients at both hospitals, and I expected to find that the private hospital was better funded and could provide patients with better treatment than that of the public hospital. I also expected that patients at the public hospital would have access to fewer resources than those at the Padre Machado. However, both hospitals experienced economic problems and supply shortages. In addition, the patient profiles were rather similar, as both hospitals serviced a mostly working-class population. Because of the country's economic instability (high unemployment and inflation), both hospitals were also seeing some middle-class patients, who before the crisis could afford private health care.

Padre Machado is run by the Venezuelan nonprofit Sociedad Anti-Cancerosa (Cancer Society). The hospital receives private funding as well as some state monies, and in terms of its policy, it is supposed to treat anyone needing oncology care, whether he or she can afford the treatment or not. Therefore, the hospital does see many patients who cannot afford treatment at a private, for-profit clinic. The Cancer Society engages in various fundraising activities, principal of which is the annual televised fundraiser mentioned previously. Unfortunately, approximately 60 percent of the women who are treated there for cervical cancer come to the hospital in what are categorized as advanced stages of cancer.[1]

Padre Machado is located across the city from Razetti, on the outskirts of Caracas city and next to one of the largest cemeteries in the city, in an area known as El Cementerio (The Cemetery). Like Razetti, Padre Machado is located near a barrio. Looking out from the top floors of the hospital, one can see the numerous small houses cramped one on top of the other on the hillsides. Because of this density, the area where the hospital is located was described to me by some of the hospital staff and patients as dangerous. In fact, in the first week that I was there, one doctor arrived agitated, explaining that a man on a motorcycle had just attempted to grab the gold chain from around his neck. Similar stories emerged at this time from others (e.g., doctors, nurses, staff) attesting to the criminal activity in the area.

Physically, the composition of this hospital is very different from that of the Razetti. The Padre Machado is a four-story building and approximately twice the size of the Razetti. It is made of brick and concrete, with none of the picturesque qualities of the Razetti. As one enters the front of the building, there is a statue depicting one of the earlier machines used for radiation treatment.

The gynecology department is located on the second floor and shares a waiting area with at least four other departments, including head and neck, mammary, and plastic surgery. There is an iron gate separating the waiting area from the various departments. A guard stands at the gate and opens it when the secretary seated across from him calls out a person's name. I was required to wear a white medical coat at this hospital as well, but I was less hesitant about wearing it here because it acted as a passport, allowing me to get back and forth through the gate with ease. That was necessary, since I was interviewing the women in an office that was adjacent to the waiting room. The waiting area held about one hundred chairs. On my first day there, every chair was taken and people were standing against the walls. There must have been about 140 people waiting that day. One of the nurses told me that it was not uncommon to see the waiting room so full. I would see it similarly crowded many more times during my tenure at the hospital. In the waiting room, there was a television set on a shelf mounted to the wall. Just to the left, in juxtaposition to the television, was a statue of the Virgin Mary encased in glass and also mounted to the wall. Next to the statue there was a picture of a saint (San Ezequiel Moreno) with an inscription underneath that read "patrón de cáncer" (patron saint of cancer).

As does Razetti, the Padre Machado hospital has a religious foundation and history. According to one of the doctors, the hospital was originally established as a home or shelter where "cancer" patients came to die and were cared for by nuns. (It is not clear whether people were actually known to have had cancer or not—they more likely had an unknown terminal disease.) It was founded by a priest, Padre Machado (Father Machado), and was in its early days known as Hogar Padre Machado. It was not a hospital, but doctors, especially surgeons, began coming to treat the sick. After many years, it was established as a hospital, and many medical specialists came to treat patients as well as to conduct research and teach.[2] The hospital now has a three-year residency program, and to be admitted to it, doctors must have training in at least general surgery. The residency is in oncology, which is further divided into two areas: surgical and nonsurgical. Nuns are still active in the hospital. They fill various staff positions and are trained as nurses as well. On occasion one of the nuns, *la hermana* Ana, would volunteer in the gynecology department, running errands and assisting with patients.

The gynecology department consisted of five small exam rooms and a conference room that surrounded one large, central main room. As one entered through the main room, there was a reception desk to the left. This main room also contained a religious artifact (as in the waiting room). There was an eighteen-inch religious statue on a shelf mounted on the wall. The room had six desks and a chair on either side of each desk. The desks were up against the walls, three on each side, and were spaced approximately seven feet apart. There was normally a pile of medical charts on each desk, and as a patient was called in, she was led to the desk of the doctor who happened to be assigned her chart that day. The conference room, which housed one large table with chairs, was also used to accommodate patients and doctors in this way. That room was also used for weekly seminars, at which the residents were required to make presentations on assigned topics. In addition, the doctors held *reuniones de médicos* (to discuss difficult cases, as at Razetti) on Wednesday afternoons. The main room also had two sinks where they could wash their hands after examining patients. Doctors could also wash in the restroom next to the reception desk. The restroom had a sign on it: Baño de Médicos (Doctors' Restroom).

The importance of this sign was made clear to me one day when I escorted one of the patients to the restroom, a woman who I had interviewed. She was in dire need of a restroom and the one in the waiting area was out of service, so I told her to go ahead and use the doctors' restroom. She was reluctant because it was the doctors' restroom, but since she was obviously desperate, I told her to use it. When she left, a nurse told me that the restroom was strictly off limits to patients. She explained that some of the patients have infections that can be transmitted (to doctors) by sitting on the same toilet seat after an "infected person" had used it. This portrayal of patients as potentially infectious and contaminating also implies danger and uncleanliness, characterizations that were later more subtly echoed (as I discuss in the next chapter) by doctors in their discussions of cervical cancer risk. Moreover, by "allowing" the patient to use the restroom, I suspect that I also breached a boundary that helps to maintain a division and hierarchy between doctor and patient.

The staff in the gynecology department included five *médicos adjuntos* (attending physicians) and various residents and *pasantes* (those doing short three-month rotations at the hospital). The *jefe de servicio* (department head) was a woman, but she was the only female attending physician in the department. There was also one female resident. Most of the doctors in the department were male. There were five female nurses, one of whom had worked at the hospital for more than twenty years. She was a quiet woman in her midfifties who, I would learn later from other staff, was known to at times take into her home some of the patients who came for treatments and could not afford to stay at a hotel. As at the Razetti, some of the doctors were there for three-year residencies in surgical oncology, and others were there for three- or six-month rotations (*pasantías*) in the training program with Maternidad Santa Ana.

The routine at Padre Machado requires that patients first go to *triaje* (triage). The doctor in triage gives the patient a general physical exam and sends him or her to a specific oncology department depending on the problem. This is the same routine discussed earlier for patients at the Razetti. However, at Padre Machado the patients do not routinely see a social worker. A social worker is usually consulted by only those patients who have difficulty affording the treatment and/or hospitalization costs. In those cases, a hospital staff person (normally a nurse, doctor, or secretary) directs the patient to the social worker, who determines how much the patient can pay and develops a payment schedule. Unlike the Razetti, the role of the social worker at Padre Machado was mainly administrative, focusing on the financial obligations of the patient. In fact, one of the patients I later interviewed said that at first she was hesitant to respond to my question about monthly income for fear that I was affiliated with the hospital and would somehow use the information to increase her payments. I always introduced myself to the women that I interviewed and assured them that I was not affiliated with the hospital and that their information would remain confidential. Because this particular woman appeared hesitant to respond to that question, I kept reassuring her throughout the interview that all information was confidential. By the end of the interview she was very open with all of the questions I was asking her. We became friendly, and I stayed in touch with her on a personal level throughout my fieldwork in Caracas. Her name is Francisca, and I introduce her story in chapter 3.

I will include more descriptions of both hospitals in later chapters as they become relevant. This general introduction of the hospitals is followed in the next section by an explanation of interview and observation methods. The final portion of this chapter is dedicated to demographic descriptions of the patients and doctors whom I interviewed.

Interviews and Observations

The sample population of patients and doctors was drawn from both hospitals (Razetti and Padre Machado). The sample of patients depended largely upon the availability of first-time patients admitted with cervical cancer. The interview language was Spanish, in which I am fluent. I conducted ethnographic interviews consisting of both open- and close-ended questions. The closed questions allowed me to gather pertinent demographic data (e.g., age, education, income, residence), and the open-ended questions allowed interviewees to develop their own categories of meaning rather than impose them a priori, and to explain their responses fully (Bernard 1988).

One of the initial goals of this research was to follow women who may have cervical cancer and their physicians throughout the treatment process. However, because of time constraints and organizational difficulties within the hospitals, the focus of this study was necessarily limited to women's first appointments at the hospitals. These constraints are elaborated on in a later section. Some women, though, were interviewed informally when possible during subsequent appointments at the hospitals, to gain some insight into the progression (or lack thereof) of their medical treatment.

In addition, because of the ambiguous nature of diagnosing cervical cancer, not all the women interviewed for this project were necessarily diagnosed with cervical cancer. Many had been referred to the hospital with no clear diagnosis, only Pap smear results indicating "abnormal" or "suspicious" cells. These results might have been found later to be precancerous, noncancerous, or cancerous. One difficulty in diagnosing cervical cancer is that the biomedical understanding of "abnormal" or "suspicious" cervical cells is not clear. Posner (1991, 173) elaborates this point: "While changes in the cervical cells resulting in an abnormal cervical smear may produce no clinical abnormality, they are recognized to be statistically and prognostically abnormal. . . . The evidence is that a proportion of cell changes, if left untreated, will regress spontaneously; a proportion will remain the same; and a proportion (approximately a third) will develop into an invasive carcinoma over a period of some years. In each particular case it is not possible to know what will happen." This lack of clarity in the meaning of "abnormal" cervical cells and the potential of being diagnosed with cancer is an integral part of understanding what the women go through as they seek treatment for what for many is an unnamed affliction. Whether or not the women whom I interviewed were actually diagnosed with cervical cancer is not of paramount importance to this project. What is of concern is understanding what women go through as they seek treatment—be it for cancer, precancer, or some other "problem" (e.g., abnormal or suspicious cells) for which they have no name. This lack of a name for their affliction carries with it anxieties of its own, which I discuss in depth in another section.

The interviews were geared toward understanding beliefs and perceptions about cervical cancer and various aspects of the treatment process, as well as toward examining larger questions of power, medicine, and knowledge, and the ways these are implicated in the construction of a "woman's disease" and the control of women's lives. First, patients were interviewed before seeing the physician for the first time. Next, the patient-doctor interaction was observed during this first visit. Finally, the patient was interviewed immediately after seeing the physician.

The interviews with physicians explore their perceptions of treatments. I compare physicians' beliefs with those of their patients. I also trace how doctors seek to relate aspects of their patients' social locations to the progress of their illness—and, specifically, how they link poverty or perceived "backwardness" to the illness.

A key part of my research—observing patient-doctor interaction in the treatment process—also entailed use of the ethnographic method of participant observation in the hospital setting (Jorgensen 1989). I also observed patients and doctors informally in various hospital settings (e.g., waiting rooms) in addition to engaging in more directed observations during examinations and treatments; patient-doctor confidentiality was of course taken into account, and I received the proper permission from patients and doctors before beginning such observations. In this latter setting I tape recorded conversations between the doctor, patient and other medical personnel who were present. This method has been used successfully by Waitzkin (1993) to see the type of knowledge that doctors share with patients, how they share it, and which knowledge is not shared. These types of questions will help illuminate the relations among power, medicine, and knowledge.

Time was also devoted to gathering information on public health programs for the prevention of cervical cancer. This has allowed me to explore the kinds of images used in "targeting" women for intervention programs. This section of the research is not intended to be an exhaustive study of public health programs; the intention is only to explore the ways in which cultural images and meanings are implicated in public health discourses of cervical cancer prevention. I interviewed public health administrators to examine how their views contribute to social configurations of cervical cancer so that I could locate the interconnections of medical knowledge and public health. In effect, I looked at the ways medical power is exercised through discourses of public health, which may ultimately carry over into policies affecting the treatment of women with cervical cancer.

The combination of methods described here—interviews, participant observation, and archival research—has allowed for macrohistorical understandings of conceptions of cervical cancer found in public health documents, as well as micro-level understandings obtained through interviews with patients, doctors, medical personnel, and public health administrators. In addition, the observation of interactions of patients, doctors, and medical personnel provided an arena for understanding the forms that power takes not only in responses generated from interviews but also in observable actions (and inaction).

After my fieldwork, I monitored news of the hospitals in online news. In 1997, the situation had gotten so bad at Razetti that an article dated June 9 in *El Universal* declared that new appointments at the hospital were to be suspended until November. However, the next day the same paper quoted the director of the hospital as saying that all patients who came to the hospital would be treated, even though she did acknowledge that the hospital was having dire financial problems, which occasionally caused the gynecology department to suspend appointments. The hospital continued struggling to keep its doors open in the face of economic upheaval, but it remained open as of 2017. The president of the Razetti Medical Society was quoted as saying, "This is the only hospital that did not abide by the medical strike. All cancer cases are emergencies and cannot be left unattended."[3]

Patients

I interviewed a total of forty-five patients. Twenty-five of the women were patients at the public hospital (Razetti) and twenty were from the private hospital (Padre Machado). Most of the women were born in Venezuela. Two were Colombian and one was Ecuadorian. I present the demographic information for the patients at the public and private hospitals separately for purposes of comparison.

Among the women who sought treatment at the Razetti (public hospital), most came from Caracas or were within a two-and-a-half-hour bus or car ride to the city. However, seven of the women did travel four or more hours by bus to get to the hospital. Nineteen (76 percent) of the women came from urban areas. Only four (16 percent) of the women described their communities as a small town (*pueblo*), and two (8 percent) said they came from *ranchos* or *campos* (countryside or rural areas).

The mean and median age of the women was forty years, with a range from twenty to sixty-four. Their years of formal schooling were on average 6.7, which represents completion of primary school education (six years) plus almost one year of secondary education.

The mean monthly income for the women was US$172 (29,174 bolivares, bs.) and ranged from $6 (1,000 bs.) to $353 (60,000 bs.), with a median monthly income of $150 (25,500 bs.).[4]

Forty percent of the women (ten) were married, 24 percent (six) were living with a partner, 16 percent (four) were divorced, 8 percent (two) were separated, another 8 percent (two) were single, and 4 percent (one) was widowed.

When asked about their occupations, many of the women (44 percent) described themselves as homemakers. Three (12 percent) worked in the informal sector, selling clothes out of their homes, and another three (12 percent) worked in positions of management. Other occupations included student, waitress, seamstress, and nurse. For a complete list and breakdown of the women's various occupations see Appendix 1.

In the earlier interviews among the patients at Razetti, I erroneously excluded the question of religious background. Given that more than 90 percent of the Venezuelan population is Catholic, I (correctly) assumed that most of the women would be Catholic. Unfortunately, I did not anticipate the degree to which a less common but increasingly popular religion among the working class, that of Jehovah's Witness, might affect a woman's illness experience in terms of medical treatment. It was not until I interviewed a woman who was a Jehovah's Witness that the question of religion took on great importance. This woman, Beatriz Tellez, had great difficulty getting the type of treatment she needed (surgery) because her religion dictates that she not be given blood transfusions. Beatriz's experience is discussed at length in another section of this work. However, I mention her here because it was only after her interview that I began asking the women specifically about religion. Therefore, the data set for this question resulted in the following: thirteen missing values, nine Catholic, two Evangelical Christian, and one Jehovah's Witness.

The other group of women I interviewed were patients at the private hospital (Padre Machado). The majority of these women came from Caracas or other urban areas within a two-hour drive of Caracas. Only four women described their communities as *pueblos*, or small towns. None of them lived in the countryside or in rural areas. Unlike some of the women at Razetti none of these women had traveled more than three hours to reach the hospital. Their ages ranged between twenty and seventy, with a mean age of 38 years and median age of 34.5. The women's years of formal education ranged from zero to twelve; the mean years of formal education were 7.05, only slightly higher than that of the women at Razetti.

However, the mean monthly income for women patients at Padre Machado, at US$255 (43,316 bs.), was significantly higher than that of the women at the public Razetti. The range of incomes for the Padre Machado patients was between $59 (10,000 bs.) and $588 (100,000 bs.), with a median monthly income of $235 (40,000 bs.).

In terms of marital status, 40 percent of women fell into the category "living together." Thirty-five percent of the women were married, 15 percent were single, and 10 percent were separated. None of the women were widowed or divorced.

As with the patients at the public hospital, the majority of the women at Padre Machado, 65 percent, described their occupation as homemaker. They described fewer occupations than the patients at the public Razetti (see Appendix 2). In addition, 25 percent of the women at the private hospital worked as housekeepers, a job not mentioned by public hospital patients.

The majority of the women at Padre Machado said that they were Catholic, one woman was Evangelical Christian, and four of the values are missing.

Appendix 3 compares mean age, income, and formal education for the women at the public and private hospitals. The variable with the greatest disparity is that of mean monthly family income ($172 and $255, respectively). Mean ages (forty and thirty-eight years, respectively) and years of formal education (6.70 and 7.05, respectively) are similar.

Moreover, the women's responses to the interview questions did not suggest any significant differences between the two groups. One reason for this is that the patients at the public hospital encompass not only the poor but the middle-class as well. Venezuela's economic and political problems over the 1980s and 1990s forced the middle class to seek health care at public institutions because they could no longer afford the cost of private health care. In addition, because the private hospital, where part of this research was conducted, actually teeters somewhere between private and public (it receives some public health funding), the population of patients at both hospitals was similar. Thus, when presenting the patients' interview data, I do not draw distinctions between the public and private hospitals, except in those cases where it may be relevant to do so.

Doctors

I interviewed a total of seventeen doctors, ten from Padre Machado and seven from Razetti. Fourteen of the doctors were male, and three were female. All the doctors were Venezuelan born. Their ages ranged from twenty-nine to forty-nine years, with a mean of 37.6 years. They had a mean monthly income of $1,732 (294,412 bs.), which ranged from $324 (55,000 bs.) to $4,118 (700,000 bs.). The median monthly income was $1,294 (220,000 bs.). Most of the doctors were married (ten), four were single, and three were divorced. Mean education was 22.5 years. A profile of each one of the doctors is broken down into two tables according to type of hospital (Appendixes 4 and 5).

For the one female and six male doctors at the Razetti, their ages ranged between twenty-nine and forty-nine years, with a mean of thirty-nine. Their years of education ranged between 18 and 27, with a mean of 22.1. Three of the doctors were married, two were divorced, and two were single. Their mean monthly income was $1,874 (318,580 bs.), with a broad range between $706 (120,00 bs.) and $4,118 (700,000).

Two of the ten doctors interviewed at Padre Machado were female. The doctors ranged in age from 32 to 74 years, with a mean of 32.8. Mean years of education were 22.7, with a range from 19 to 27. Again, the majority of the doctors were married (seven), two were single, and one was divorced. Monthly incomes ranged between $324 (55,000 bs.) and $2,941 (500,000 bs.), with a mean monthly income of $1,632 (277,500 bs.).

Appendix 6 compares mean age, mean monthly income, and years of formal education for the doctors at both hospitals. The profiles of the doctors at both hospitals were very similar. In fact, three of the doctors worked at both hospitals. Two of them were *pasantes* (doing short-term rotations at the hospital) who had done a prior rotation at Razetti before I interviewed them at Padre Machado. One of the doctors was a *médico adjunto* (attending doctor) at both hospitals concurrently. The medical backgrounds of the doctors at both the public and the private hospitals are also similar (Appendix 6).

In addition, most (fifteen) of the doctors stated their religion as Catholic. The exceptions were a forty-nine-year-old male who had no religious affiliation and a thirty-two-year-old male who was a Jehovah's Witness. Interestingly, the latter doctor, an OB/GYN resident at another hospital, was very concerned that the other doctors would find out his religion; he was worried that they would ridicule him. I reassured him that all the information he provided would remain confidential. Because their religion prohibits them from receiving blood transfusions, being a Jehovah's Witness places him in an awkward position with other colleagues, as he felt they might belittle his belief. His concern was likely well founded, given that most of his colleagues are surgeons, who place great value in blood transfusions for their practice.

All the doctors whom I interviewed graduated with the medical title *médico cirujano*, or surgical doctor. However, they all pointed out that the title does not necessarily mean that they are trained as surgeons. In fact, they explained that the title is misleading and actually reflects training in general medicine. Most of the doctors, however, did have surgical training. Sixty percent of the doctors at the private hospital had medical specializations in general surgery. In addition, 67 percent also had specializations (or were in the process of specializing) in either gynecological or surgical oncology (see Appendix 7).

At the public hospital, the medical backgrounds of the doctors were similar to those at the private hospital. Seventy-one percent of doctors had specializations in general surgery. All but one, who was in the process of specializing in surgical oncology at the hospital at the time of this research, had specializations in surgical oncology as well. In addition, all but one of the doctors that I interviewed at Razetti and Padre Machado were trained in Venezuela. The exception was a forty-seven-year-old male doctor, who had studied medicine in Brazil and then specialized in general surgery and later surgical oncology in Caracas. Two of the doctors also had some short-term training outside of Venezuela. One was a forty-three-year-old male doctor who had taken a one-month course in France in laparoscopic surgery. At the time of this research, he was in the process of applying for a surgical resident fellow program in the United States. The other doctor, a forty-six-year-old male, completed a six-month program in gynecological oncology in Houston, Texas.

In addition to working at either the Razetti or the Padre Machado, all but one of the doctors worked concurrently at other hospitals and/or private practices. The *médicos adjuntos* tended to work in private practice, while the residents tended worked at other state hospitals. At Razetti, for example, two of the doctors (IDs 205r and 211r; see Appendix 9 for workweek hours) were also residents at Hospital Maternidad Santa Ana, where they were specializing in gynecology and obstetrics at the time of this research. They were required to work a shift of approximately twenty hours one day a week at that hospital in addition to their rotation at Razetti. They were doing a three-month rotation at the Razetti as part of their training to learn how to administer a Pap exam and biopsy and to spot potentially cancerous lesions.

The doctors' mean workweek at Razetti was twenty-six hours. Their total mean workweek (including other hospitals and private practice) was fifty-one hours. Additionally, the amount of time the doctors had worked at Razetti at the time of this research ranged from one month to twenty years. The doctors doing *pasantías* of course had been there the least amount of time and the *médicos adjuntos* had been there the longest.

For the private Padre Machado, the workweek hours are summarized in Appendix 10. Mean hours at Padre Machado were thirty-eight per week—twelve hours more per week on average than those at Razetti. This difference in hours is likely at least in part a reflection of the better funding available to Padre Machado. Unlike Razetti, Padre Machado has functioning radiation machines. Because of this, doctors there see a greater number of patients than at the Razetti, where at the time of this research radiation treatment was unavailable. (Although I would be hesitant to describe the conditions at Padre Machado as good, as the hospital also lacked basic supplies.) The doctors' work hours ranged anywhere from fourteen hours to seventy per week. The total mean workweek (including at other hospitals and private practice) was fifty-seven hours. As with the Razetti, the amount of time the doctors had been working at the Padre Machado ranged greatly from one week to twelve years. Again, this difference is indicative of the positions that the doctors hold in the hospital, with *médicos adjuntos* having long-term positions and residents having short-term placements.

In terms of analyzing data from both hospitals, as with the patients, distinctions are made between the two groups of doctors only where relevant. However, what is of interest for this work is the extent to which patients are treated differently by doctors in the two hospital settings. This is explored in later chapters.

Next Steps

In this chapter I have given an account of my early experiences in the field and an outline of some important contemporary social, political, and economic issues for Venezuelan society in order to place this research in context. I also provided descriptions of the hospitals where this fieldwork was conducted and demographic information on those whom I interviewed. The next chapter will focus on doctors' and patients' perceptions of risk for cervical cancer. A discussion of risk is important for laying out the ways in which cervical cancer is configured in Venezuela and for understanding how people or groups are perceived in relation to this disease, bringing to the forefront questions of power, control, medicine, and morality. The following chapter on cervical cancer risk also sets up the analysis of public health and cervical cancer in Chapter 3 and provides insight into understanding doctor-patient interactions in the medical encounter, which are explored in Chapter 4.

2 The Ambiguities of Risk
Morality, Hygiene, and the "Other"

> Cultural theory brings us somewhat nearer to understanding risk perception.... Instead of isolating risk as a technical problem we should formulate it so as to include, however crudely, its moral and political implications.
> *Mary Douglas (1992, 51)*

Culture and Risk

In her monograph *Risk and Blame*, Mary Douglas (1992) points to the domain of health "risks" as an area in need of problematizing within an anthropological framework. She argues for locating scientific risk factors within a wider social, cultural, and political climate. Similarly, Tesh (1988:3) notes: "The point is not that values contaminate science. Instead there is an inextricable interrelationship between facts and values.... I argue not that values be excised from science and from policy but that their inevitable presence be revealed and their worth be publicly discussed." Health "risk" is one area in which this interrelationship between facts and values is being examined.

The study of risk from an anthropological perspective is gaining importance as scholars address the cultural construction of various languages of risk: epidemiological, clinical, and lay (Balshem et al. 1992; Frankenberg 1993; Kaufert and O'Neil 1993; Gifford 1986). Gifford (1986), in particular, has focused on the ambiguities in lay versus medical definitions of breast cancer risk. She argues that "it is more appropriate to speak of a 'language of risk' in that the term is used to convey a constellation of meanings some of which are intended and some of which remain largely unconscious" (214). This attention paid to the study of risk—with social, political, and cultural implications—opens up opportunities for exploring the ways in which risk factors may reflect moral beliefs about proper and acceptable behaviors. Critical analyses of risk should regard the classifications of risk not simply as descriptive taxonomies of naturally occurring phenomenon but rather as ideologically produced conceptual systems whose history and political function can be uncovered.[1] Such a critical perspective seeks to understand the sociohistorical context in which risk is constructed, and in that way question the taken-for-granted assumptions that arise in interpretations of epidemiological profiles of risk of disease.

Historically, morality played a central role in medical definitions of risk of disease. As Turner (1984, 264) has noted, "Health depended on morality because improper lifestyles constituted the root of personal illness and the immorality of the individual was a product of social disorder." As a consequence, the explicit and implicit prescriptions for health were based on a moral lifestyle.

While contemporary medical researchers and doctors have consciously moved away from issues of morality and have focused on the biological functioning of the body, it is still apparent that morality plays a key role in the medical language of risk in sexually transmitted diseases, such as AIDS (Farmer 1992). For example, scholars have analyzed discursive constructions of sexually transmitted diseases such as syphilis, gonorrhea, and AIDS (Sturma 1988; Fee 1989; Farmer 1992). In doing so, they have addressed questions of risk, blame, hygiene, and morality with which these diseases have come to be associated (Turner 1984; Farmer 1992). As Brandt and Rozin (1997, 5) note, "Cultural beliefs and practices about disease are revelatory of a society's most basic moral beliefs and practices. The meanings and moral configurations, in turn, have a dramatic impact on both the care of those who are sick and on broader social and political policies."

However, little attention has been paid to the ways in which cervical cancer, in particular, seems to move between concepts of contagion (as an STD) on the one hand and incommunicability (as cancer) on the other. Given the accepted epidemiological risk factors for cervical cancer (e.g., HPV, sex at an early age and multiple sexual partners), this study looks at how risk, blame, and morality figure into social constructions of cervical cancer and how they may extend from interactions of patients, doctors, and medical personnel into the lives of women in subtle and pervasive ways.

Hygiene and Risk

Histories of medical science have shown us the methods of classification that medical science has developed to control not only disease but also the people who are categorized as potential agents of disease. Medical notions of hygiene, in particular, have been historically linked to processes of colonization and modernization (Anderson 1992; Comaroff and Comaroff 1992; Burke 1996). In speaking of Western Europe during the first half of the nineteenth century, Burke (1996, 22) notes:

> In England, cleanliness was an important part of an interlocking network of Victorian and Edwardian figurations of bodily propriety, purity, sanitation, sexuality, medicine and domesticity, a network with powerful formative influence on class, national, gender and religious identity. . . . The intensive promotion of various forms of social and personal hygiene in England was distinctly the product of what Frank Mort has called the 'medico-moral politics' of the nineteenth and twentieth centuries. These politics produced new images and ideals, such as the depiction of the new working classes as 'unwashed' and the envisioning of women as the guardians of domestic space.

In this case, class and gender played important roles in delineating who and what counted as clean—and therefore dirty—and also whose task it was to monitor hygiene and morality: women. Who better than women, it was argued, should recognize the importance of maintaining cleanliness and thus orderliness?

In contemporary times, the linking of morality and cervical cancer has been receiving increasing attention. In a recent study of public health campaigns to decrease rates of cervical cancer, Posner (1991, 181) suggests that the medical risk factors for cervical cancer are interconnected with issues of morality, stating: "The physical state of a woman's cervix has been taken as a reflection of her sexual history, her integrity as a woman bound up with the integrity of her cervix. Examining the state of the cervix has been a process of revealing hidden defects and symbolically exposing secret transgressions—magnified for medical examination." Similarly, Martínez, Chavez, and Hubbell (1997) explored the moral dimension of physicians' and women's beliefs surrounding the risk factors for cervical cancer. They found that physicians' perceptions of risk at times included moral judgments about women's behavior. When listing risk factors, their use of the term *promiscuity*, as opposed to *multiple sexual partners*, in particular, suggested the value-laden nature of the discourse surrounding this disease.

If we are to understand the construction of hygiene as a medicalized risk factor, we must first understand hygiene as concept mediated by culture. Douglas's (1966) work has had a profound impact on our understanding of hygiene and the body as products of culture. I argue, as does Douglas, that "the unclean is a by-product of our classification of the world; things that do not fit in, or things in the wrong place" (Douglas, as cited in Linde-Laursen 1993, 277). However, unlike Douglas, who argues that that which represents the unclean is also that which escapes classification, I argue that in classifying cleanliness, one also binds into classification that which is unclean (i.e., by-products are also classifications).

Hygiene has figured in medical discourses of cervical cancer risk (Herrero et al. 1990; Jayant et al. 1987). In a study of cervical cancer risk, medical researchers pointed to the role of the personal hygiene of women in risk of cervical cancer (Herrero et al. 1990; Jayant et al. 1987). Interestingly enough, these studies focus on personal hygiene in Latin America and India. The possible connection of hygiene to cervical cancer appears to be of concern only in so-called underdeveloped regions. Researchers in India stated the importance of investigating hygiene in relation to cervical cancer: "In the etiology of cervical cancer, personal hygiene of the woman is one of the factors believed to be of importance. However, there is hardly any data on this aspect" (Jayant et al. 1987, 47)." Why hygiene is believed to be of importance, however, is left unstated. Similarly, researchers in Latin America argued with respect to hygiene that "few studies have analyzed the role of specific factors in this region" (Herrero et al. 1990, 380).

Although one might argue that the basis for such an analysis of risk is rooted in "scientific" concerns for the advancement of etiological knowledge—which I do not propose to contest or support—questions of how and why it is that this risk factor is associated with particular geographical locations is unclear. Why is it that personal hygiene is not a concern in "developed" countries? Again, one could argue that underdeveloped countries lack resources such as clean water, adequate sewage, and so on, and therefore make hygiene of tantamount concern in relation to cervical cancer. However, by treating these categories of "developed" and "underdeveloped" as homogeneous and *natural* units of analysis, we ignore the fact that resources and lack of resources have no bounds—both are found in so-called developed and underdeveloped areas. I suggest that a more fruitful avenue of analysis would seek to understand how these categories of "underdevelopment" and "third world" come to be associated with notions of disorderliness, uncleanliness, and general backwardness. In this way, we can conceptualize hygiene not as an essentialized and objective category, but as a category with historical, political, and sociocultural referents (Butler 1993).

In analyzing representations of hygiene from a cultural perspective, we need to reconsider the naturalness and determinism of the concept of hygiene, particularly as it relates to medicalized risk. Only in this way will it be possible to uncover the ways that scientific and authoritative definitions of hygiene intersect with and mask such categorizations as "modern" versus "traditional," "first world" versus "third world," and "developed" versus "underdeveloped," among others.

I return my attention to the study conducted in Mumbai (at the time Bombay; Jayant et al. 1987) by the Epidemiology Unit of the Cancer Research Institute at Tata Memorial Centre to begin to consider some of the questions posed here. The research looked at personal hygiene in groups with varied cervical cancer rates. Two hundred women belonging to a low socioeconomic group were interviewed. According to the study, there are differences in cervical cancer rates among several religious groups: the age-adjusted rate for Hindus is 27.7 percent (per 100,000), for Muslims it is 15.7, and for Christians it is 17.7. The researchers' questions elicited information on the availability of clean water, daily bathing, bathing in the nude, bathing in an enclosed bathroom, washing genitals, washing after micturition, removal of pubic hair, washing after coitus, daily bathing during menstruation, and abstinence from intercourse during menstruation. Women were also asked about the personal hygiene of their husbands: whether they bathe in an enclosed bathroom, wash before and after coitus, and whether they are circumcised. The researchers concluded that the role of women's hygiene in the etiology of cervical cancer has perhaps only a minimal role in the evolution of the disease, but they emphasized that further research needs to be done in this area. No consistent associations for risk were established for the specific hygienic practices described above.

Another study of hygiene practices, sexual behavior, and venereal diseases was carried out in "high-risk populations" in four Latin American countries: Costa Rica, Panama, Mexico, and Colombia (Herrero et al. 1990). The authors pointed out that most of the epidemiological research on cervical cancer up to that point had been conducted in developed countries, which have seen a significant decline in rates over the past fifty years. Moreover, few studies have looked at the role of specific risk factors in Latin America, which continues to be a "high-risk area for invasive cervical cancer" (Herrero et al. 1990, 380). In this study investigators asked women with invasive cervical cancer and controls about their sexual behavior, histories of specific venereal diseases, and hygiene practices. In terms of the latter, they were asked about frequency of bathing, frequency of washing the genital area, frequency of washing the genital area during menstruation, use of sanitary napkins during menstruation, use of tampons during menstruation, and douching practices. The authors concluded that hygiene practices do not play a significant role in the etiology of cervical cancer. Only the frequent washing of the genitals during menstruation was associated with a reduced risk. However, they also found an increased risk in women who washed their genitals more than twice a day. This incongruous finding was explained as a possible reflection of "increased sexual activity" (1990, 385). Hygiene, therefore, in the latter case, is thought to signal increased sexual activity, which would explain the increased risk associated with washing one's genitals more than twice a day. What may be described as excessive hygiene, then, is assumed to correspond with heightened sexual activity. The one way in which the authors chose to interpret this finding (they offer no other possible explanation) is to focus on women's sexual behavior. In the end, the authors concluded: "The high incidence of cervical cancer in Latin America is probably influenced by the lack of adequate cytological screening programs and the high prevalence of early sexual activity" (1990, 385). Hygienic practices, then, do not appear to play a large role in the etiologic profile of cervical cancer.

However, both studies leave unclear the question of why the hygienic practices of women in "underdeveloped" areas such as India and Latin America are of particular concern. Studies of hygiene and cervical cancer risk among women in "developed" countries do not seem to be of equal interest. I suggest that this difference in the approach to hygiene and cervical cancer is at some level related to the ways in which developed, underdeveloped, and developing regions are conceptualized. The so-called third-world poor, in particular, are often configured as unhealthy, backward, disorderly, and unhygienic—concepts that have also been associated with regional descriptions of the third world. In other words, it is in "underdeveloped" areas that hygiene is conceptualized as problematic. These categories carry powerful meanings that are used in the construction not only of regions and nations but also of people.

That representations of hygiene and pollution are linked in opposition, through relationships of power, to those essentialized and taken-for-granted constructions that are the so-called third and first worlds has not been adequately addressed. We must understand why and how it is that concerns for proper hygiene and cleanliness manifest in relation to distinctions made among class, race, first versus third world, and developed and underdeveloped. The problem with these classifications is that they serve to essentialize and to create distinct bounded entities that have no referents to social, historical, and political interconnections between the ostensibly discrete objects. As Coronil (1996, 52) has noted, "Although it is not always clear to what these terms refer, they are used as if there existed a distinct external reality to which they corresponded, or at least they have the effect of creating such an illusion." The resulting classifications are not simply a problem of labeling or naming; they speak to larger questions of representation and control.

As Foucault (1970), and later Anderson (1991) have argued, labels are historical constructions that become concretized. At the core of such labeling are efforts to control. Orders of classification do not exist naturally in the world but are created as "natural" orders, which serve as mechanisms of control for those in positions of power. In this way, people are restricted from moving in and out of identities because of the fixity of labels that use "tradition" or "backwardness" to mask histories of displacement and dispossession (Malkki 1995). At the same time, however, these categories of "underdeveloped," "natural," and "third world" also evoke idealized objects of development such that notions of change are coded in the language of modernization, progress, development, and education. Thus, movement and change are perceived as evolutionary trajectories.

If we are to understand the political, social, and cultural meanings and representations attached to cervical cancer in Venezuela, it is necessary to treat these meanings and representations as processual and discursive in nature. This includes, but is not limited to, deconstructing the languages of risk, morality, the body, modernization, third world, and underdevelopment.

The Body: An Anthropological Project

The body is not opposed to culture, a resistant throwback to a natural past; it is itself a cultural, the cultural, product.
E. A. Grosz (1994:23)

To continue with a discussion on the meanings and perceptions of cervical cancer risk, it is first necessary to problematize that object onto which discourses of risk are mapped: the body. In other words, risky behaviors get reconfigured as risky bodies and bodies at risk. As we shall see, the power to define risk is intimately tied to the power to define bodies.

In a review article, Lock (1993, 133) points out that the body has remained largely unproblematized in anthropological research despite its ostensible centrality to the "anthropological endeavor." According to Munn (1992, 93), the body's explicit appearance has been sparse and often "handmaiden to other anthropological frames and issues" (as cited in Lock 1993, 133)—even though (or perhaps because) its importance seems unquestionable given that "the body mediates all reflection and action upon the world." The body is also, as Mary Douglas (1970) has argued, a strong symbolic form.

Over the past few decades this lacuna is being addressed by those anthropologists and other scholars interested in theorizing the body not as a natural category but as a politicized terrain where power is exercised, contested, and resisted (Bordo 1997; Ryan and Gordon 1994; Lindenbaum and Lock 1993; Lock 1993; Haraway 1993; Arnold 1993; Schilling 1993; Butler 1993; Turner 1992; Comaroff and Comaroff 1992; Anderson 1992; Balshem 1991; Vaughn 1991; Jacobus, Keller, and Shuttleworth 1990; Martin 1990, 1987). It is necessary to introduce some theorizing on the body that is useful in addressing questions of power and control in the definition, and ultimately regulation of bodies (as described in Chapter 4).

Scholars of colonialism in particular have looked at questions of power within the historical particularities of colonial domination and the ways in which colonized bodies have been marked and defined in the process (Vaughn 1991; Comaroff and Comaroff 1992; Anderson 1992; Arnold 1993). These works focus at least partly on the role of medicine, both subtle and overt, in controlling and subjugating native populations through scientific discourses of biological difference. Comaroff and Comaroff (1992, 215), for example, argue that:

> the rising hegemony of biology in Europe can be read in the control of threatening populations at home and abroad—and, more generally, in the regulation

of relations between the "civil" and the "unruly." But the expanding empire also fed the new science with essential "raw material" and with a natural rationale for its emerging vision of physical man. As an object of European speculation, "the African" personified suffering and degeneracy, his environment a hothouse of fever and affliction.

This control of populations through biology was also fed, as they point out, by the construction of "African bodies" as "raw material," which also served to distance and differentiate white bodies from black bodies within a schema of evolutionary racism. Colonial studies in other parts of the world point to similar ideas about the body of the "Other" (Anderson 1992; Arnold 1993; Stoler 1997). For example, Warwick Anderson's (1992, 508) account of American colonization in the Philippines explores the ways in which laboratory medicine served as a tool in asserting scientific understandings of biological difference: "The Filipino emerged in this period as a potentially dangerous part of the zoological realm, while the American colonizer became a resilient racial type, no longer inevitably susceptible to the tropical climate but vulnerable to the crowd of invisible, alien parasites newly associated with native bodies."

These critiques center largely on the construction of the "native" or colonized body in juxtaposition to that of the colonizer through the creation of authoritative and "official" knowledge (Mani 1990; Vaughn 1991; Anderson 1992; Arnold 1993). This concept of official knowledge, taken from Mani (1990), helps conceptualize how medical and other "authoritative" knowledge of the body, particularly women's bodies and diseases, is constituted. Moreover, these accounts of colonial domination through constructions of biological difference may help illuminate contemporary conflicts surrounding representations of diseased bodies within a context of power relations. Because I analyze patient-doctor interaction during the treatment process, as well as public health campaigns to combat cervical cancer, questions of power, control, and conflict in the construction and dissemination of official knowledge are of direct relevance to this project.

In addition, I locate other "unofficial" or submerged discourses of the body, principally those of women patients. This locating of nonauthoritarian, submerged, or subjugated knowledge has been privileged by feminist scholars. As Haraway (1991, 190–191) argues:

> Many currents in feminism attempt to theorize grounds for trusting especially the vantage points of the subjugated; there is good reason to believe vision is

better from below the brilliant space platforms of the powerful. . . . The standpoints of the subjugated are not "innocent" positions. On the contrary, they are preferred because in principle they are least likely to allow denial of the critical and interpretative core of all knowledge.

Haraway refers to this "marked" and "partial perspective" of the subjugated as "situated knowledge." While she warns against a romanticization of this partial perspective, she also argues that this critical positioning can open up possibilities of meaning—as opposed to those totalizing perspectives that recognize only "unmarked" or dominant forms of knowledge. This approach allows for the illumination of a multiplicity of meanings of the body and for posing questions geared toward understanding the ways in which women's cultural perceptions of the body inform beliefs about illness.

Cervical Cancer Risk in Venezuela: Doctors' Beliefs

In interviews, physicians and patients mentioned a number of risk factors for cervical cancer. For both physicians and patients, some risk factors are consistent with those found in epidemiological studies of cervical cancer risk, whereas others are not.

At the time of my initial fieldwork in the mid 1990s, epidemiological studies had identified various behavioral risk factors associated with cervical cancer, most notably multiple sex partners and early age at first sexual intercourse (Franco 1991). Other risk factors found in this literature included smoking, low socioeconomic status, and multiparity. The consistent finding of an association of cervical cancer risk with sexual behavior suggested that a sexually transmitted infectious organism was the cause. Herpes simplex virus (HSV) and the human papillomaviruses (HPVs) have been the most investigated "suspects" (Herrero et al. 1990). As a result of the focus on these two sexually transmitted viruses as possible causal agents, cervical cancer was increasingly being categorized along with gonorrhea and syphilis as a sexually transmitted disease (Martínez, Chavez, and Hubbell 1997). Since then two types of HPVs have been found to account for 70 percent of all cervical cancers.

In Venezuela, the official profile of cervical cancer included those factors that "all epidemiological studies have demonstrated to be . . . unquestionably related to sexual activity" (MSAS 1987a:8). These are sex at an early age, sexual promiscuity of the woman or of her husband, and multiparity. The

MSAS publication mentions Stern's Italian study, which showed an absence of cervical cancer in nuns, to highlight the sexually transmitted nature of this disease. In addition, illiteracy, poverty, and "deficient hygienic habits" are described as indirectly related to the first set of factors (those having to do with sexual activity) because "they favor their existence." In other words, illiteracy, poverty, and deficient hygienic habits are thought to indirectly signal promiscuity, sex at an early age, and multiparity. The use of the phrase "deficient hygienic habits" is particularly vague, and no attempt is made to explain its meaning. Two other publications put out by the MSAS (1987b, 1991) included "deprived culture" and "low cultural level" in their profiles of cervical cancer. Risks having to do with hygiene and culture, in particular, are asserted and presented as common wisdom without clear explanations as to what the terms mean and without reference to the epidemiological literature. Underlying these risks is an implicit connection among class, behavior, and disease. The result is that an image is created of those who get cervical cancer: promiscuous, poor, and unhygienic women. Taken-for-granted associations are created, as promiscuity, sex at an early age, poverty, lack of hygiene, and lack of culture come to connote one another. As we will see, doctors in Venezuela also included the epidemiologically unsupported factors of lack of hygiene and low cultural level in descriptions of at-risk behaviors for cervical cancer.

The most frequently mentioned risks among the doctors I interviewed were sexually transmitted infections, promiscuity (or multiple sexual partners), sex at an early age, lack of personal hygiene, heredity, lack of medical attention, low socioeconomic status, and multiparity. For an overview of the risks, I combine the results for doctors at both hospitals (see table 2.1).

As one might expect, sexually transmitted infections are frequently cited by the doctors as a risk for cervical cancer. This risk includes infection with HPV, sexually transmitted infections (in general), infection with herpes, and recurrent venereal infections. All but two of the doctors included sexually transmitted infections as part of their etiological profile. In some cases, doctors mentioned more than one of these risks, which were coded as single responses under the larger category of "sexually transmitted infection" (see table 2.1 for the breakdown of sexually transmitted infection risks).

The most commonly mentioned risk was promiscuity or multiple sexual partners. As stated earlier, the sexually transmitted disease etiology for cervical cancer is correlated with the risk factor of multiple sexual partners. Medical research (most research having been done on women's sexual behaviors in

TABLE 2.1 Percentage of Doctors at Both Hospitals Who Mentioned Each Cervical Cancer Risk Factor

Risks	Doctors who mentioned each risk (N=17)	
1 Sexually transmitted infections	(15)	88%
Breakdown of sexually transmitted infections:		
Infection with HPV	(13)	76%
Sexually transmitted infection (general)	(05)	29%
Infection with herpes	(04)	24%
Repetitive venereal infections	(03)	18%
2 Promiscuity	(18)	106%[a]
3 Promiscuity of spouse or partner	(01)	6%
4 Sex at an early age	(09)	53%
5 Lack of personal hygiene	(08)	47%
6 Heredity	(08)	47%
7 Lack of medical attention	(08)	47%
8 Low social, cultural, economic status	(07)	41%
9 Multiparity	(06)	35%
10 Poor nutrition/immunological deficiency	(05)	29%
11 Smoking	(03)	18%
12 Birth control pills	(02)	12%
13 Black race	(02)	12%
14 Nul parity	(01)	6%
15 First time sexual relations late in life	(01)	6%
16 Male factor (semen)	(01)	6%
17 Medical contamination during surgery	(01)	6%

[a] One doctor included both promiscuity and a woman who has many husbands as separate responses.

relation to cervical cancer) suggests that sexually transmitted infections are more likely to occur among those women who have multiple sexual partners than among those in monogamous relationships (I return later to the problematic assumptions inherent in uncomplicated juxtapositions of monogamy and promiscuity) (Azocar et al. 1990). In other words, in terms of specific causal agents, sexually transmitted infections (i.e., certain strains of HPV and herpes) were the primary suspects, with multiple sexual partners being a secondary risk. Interestingly, although sexually transmitted infections were the primary suspects, two of the physicians I interviewed did not mention this risk, whereas none of them failed to mention promiscuity as a risk factor. In most cases the promiscuous behavior of the woman was implied. For example, this response by a thirty-eight-year-old male doctor at Razetti was typical in content of the doctors' replies when asked about the risk factors for cervical cancer:

> First, the infection by the human papillomavirus, it's a necessary condition but not sufficient. Two, . . . promiscuity, the more partners a woman has, the greater her risk of cancer. . . . Why? Because it's a statistical correlation. The patient who has more partners has a greater risk of acquiring cervical cancer. That is probably because they have a greater risk of being contaminated with an aggressive human papillomavirus. There are papillomaviruses that are more related with, that have the capacity to develop, to induce the production of tumors and others [human papillomaviruses] that don't.

In two cases, doctors added other variations of promiscuous behavior when discussing their beliefs of cervical cancer risk. For example, a thirty-three-year-old male doctor stated that in addition to a woman's promiscuous behavior, a promiscuous man could expose a woman to HPV and thus put her at risk for cervical cancer. In another case, a forty-four-year-old male doctor included "a woman who has many husbands" separately from his generally stated risk of promiscuity. Here, the emphasis is evidently placed on the "risky" sexual behavior of the woman.

Some of the doctors also brought up promiscuity in relation to low socioeconomic status in their discussions of cervical cancer risk. They described the poor as having many more sexual partners and, therefore, engaging in more promiscuous behavior than those from the middle or upper classes.

The characterization of the poor as sexually promiscuous has been commented on by various scholars. Many have focused on the discourses of sexual morality and disease in accounts of the colonizer and colonized (Whitehead 1995; Anderson 1992; Arnold 1993; Gilman 1988). Gender has been a key factor in these discussions, which, for the most part, point to the production of "native" women as pathologically promiscuous—as dangerous. In many cases, these constructs were a result of the medical discourses, which were used to construct and legitimate bodily difference. However, understandings of contemporary issues in the intersection of class relations, gender, public health, and disease need to be more adequately addressed.

The Venezuelan doctors' medical discourse of cervical cancer risk reveals the ways in which social class, gender, and disease overlap. For example, one thirty-eight-year-old male doctor commented on the relationship between low social status, promiscuity, and cervical cancer in the following way:

> They have multiple partners . . . they have a low socio-economic status, do you understand? Or in other words, they have more needs because they have to look for a partner or two and tomorrow another one. Their hygiene isn't adequate. They don't have orientation, it's a lack of understanding of what illness is.

It's not clear whether *needs* refers to a hypersexual drive or to a partner "needed" for economic stability. However, the next comment referencing hygiene leads me to believe that he was making a judgment about her sexuality, alluding to the promiscuity mentioned by all the doctors as a risk for cervical cancer. Coupling low-socioeconomic status with "needing" one partner after another in an imagined unending stream also plays to the idea that poor women are sexually out of control.

One of the doctors whom I got to know well was forty-four-year-old Dr. Cortez from Razetti. I ended up spending more time at this hospital because it is where I started my fieldwork, and it is also the group of people with whom I would sometimes go out to lunch. As a result, I got to know the doctors at Razetti better than those at Padre Machado. Dr. Cortez was younger than his gray and white hair indicated. He had an engaging personality and liked to joke around. Unfortunately, many of his jokes, not unlike some of the ones told by other male doctors, were sexual in nature and would today be considered sexual harassment in the workplace. At the same time, he was one of the doctors who consistently showed up at the hospital to treat patients and teach medical students. Recall the big meeting I described when I had first arrived at which doctors were being called out for missing work and collecting a paycheck. Dr. Cortez, like a majority of the attending physicians who had been at the hospital the longest, was resistant to my interviewing him. He kept putting me off until I was getting close to leaving for the United States. He told me:

> In the low class the patients can't go to a hospital, they can't constantly go and have gynecological check-ups and as a result, the risk of cancer increases in that patient and in fact in the low class is where you see promiscuity, you see the use of multiple husbands. Are we clear?

As his quotation suggests—and as will become more obvious below—poverty, as a risk factor, was often interwoven with other perceived risks, such as lack of hygiene, promiscuity, and multiparity.

A third risk factor, sex at an early age, is also correlated with multiple sex partners and sexually transmitted infections. The medical theory here is that the younger a person is when she has sexual relations, the greater number of lifelong partners she will have, as compared to those who start having sexual relations later in life. It is still not entirely clear what other role this risk might play in the etiology of cervical cancer. However, it has been suggested that the adolescent cervix, which is not fully developed, is susceptible to "coitus-related carcinogens" (Rotkin 1967, as cited in Herrero et al. 1990). Nonetheless, sex at an early age, multiple sexual partners, and sexually transmitted infections are all interrelated in this profile of cervical cancer. However, despite its wide recognition in the medical research, not all the doctors cited this risk. Only nine of the seventeen, or 53 percent (just over half), of the doctors mentioned sex at an early age in their free-form responses.

Moreover, it is unclear what sex at an early age actually means in medical and/or practical terms. A few of the doctors provided different interpretations as to what age is an "early" one for sexual relations. For example, one described sex at an early age as younger than fifteen. Another doctor placed the cutoff at younger than sixteen, and two other doctors stated a more conservative age of twenty. The others who mentioned this risk did not specify an age.

Lack of hygiene, a risk factor that is not epidemiologically supported, but is found in Venezuelan medical literature, was mentioned by eight of the seventeen doctors (47 percent). In their descriptions of this risk, they included such things as not douching or not washing the vaginal area properly, especially after menstruation, and at least one doctor included lack of medical examinations as an example of an unhygienic practice. Importantly, discussions of hygiene or, more specifically, lack of hygiene, sometimes referred to as *desaseo* (uncleanliness), were always centered on descriptions of the habits of the lower classes.

For example, the comments from a forty-four-year-old male doctor at Razetti reveal his perspective on social class and hygiene:

> DOCTOR: In the low social class is where you see dirtiness [*desaseo*] . . . also less medical control or no medical control.
> RM: What do you mean by dirtiness?
> DOCTOR: It's a lack of hygiene, little hygiene in that person.
> RM: Hygiene in what sense?
> DOCTOR: Douching, all of those things.

A thirty-two-year-old male *pasante* at the private hospital remarked similarly about the relationship among cancer, class, and hygiene:

> Generally, we speak of educational level, of formation. People of low economic status don't have the cultural level or understanding . . . or the hygienic habits, [they] lack daily genital cleanliness . . . not douching and washing themselves.

A thirty-four-year-old female *pasante* at the public hospital said:

> Well, really it depends on the cancer that we are talking about. The majority of cases are related to low socioeconomic factors, number one, and people of older age, this is in general because every cancer has its particularities, no? Bad hygienic habits, environmental factors . . . for example, there can be cancer in the lung like there can be cancer of the cervix, which results from promiscuity, *aginamiento* [many people living together in a cramped space], and these types of habits.

A thirty-three-year-old female resident at the private hospital who was doing a residency in surgical oncology stated:

> RM: What do you think can cause or increase the chances of a person getting cancer, cancer in general?
> DOCTOR: . . . some of the patients' habits like smoking, lack of hygiene, a diet rich in carbohydrates and fat, promiscuous sexual activity, lack of hygiene.
> RM: Lack of hygiene? In what sense?
> DOCTOR: Most importantly in a gynecological sense because already if a patient is promiscuous, has multiple sexual partners, the consequence can be a malignant disease. Not taking care of oneself, of having sexual activity with different [people] without using condoms, and not maintaining local hygiene. Also, the man's penis, lack of hygiene in the penis . . . hygiene is important, both internal and external.

The doctors who mentioned douching are of particular interest because that practice has been critiqued in gynecological medicine since the 1980s, as it disturbs the balance of vaginal flora and leads to infections and other health problems. Yet doctors in Venezuela regularly recommended it and linked its perceived absence among poor women to cervical cancer risk. Low socioeconomic status was also intertwined in many cases with other risks such as a lack of medical attention and poor nutrition or immunological deficiency.

The following exchange between myself and a thirty-three-year-old male doctor from Padre Machado illustrates these points:

> DOCTOR: Well, there's talk of a sexually transmitted disease, a virus, HPV, that is the human Papilloma . . . of course the sexually promiscuous comportment, that is, with various partners, that is a risk factor because there are more possibilities of exposing a given person to this virus that produces cancer. Right? There is also talk of the "at-risk partner." In that case, it's not the woman who has sexually promiscuous comportment but the man and he exposes her. Smoking. . . . Other factors as well, like nutrition, which is related to economic [factors]. I think this is more closely related to the factors I mentioned before . . . with everything, with sexual promiscuity, and sexual comportment that can transmit the virus.
>
> RM: These things are related to what?
>
> DOCTOR: To low socioeconomic status . . . with one, two, three, and also seven.
>
> RM: So then, related to low socioeconomic status? They have more partners?
>
> DOCTOR: [Nods] And more pregnancies . . . yes, its more frequent that they have, the women at least in this country, that they have a social comportment that is more or less epidemic. She has a partner and has children with him. This one leaves her and then she gets another partner who demands that she have his children for him to stay with her and she has another one [child], one or two children. This partner leaves and now she has four children. She gets another partner who demands that she have his children. She already has four, now she has to have one of his . . . the result is many children, many partners and no stability, instability.

Another doctor, a forty-nine-year-old male, characterized cancer in relationship to poverty in a similar fashion:

> Any type of person can get cancer, there are some cancers that have a predisposition in certain types of people. For example, genital cancers are more frequent in low socio-economic groups. Maybe in this low socioeconomic group the majority of the risk factors that can lead to cancer, for example cervical cancer, conjoin. The people who are in a low socioeconomic position have more offspring, many more offspring, they give birth much more than those people from an elevated socioeconomic class. The possibility of multiple partners, many companions is seen more in the low social class than in the upper class.

> The possibility of genital infections from a lack of care, because of a lack in the ability to treat it, is seen more in the low class than in the upper class.

For another doctor, a forty-three-year-old male, poverty, promiscuity, hygiene, and cervical cancer become almost self-referential, as is evident in his response to the question of who gets cancer. He said the following:

> In Venezuela almost all the poor people get cancer. The people who are immunodeprived, that have poor nutrition, that don't go have check-ups, don't have Pap exams with regularity. Those are the people who get cancer. The people who are *descuidadas* (not take care of oneself) and promiscuous . . . promiscuity is an important factor. Those people get cancer because they don't have important control, right? Because at least every year she should have her cervix examined. . . . Almost all are poor. Promiscuity is among people who are unclean and poor. If you look at the upper classes, you see very little cervical cancer. They have other kinds of cancer—ovarian, uterine—but not cervical. Cervical [cancer] you see in the poor. Those who have cervical cancer have multiple sexual partners, a lot of boyfriends or *mari-novios* . . . they are boyfriend-husbands.

In his perception of risk, poverty, hygiene, and promiscuity converge to characterize the poor in moral as well as medical terms. Poor women come to connote a disease, which the doctor points out is not seen in the upper classes. Poverty, then, is interpreted as indicating a series of different things: promiscuity, lack of culture, and lack of hygiene. Having cervical cancer can mark a woman in a number of ways as judgments are implicitly made about her moral standing.

Moreover, only infrequently did doctors discuss poverty and lack of access to medical services in terms of the structural obstacles to health care. Instead, when poverty was discussed, women were still blamed for not getting checkups and generally for not taking proper care of their bodies. Thus, poverty was described as a personal flaw rather than a hardship born of political, social, and economic circumstances.

Risk, "Culture," and Class

A common theme that runs through these doctors' quotes is an assertion that their low-class patients lacked competency in maintaining their health. This lack of competency was very often expressed in terms of a "lack of culture."

The meaning of *culture* in these comments is somewhat vague, often mentioned in conjunction with a lack of education and conditions of poverty, yet not reducible to these descriptions. Consider the response from a thirty-two-year-old male doctor at the private hospital when asked about the risk factors for cervical cancer: "Generally we speak of the educational level, no? Of one's formation. People of low socio-economic status do not have the cultural level or understanding." Moreover, when asked about the ways women could avoid getting cervical cancer, he said, "Better the culture of the population, avoid promiscuity, and have frequent gynecological control." In my discussions with them about their hospital patients, doctors often used the terms *culture, education,* and *class* interchangeably in describing their patients as lacking these things. In formal open-ended interviews with doctors, 35 percent referred to "culture"—either "low cultural level" or "lack of culture"—in relation to cervical cancer risk. As we will see in the examination of public health and cervical cancer in Venezuela (Chapter 4), the concept of culture is interwoven with discourses of nation, health, and progress.

The invocation of culture by the doctors has more to do with perceptions about what it means to be "cultured" in a class sense (i.e., educated, sophisticated, worldly) than what one might think of in an anthropological sense. However, one epidemiological study on cervical cancer in Venezuela draws on cultural difference by comparing indigenous women and "urban" women. The researchers analyzed differences in cancer rates among the indigenous group, described as monogamous in their sexual behavior, and the urban women, who are characterized by their nonmonogamous behavior (having multiple sexual partners) (Azocar et al. 1990). The indigenous women have lower rates of cervical cancer than the urban women. In this case, the indigenous are treated as a distinct cultural group whose monogamous behavior is described as non-Western:

> The populations reported here have the advantage of being women with well-defined sexual behavior. Members of the non-monogamous group have histories of multiple sex partners, while those in the other group, the aboriginal women, are monogamous. Monogamy is a well-studied and identified cultural pattern in the Piaroa aboriginal culture (Kaplan, 1975), as long as it remains free from Western influences. (Azocar et al. 1990:623)

At the same time, this statement suggests that "Piaroa aboriginal culture" is free from Western influence, whatever that may mean, and in danger of losing its cultural distinction if it does not remain "free from Western influences" (in other words monogamy may be threatened). The use of the term *aboriginal* is unusual here, and it remains unclear as to why the researchers use it instead of the usual term, *indigenous*. Perhaps it was meant to draw on a romantic trope of the aboriginal untouched by Western influences in this biomedical construction of risk. Similar to this cultural differentiation between aboriginal and urban women, which draws on medical and social science, Vaughn (1991, 7) notes in her study of medicine in colonial Africa that "what is striking about so much of the medical knowledge produced in and about colonial Africa is its explicit concern with finding social and cultural 'origins' for disease patterns. Biomedicine drew for its authority both on science and on social science." Here we see risk problematized in relationship to culture, drawing on ideas about "a people"—in this case what has been connoted as a Western-free practice of "Piaroa aboriginals" (monogamy).

Culture, then, takes on various meanings in relation to cervical cancer risk. The doctors I interviewed focused not on an understanding of culture as "a people" or distinct cultural group, which carries its own set of questionable assumptions, but on the problematic construction of culture as a concept mediated by class (so-called "cultured" and "uncultured" peoples). The concept of culture did not, however, come up in patients' discussions of risk. In the next section I explore those cervical cancer risks that patients did mention.

A "Woman's Disease"

Under neoliberalism in Venezuela, women, in particular, have borne the brunt of the connection that is drawn between promiscuous sexual behavior and cervical cancer, as the medical configuration of this disease places emphasis on the sexual practices and moral transgressions of women—poor women. In addition to promiscuity, the moral connotations of this disease were also expressed in the focus of both doctors and public health campaigns, as we shall see in Chapter 3, on hygienic practices. Risks having to do with hygiene and culture, in particular, were asserted and presented as common wisdom without clear explanations as to what the terms mean and without reference to the epidemiological literature. Underlying these risks is an implicit connection among class, behavior, and disease. An image is created of those who get cervical cancer: promiscuous, poor, and unhygienic women. Taken-for-granted associations are created as promiscuity, sex at an early age, poverty, a lack of hygiene, and a lack of culture come to connote one another.

The Venezuelan doctors' medical discourse of cervical cancer risk reveals the ways in which social class, gender, and disease overlap. The cultural politics surrounding this "woman's disease," then, are imbued with the medical legitimacy and authoritative knowledge to represent it as a disease of uncultured, unhygienic, and unregulated habits of low-class women. A key component of this configuration is that of control. The term *control* is used in the medical setting to refer to medical checkups or examinations. Thus, a woman's annual Pap smear examination was often referred to as her "annual control." The phrase "lack of control," while used in the medical setting with a particular meaning, also gives way to a broader social referent. Many of the risk factors for cervical cancer that were mentioned by the doctors, social workers, and public health administrators (e.g., multiple sexual partners, sex at an early age, repetitive venereal infections, lack of medical control) produce an image of working-class women as "out of control." They have too many sex partners at too early an age, producing too many children and living in houses that are too crowded. In addition, a lack of hygiene also contributes to this image of being out of control—not having proper control over one's body. Moral judgments and characterizations about lower-class women's unruly behavior and the need to somehow control and regulate them were a part of the medical construction of this disease in Venezuela.

Cervical Cancer Risk: Patients' Beliefs

Some of the cervical cancer risk factors mentioned by patients were similar to or the same as those mentioned by the doctors, but others were unique to the women. I use the language of risk to parallel the responses of the doctors, but I realize that the language of risk is a product of the social construction of biomedical knowledge about disease. For example, the eight most common risks cited by the women were lack of medical attention, sexually transmitted infections, lack of personal hygiene, multiple sex partners, intrauterine devices, vaginal infections from dirty toilets, the ubiquitous nature of cancer, and sex at an early age (see table 2.2 for a complete list of risks and their frequencies). All but three (intrauterine birth control, vaginal infections from dirty toilets, and the ubiquitous nature of cancer) were mentioned by the doctors as well. In addition, the women listed twice as many risk factors as the doctors. They mentioned a total of thirty-two different risks, whereas the doctors named sixteen.

TABLE 2.2 Percentage of Patients at Both Hospitals Who Mentioned Each Cervical Cancer Risk

Risks	Patients who mention each risk (N=45)
1 Lack of medical attention	15 (33%)
2 Sexually transmitted infections	14 (31%)
Breakdown of sexually transmitted infections:	
Sexually transmitted disease (STD)—general	06 (13%)
STD from husband/partner	06 (13%)
Infection with human Papilloma virus (HPV)	01 (2%)
Repetitive venereal infections	01 (2%)
3 Lack of personal hygiene	06 (13%)
4 Multiple sex partners (promiscuity)	05 (11%)
5 Intrauterine birth control devices	04 (8%)
6 Vaginal infection from dirty toilet	03 (6%)
7 Everyone has cancer cells (ubiquitous)	03 (6%)
8 Sex at an early age	03 (6%)
9 Rough sex	02 (4%)
10 Having sexual relations with vaginal infection	02 (4%)
11 Sex during menstruation	02 (4%)
12 Debilitated cervix due to childbirth	02 (4%)
13 Not following proper diet after giving birth	02 (4%)
14 Heredity	02 (4%)
15 Birth control pills	02 (4%)
16 Poor diet	02 (4%)
17 Abortion	02 (4%)
18 Inflammation	02 (4%)
19 Ulcerous lesion	02 (4%)
20 Prolapsed uterus	01 (2%)
21 Fibroid	01 (2%)
22 Too much sex	01 (2%)
23 Too much douching	01 (2%)
24 Eating acidic things during menstruation	01 (2%)
25 Blood coagulation	01 (2%)
26 Hemorrhaging	01 (2%)
27 Bad menstruation (more than once a month)	01 (2%)
28 Having many children (multiparity)	01 (2%)
29 Pregnancy can accelerate the process	01 (2%)
30 Doctor damaging cervix during childbirth	01 (2%)
31 Tubal ligation	01 (2%)
32 Fungal infection that is not treated	01 (2%)

The single most commonly mentioned risk factor by the patients was lack of medical attention. It was cited by 33 percent of the women and accounted for 17 percent of total risk. The women mentioned this risk factor in terms of both a lack of resources (e.g., money, transportation) and a lack of personal initiative due to either apathy or fear. Consider this response from a twenty-six-year-old woman whom I interviewed at the public hospital: "One doesn't go to the hospital for fear of the doctor and because one can't afford to buy the medicine.... There are many people who deprive themselves of those things [health care] because they are afraid and they don't have any [money]." She discussed these issues in terms of a lack of medical attention and combined both the obstacles of fear and of a lack of material resources. Another woman, a fifty-seven-year-old patient at the public hospital, provided a more general and common response: "What can increase the risks [of acquiring cervical cancer]? Well, not having an exam, like the doctor indicates and then that can cause it [cervical cancer]. I don't know, but increase the chances, well, not going to see the doctor because, for example, a person has the beginnings of cancer and the person doesn't take care of it, the person will end up with a cancer that can't result in anything good; in other words, that can be diagnosed so that the person can be healed." A thirty-one-year-old public hospital patient echoed that statement with a similar observation: "Not seeing a doctor would increase the risk and that would be fatal." These explanations warn of the negative consequence of not following doctor's orders: not catching cancer early enough for effective treatment and eradication. They emphasize individual responsibility in seeking health care. Another woman, a thirty-eight-year-old patient at the private hospital, gave the example of her sister who had died of cervical cancer to underscore the importance of preventive medical attention. She said, "I don't know because when she died there wasn't a lot of information about it [cervical cancer], but I think my sister died because of her own lack of personal care. I think, because by the time she went to the doctor, she already had it [cervical cancer] . . . it [medical exam] wasn't constant." She, like many of the women who mentioned lack of medical attention as a risk factor, emphasized personal responsibility in preventive care by getting annual Pap exams. Few women spoke of the obstacles to medical care in terms of cancer risk. However, as I show in Chapter 5, in the discussion of public health and cervical cancer in Venezuela, the women did relate their own stories of obstacles to treatment, but ultimately many stressed personal accountability for their health problems.

The second most commonly mentioned risk factor by the women was sexually transmitted infections. Take, for example, this comment by a forty-two-year-old woman:

> Well, a few days ago when I saw the program *A puerta cerrada*, a risk for women is when they never have a Pap exam, when they never go to the gynecologist and also infections . . . venereal infections.

She got her information of cervical cancer risk from a Venezuelan talk-show program that covers various topics, including health.[2] She cited both a lack of medical attention and sexually transmitted infections, specifically stating venereal infections, in her explanation of cervical cancer risk. Other women specifically talked about the role of husbands or partners in the transmission of an infection that could lead to cervical cancer. One thirty-eight-year-old woman at put it this way:

> Well, avoiding for example, if my husband was going to have sexual relations with another woman, with another person, he could give it [infection] to me . . . having sex relations with a woman who has that problem [infection] and passing it onto me, that can be passed on to another person.

Another young woman, age twenty-four, said, "It [cervical cancer] can be gotten because of your partner, from X disease, you develop it [cervical cancer]. You are not aware that you have it and a little wound/sore [*llaga*] forms and then you get it from there." A forty-five-year-old Ecuadorian-born woman echoed this belief: "sexual contact . . . in that the other person can have some kind of problem [infection] and if you have a problem in your cervix, then it makes it worse. The man can have a disease and give it to you." In this explanation, a woman's partner can make an already-existing condition even worse by transmitting an infection.

The women's concern for the role of partners in the risk of cervical cancer is noticeable. Of those who mentioned sexually transmitted infection risks, 13 percent (six of forty-five) referred to the role of the partner (see table 2.2). Comparably, only one of the doctors brought up the role of a partner in the risk etiology. Similarly, in their study of risk beliefs for cervical cancer among Latinas and physicians in North Orange County, California, Martínez et al. (1997) found that Latinas tended to mention sexual behavior of their husbands or partners in perceptions of cervical cancer risk, whereas physicians focused on the sexual behavior of women, not on that of their partners.

As with the doctors, some of the women also considered lack of hygiene to be a risk factor for cervical cancer. Although it was the third most commonly mentioned risk factor among them, it was mentioned by 13 percent of the women, as compared to 47 percent of doctors.

When women are told by physicians that their cervical cancer is caused by lack of hygiene, problems arise. For example, Isabel, a twenty-four-year-old single woman, was a patient at Padre Machado and was told by a doctor (at another hospital) that lack of hygiene was a risk factor for cervical cancer. Isabel was born in a *pueblo* (small town) in the northeastern Venezuelan state of Monagas, and at the time of the interview, she resided in Caracas and worked as a receptionist. She had never had any type of gynecological exam before, and when she felt some painful cramping in her ovaries and uterus a friend of hers told her she should have a gynecological exam. She went to a social security hospital, which she had access to because of her job. The doctor there gave her a Pap exam and, when the results came back, told her that she had cancer. When I asked her what she thought might have caused it she related the following exchange between herself and the doctor at the social security hospital:

> ISABEL: He told me that it could be because of a lack of cleanliness but he didn't really tell me exactly what it came from. There are doctors who explain, especially when one ignores the circumstances, so that one can take preventative measures.
>
> RM: What do you think about that?
>
> ISABEL: That no, because I am very, what I mean is that in the personal aspect, that is something that I was inculcated with from the time I was a child.
>
> RM: Did you discuss this further with the doctor?
>
> ISABEL: No, I didn't say anything to him because he's one of those people who tell you things and then don't want to clarify, I don't know. For me, they don't have professional ethics because a professional will tell you, "Look this happens because of this, that and the other," and he explains, he tells you why these things happen, but not this doctor. He limited his discussion to tell me, "Look you have cancer, you need an operation and if you don't want it, well, you'll have to see what you do."

She rejected the doctor's suggestion that her illness could be due to a lack of cleanliness. She countered with a declaration of having been inculcated with cleanliness as a child, assuring me that her cleanliness is an integral and lifelong part of her person. Isabel's tone was agitated at my mention of the doctor whom she felt had implicitly regarded her as "unclean." Moreover, she regarded his explanation as incomplete and unprofessional. Her interaction with this particular doctor did not correspond with her view of how a doctor should treat patients. Thus, rather than viewing Isabel's lack of communication with this particular doctor as an example of apathy in the face of authority, one should recognize that she evaluated her situation (and the doctor) and decided against pursuing any discussion with him. Although she might not have voiced her opinions to the doctor, as she felt that to do so would be ineffectual, Isabel was anything but satisfied with the interaction. She concluded that since she was getting a referral for Padre Machado and would therefore not need to interact with this particular doctor anymore, she would forgo talking with him about her condition, knowing that she could wait to ask questions of the doctors at Padre Machado. Some might interpret Isabel's actions as passive. However, I believe that she was making a calculated decision. She did not agree with the doctor's interpretation, nor did she internalize any shame regarding his suggestion that a lack of hygienic practices on her part played a role in her cancer. Instead, she was forthright with me about his causal explanation and summarily rejected it. If she had internalized his reasoning, I doubt she would have shared the exchange with me. I take Isabel's openness with me in relating the patient-doctor interaction as an indication of her agency, demonstrating confidence in her willingness to reject an etiology that went against her own knowledge of self.

Other women brought up the subject of hygiene themselves in response to my inquiry about the risks for cervical cancer. Consider the following quote from a forty-eight-year-old woman who came to the public hospital with a diagnosis of a uterine fibroma:

> Well, I think it's also a question of hygiene. Hygiene is very important. Even though that is an area that cleans itself, no? It cleans itself but in another way because an excess of hygiene is also bad.

For her, both extremes—not enough hygiene and too much hygiene—presented problems.

At least three other women discussed hygiene in reference to sexual relations. Carmen, a thirty-seven-year-old Caraqueña, did not have a referral but came to Padre Machado through a contact person, a family friend who worked at the hospital. She was concerned because she had gotten two different results on Pap smears that she had taken with different doctors. One result indicated that she had inflammation and the other NIC I (cervical intraepithelial neoplasm, abbreviated as NIC in Spanish). She didn't know what NIC I meant, but the contradiction in the results led her to seek advice from her family, who, with the help of the family friend, was able to get her an appointment at the private hospital, Padre Machado. When asked about the risks for cervical cancer, Carmen mentioned a lack of hygiene but emphasized not only a woman's hygiene but also that of her sexual partner:

> Well, lack of hygiene could be one . . . not douching, for example. When you are going to have sexual relations and you don't tell your partner to clean himself before and that sort of thing. That [lack of hygiene] can bring on infections and that is when cancer forms in my opinion.

Similarly, another woman, a forty-nine-year-old patient at the public hospital, spoke of hygiene in terms of a potential diseases passed on by a husband: "It can be because of a lack of cleanliness, because the husband could have some kind of disease and pass it on and she doesn't take care of herself." In this case, a lack of hygiene does not simply refer to a deficiency in cleaning oneself; it encompasses the idea that disease itself is dirty. In other words, a husband who contaminates his wife with disease is unclean. However, at the same time, she is responsible for "taking care of herself," which in this context may also mean cleaning herself (possibly douching) to try to rid herself of the disease or dirt and/or going to the doctor for a checkup. Although it is not exactly clear what is meant by the phrase "taking care of herself," other women whom I interviewed often used similar phrases when talking about having regular Pap exams and by doing so maintaining "proper" health care.

Another patient, a single woman in her late forties, emphasized the hygienic practices that she deemed necessary after engaging in sexual relations. She made the following comment in response to the question of cervical cancer risk:

> Well, I don't know. What I'm going to tell you is my opinion that a woman uses, at least to not get pregnant, uses special tampons [*tapones*] that she forgets about after having a [sexual] relation and doesn't have the necessary hygiene that is necessary after a sexual relation. Because many women after they are fin-

ished, had their [sexual] relation and had their orgasm, they get up when they are finished, but then comes needing to wash yourself, doing a vaginal douche, and all of those things, that is what I understand.

Her quote, while emphasizing the need for a woman to clean herself by douching after engaging in sexual relations, also contains a moral undertone that suggests that those women who try to prevent pregnancy through the use of a barrier form of birth control are likely to forget about its presence, not engage in proper hygiene, and ultimately put themselves at risk for cervical cancer.

Overview of Doctors' and Patients' Beliefs

Overall, the women mentioned twice as many different risk factors as the doctors, thirty-two and sixteen, respectively. This is likely because the doctors tended to mention risks that are a part of the biomedical model for cervical cancer in general.[3] Women, in contrast, included biomedical risks, but they were also more likely to draw on life experiences outside of what the medical model would posit as cancer risk. The risk factor most often mentioned by the women, 33 percent of them, was a lack of medical attention. Sexually transmitted infections was the second most-stated risk, mentioned by 31 percent of women, followed by a lack of hygiene, stated by 13 percent of women, and promiscuity, mentioned by 11 percent of women. For the women, all of whom came from working-class backgrounds, a lack of medical attention is likely the factor they believe was most directly relevant to their own situations.

Although lack of medical attention was most often mentioned by the women, sexually transmitted infections and promiscuity were the factors most often stated by the doctors. All the doctors mentioned promiscuity as a risk factor, and 88 percent of them mentioned sexually transmitted infections. Another risk for cervical cancer that is found in the biomedical literature, sex at an early age, was mentioned by 53 percent of doctors. Lack of medical attention, heredity, and lack of hygiene were each stated as risks by 47 percent of doctors. Somewhat surprisingly, lack of hygiene, a risk factor not supported in the medical literature, was mentioned by almost half of doctors. Their discussions of a lack of hygiene, sometimes referred to as *desaseo*, were always centered on descriptions of the habits of the lower classes. Often, sexual hygiene, sexually transmitted infections, uncleanliness, and poverty were intertwined and came to connote one another. The working class and poor are defined in terms of these habits (promiscuous and lacking hygiene), whereas the more affluent are characterized in opposition to them—as monogamous and clean. Having cervical cancer implicitly calls into question the moral standing of poor women. Cleanliness, though discussed in terms of medical risk, is a moral category with social and cultural referents; it goes beyond a simple reference to bodily hygiene into judgments about one's character. As is evident from many of the doctors' comments, ideas about cleanliness are interwoven with those of promiscuity, culture, disorderliness, and moral standing in general.

It is important to underscore that hygiene, while emphasized in many of their discussions of risk, is not supported by the epidemiological literature. Yet, as I have demonstrated, it is still an integral part of the official discourse on cervical cancer in Venezuela, not only stated by physicians but also found in medical publications and at conference presentations. This is precisely where we can see class, medicine, and relationships of power coming into play, defining and categorizing women and disease. Ideas about risk, disease, and women (subaltern and elite alike) are drawn from a sociocultural context, yet presented as value-free and scientifically neutral. The official, authoritative, and medically legitimate profile of cervical cancer in Venezuela blends the epidemiology of cancer with the ideology of cancer. In the configuration of disease (and diseased bodies), the boundaries between epidemiology and ideology are blurred, and moral judgments about the character of poor women are being made.

In contrast, while doctors tended to place the onus of hygiene and promiscuity on the behavior of poor and working class women (although one doctor mentioned the hygiene of the penis and another discussed the role of the woman's partner), the women often discussed the risks of promiscuity and sexually transmitted infections in relation to the behavior of male partners. Even when lack of hygiene was mentioned (e.g., by 13 percent of patients compared to 47 percent of doctors), it was discussed in terms of needing to take care of oneself after sexual relations (e.g., poor hygiene on the part of one's sexual partner, douching to reduce the risk of an infection from one's partner). At least one woman remarked that she was insulted by a doctor's suggestion that lack of hygiene could be a risk for cervical cancer. She took this personally as an insinuation that her own cleanliness, and possibly even her moral character, were being called into question.

Moreover, although morality did play a role is women's discussions of cervical cancer risk, unlike doctors, class difference was not a part of their moral profile of cancer. Class, in the women's discourse of risk, was implicated only in regard to access to medical care, not in relation to behavior (promiscuity and uncleanliness), as can be discerned from many of the doctors' profiles of cervical cancer.

3 Targeting Women

Bodies out of "Control," Public Health, and the Body Politic

> [Lower-class] patients can't go to a hospital, they can't constantly go and have gynecological checkups, and as a result, the risk of cancer increases in that patient and, in fact, in the low class is where you see promiscuity. You see the use of multiple husbands. Are we clear? In the low social class is where you see uncleanliness [*desaseo*] . . . also less medical control or no medical control.
> Doctor at Razetti, interviewed July 10, 1995

Women, Public Health, and Latin America

Women, in particular, have historically been the targets of public health campaigns seeking to monitor and change behavior with the ostensible goal of eradicating disease. Many scholars have pointed out that women's bodies, particularly those bodies of the poor and otherwise socially marginalized, have often been seen as the root of moral societal breakdown, leading to disease, contagion, and the need for public health intervention (Guy 1990, 2000; Douglas 1992; Patton 1992; Gilman 1992; Whitehead 1995). In the context of Latin America, Donna Guy (1990) has provided an important historical analysis of public health campaigns in Buenos Aires, Argentina. She argues that *higienistas* (hygienists) played an important role in the regulation and policing of the body politic at the turn of the nineteenth century. These hygienist-physicians were working at a time of mass European immigration and economic growth in Argentina and acted as tools of governance during an era of great social, political, and economic transformation (Rodriguez Garcia, van Voss, and van Nederveen Meerkerk 2017). According to Guy (1990, 297), "*higienistas* believed that inappropriate behavior by the few could endanger the health rights of all, they established different criteria for diagnosing illness among rich and poor, female and male." As they implemented their programs, "capitalism, gender, and morality became inextricably linked as pubic health became one means of denoting the limits of one's place and one's rights within civil society" (Guy 2000, 123). In this account, prostitutes and laundry women were subjected to health monitoring so as not to spread sexually transmitted diseases, in the case of prostitutes, and cholera, in the case of laundry women. Laundry women, it was argued, could spread cholera through the water they used in washing. Ironically, they were suspected of being unhygienic and unclean because of the status of their work. This regulation of lower-class women who were marginalized in terms of social and geographical space was meant to improve mortality statistics but also to ensure the health and the promotion of the nation—the healthy nation, particularly to avoid contamination of the upper class by the presumed immoral and unhygienic practices of the dangerous poor. Blame was directed at the poor rather than the social conditions that made them susceptible to disease. As Guy (2000, 124) states, "By conflating social and economic marginality with physical pathology, physicians directly linked pubic health with class-specific political programs aimed at social control." Although she is speaking about nineteenth-century Argentina, similar moral ideologies of disease based on class distinctions remain present in Latin America today.

Writing on the same topic of *higienistas* in Argentina and Chile during the nineteenth and early twentieth century, Manuel Alejandro Duran Sandoval (2012) illustrates the various ways in which medical regulation of women was established through sexuality and reproduction. The *higienistas* argued that the role of women is limited to reproduction and motherhood and contrasted these expectations to the dangers of an "overflowing sexuality and unbridled excitement." In this context "the female reproductive model was associated with passivity as a natural essence of her sexuality and pleasure was not only an obstacle to the proper development of a pregnancy, according to some thinkers, but downright harmful" (Duran Sandoval 2012, 167–168). The regulation of women served to maintain a patriarchal social order, which relied on women reproducing workers needed for capitalist production and ensuring those workers' survival through their domestic duties.

Although *higienistas* played a large role in Latin America during the nineteenth century, their ideas weren't limited by place. Similarly, in a study of nineteenth-century sanitary legislation in India, Whitehead argues that sanitation reforms were mainly intended to monitor and control the social and sexual relations between male British colonialists and the potentially disease-ridden female natives. Indian prostitutes in particular were popularly imagined by the colonial state as being "the epitome of dangerous contagion and exotic sensuality" (Whitehead 1995, 41). Notably, the Contagious Diseases Act implemented in the latter part of the nineteenth century "introduced a new form of bodily regulation, in which the moral division between unrespectable and respectable women in India began to be detached from a sacred social hierarchy and became, instead, expressed through Western medical metaphors of health and disease" (Whitehead 1995, 41).

Fertility, Family Planning, and the State

Jumping back to Latin America and ahead to the mid-twentieth century, reproduction and fertility became a central concern of public health throughout the region. The mass movements from rural to urban areas in Latin America played a role in state efforts to control fertility. In Chile in the 1960s, for example, the Association for the Protection of the Family (APROFA) was very active in family planning; the association disseminated information, held seminars, and met with health educators, social workers, and labor leaders (Pieper Mooney 2014). They concentrated their efforts on poor women and in poor neighborhoods. The success and strength of APROFA, which attracted hundreds of women to community family-planning meetings and provided birth-control devices free of charge, lay in its combination of prolife discourse and population planning for the purpose of modernization. Moreover, a film titled *The Abortion* was made to warn poor women of the hardships they could face with uncontrolled fertility and of the positive role they could play as saviors of the nation if they acted responsibly by using birth control. Jadwiga Pieper Mooney (2014) analyzes the message of the film as follows:

> Without birth control, the woman not only endangered her own life, but also threatened the survival of her family and her community. Either women would

increase the misery and discomfort of poor urban life by not limiting the number of children they raised; or women could use family planning methods, the only way out of individual, communal, and national distress.

By the same token, if women did not control their fertility, they risked being vilified as symbolic and real threats to modernization and national development. It is also no surprise that fertility efforts were directed at women. Their role as nurtures and caretakers of families was extended to symbolically encompass the nation.

In addition to Chile, fertility and family planning were also being taken up in the 1960s and 1970s in other South American countries like Venezuela (Freitez n.d.), Argentina (Felitti 2008), Colombia (Seltzer and Gomez 1998), and Peru (Necochea López 2014). Although it cannot be said that the social, economic, and political discourses surrounding population that were circulating in the United States at the time greatly shaped concerns in Latin America, scholars have documented the role of the extremely popular book by Paul Ehrlich, *The Population Bomb* (1968). In it he warned of the catastrophic social, economic, and environmental doom facing the world with "overpopulation." Public health and other agencies in the United States influenced by Ehrlich's work took great interest in Latin America, as it was seen as comprising third-world countries whose explosive population growth could endanger the planet. In a report prepared for the International Planned Parenthood Federation titled *Population and Family Planning in Latin America* (dated 1973), the author, Phyllis Piotrow, warns of the "population explosion" occurring there:

> Analysis of Latin America's demographic situation has led many to believe that the present rapid rates of population growth, the highest anywhere in the world, must be reduced in order to prevent catastrophe. Family planning associations, affiliated with the International Planned Parenthood Federation (IPPF) have been organized in 29 Latin American countries. The Victor-Bostrom Fund has provided millions of dollars annually to IPPF; and with the base provided by these funds and private contributions, IPPF has obtained support from 13 governments and the United Nations Fund for Population Activities.

This report was generated from a Washington, DC–based organization and confirms that large amounts of funds were being poured into Latin America for the purposes of family planning. The use of the word *catastrophe* resonates with the "population bomb" discourse prevalent at the time. Another part of the report engages in a gendered respectability discourse that marks women as the cultural keepers of society: "Ignorant of any contraceptive method, many women, the most responsible element in Latin society, have resorted to illegal induced abortion, a practice in Latin America that has reached epidemic proportions" (Piotrow 1973, 6). Those women who transgress social norms by seeking abortions are seen not as having agency in decision making, but as victims of their own ignorance, causing them to act against their "respectable" and "responsible" nature.

These works show how public health has functioned as a disciplinary form in the definition and regulation of respectable femininity, respectable reproduction, and respectable sexuality through the socio-medical control of women for the ostensible greater good of the social body. This is not so say that women didn't benefit from some of these programs, such as family planning. In fact, they also demanded them. Instead, my purpose is to highlight how public health projects fit state goals related to such efforts as modernization, capitalism, and colonialism.

This brief sketch of literature connecting historical accounts of institutional regulatory practices of public health in Latin America to the formation of a healthy body politic intersects at many points with the discussion in the previous chapter of marked bodies. Common to most of these health policies is a dual gender or class marking of particular bodies, which are then represented as inherently polluting, diseased, and ultimately dangerous. Despite the historical situatedness of these policies, they are significant for understanding the ways in which women are targeted in Venezuelan public health campaigns. Before delving into an analysis of public health pamphlets on cervical cancer, I discuss the barrios where most of the women who I interviewed lived. Because the barrios figured so greatly in doctors' discourses on cervical cancer and in public health concerns, a focus on the barrios is necessary to situate the medical encounters I analyze in the next chapters. Women in the barrios were described in ways that reduced them to classist and sexist stereotypes. The discourses of medical practitioners evoked similar concerns about dangerous hypersexuality, reproduction, and uncleanliness that *higienistas* articulated in nineteenth-century Latin America. The women's own subjectivities, as traced through popular sector social movements, challenges these constructions and helps make visible the agency they exhibit in medical encounters.

Cancer, Control, and Class

Recall the epigraph to this chapter. This quote from a doctor at the public hospital draws on a number of characteristics that were used to describe the "lower class" patients. I very often heard these types of descriptions not only in interviews with doctors (as was evident in the previous discussions of cancer risk) but also in my daily observations at the public and private hospitals. This particular doctor's excerpt indicates a concern for a lack of resources to obtain gynecological exams, but at the same time, the individual is blamed for bringing cervical cancer upon herself due to her promiscuity and her uncleanliness. The use of the phrase "multiple husbands" at once draws us to the conclusion that the doctor is speaking specifically and deliberately of women's sexual behavior.

Moreover, as this doctor's quote exemplifies, he is concerned with the lack of medical control of his lower-class patients. As stated earlier in this work, the term *control* is used in the medical setting to refer to medical checkups or examinations. Thus, a woman's annual Pap smear was often referred to as her "annual control."[1] The phrase "lack of control," while used in the medical setting with a particular meaning, also gives way to a broader social referent. Many of the risk factors for cervical cancer that were mentioned by doctors, social workers, and public health administrators (e.g., multiple sexual partners, sex at an early age, repetitive venereal infections, lack of medical control) produce an image of working-class women as being "out of control." They have too many sex partners at too early an age, produce too many children, and live in too-crowded homes.

Living in crowded conditions, or *hacinamiento*, was brought up by a doctor at the public hospital as a risk for cervical cancer. She spoke generally of the "dirty" and "unhygienic" conditions that can lead to disease. In addition, a social worker at the public hospital noted that *hacinamiento* leads to sexual abuse and incest. She said that one of the reasons workers ask patients about the number of people living in their household is because it clues them in to sexual abuse: "You have all of those people—three, four or five people—crowded, piled one on top of the other, adults and children in one bed. Adults having [sexual] relations in front of children and there is very likely to be sexual violations of children—incest going on there." Thus, living in what is deemed to be "too crowded" conditions automatically places the poor—the people who are most likely required to live in multiple households because of economic constraints—in a position of being suspected of morally reprehensible and criminal behavior. These excesses (too many children, too many people in one house, too many sex partners) configure bodies as lacking restraint, physically and socially. In this way, the perception of "the informal sexual practices of the lower and climbing classes are [viewed as] threatening the foundations of civil society" (Povinelli 1997, 516) through unhealthy behaviors, ultimately figured as what I term a *pathology of subaltern excess*, that is, a medico-moral discourse that frames so-called sexual, social, and reproductive irresponsibility as a property of the most marginal.

Marginality and Modernity: Barrios and Favelas in Latin America

Barrios and favelas in Latin America have long drawn the attention of scholars seeking to understand these "informal settlements," from among a number of perspectives, including, but not limited to, anthropological, psychological, sociological, historical, and medical (Blanco 1993; Scheper-Hughes 1993; Wiesenfeld 1997a, 1997b; Holston 1999, 2008; Caldeira 2000; Fernandes 2007; Velasco 2011, 2015; Rial y Costas 2011; Cooper 2015b; Moreno 2016). For example, anthropologist James Holston's book *Insurgent Citizenship: Disjunctions of Democracy and Modernity in Brazil* (2008) is one of the most important works on peripheral neighborhoods, the state, and citizenship. He traces the development of what he calls "insurgent citizenship" in Brazil, shedding light on the plight of urban poor in their struggle for economic, political, and social inclusion. Holston's ethnographic fieldwork in São Paulo—the largest metropolitan area in South America—documents the rise of favelas (shanty towns), or peripheral neighborhoods. The incredible movement from rural to urban areas that took place from the 1950s onward in Brazil led to the proliferations of these peripheries. He argues that "the autoconstructed peripheries ... fueled an irruption of an insurgent citizenship that destabilizes ... they are also the conditions of its subversion, as the urban poor gained political rights, became landowners, made law an asset, created new public spheres of participation, achieved rights to the city, and became modern consumers" (9). Importantly, "the lived experiences of the peripheries became both the context and the substance of a new urban citizenship. In turn, this insurgence of the local transformed national democratization" (9). The peripheral neighborhoods, then, are important sites for his understanding of citizenship as a "relation between state and society." The residents of these neighborhoods mobilized a social movement not through labor or similar well-known struggles but rather through the construction of illegal homes and conflicts over land. As they forged this democratized urban space beginning in the 1970s and gained a foothold in political democracy, they also experienced increased violence and injustice meant to erode their progress. But as they constructed their citizenship in these urban peripheries, the state was required to recognize new forms and sources of citizen rights. Relevant to my interests is that residents asked for special compensatory rights for women like maternity leave. Moreover, citizen rights also included access to medical care and the right to health.

The rapid urbanization that Brazil experienced also paralleled what was happening in Venezuela in the mid-twentieth century and beyond. As with Brazil, this also led to the proliferation of peripheral urbanizations known as barrios. In a later section (Barrios: Locating Political Mobilization) I further explore the idea of social movement activism and mobilization introduced here through Holston's work. I focus, of course, on Caracas, the geographical subject of my ethnography. The popular sector in Caracas, through grassroots mobilization, played a central role in electing Hugo Chávez, who ushered in sweeping health-care reforms that would benefit the residents of the barrios. First, however, I return to the ethnographic vignette that provides insight into how health practitioners viewed the barrios in the context of medicalized discourse.

Fieldnotes, September 21, 1994
In September 1994, during my preliminary field investigation, I spoke with Dr. Lomas at his home and the subject of public health campaigns in Venezuela emerged. Dr. Lomas is a retired physician who was the former medical director of the public hospital, Razetti, where I conducted my research. He was a friendly man with poor eyesight who appeared to be in his seventies. His home was in one of the more wealthy and exclusive areas of Caracas, and its decor in the French provincial style reflected this affluence. After the customary offering of coffee and pastries, Dr. Lomas asked about my research, offered his assistance in any way, and began recounting some of his experiences at Razetti.

He told of how he was removed from his position as medical director of the hospital for "political reasons." The reasons he gave had to do with his active involvement with hospital patients, many of whom resided in the barrios. He organized a group of volunteers who would go with him to the barrios to attend to those persons with advanced cancers who could not go out, much less make it to the hospital. He did not elaborate much further, only to say that his connection with the people of the barrio, his affect for them, was viewed by some administrators as "unscientific" and lacking in "objectivity." This situation, he said, led to his being replaced as medical director.

Dr. Lomas spoke of some of the public health problems that he noticed with the people who live in the barrios. First, he outlined some general characteristics to describe the people who live in the barrios: they come from *ranchos* or *el campo* (rural areas), they are "illegal," they are illiterate, they are timid and lacking in self-confidence, and they are embarrassed about their "low" or "lacking" vocabulary. He stressed and elaborated on this latter point, referring to them as being "without vocabulary." To describe what he meant by this phrase, Dr. Lomas recounted a study that he carried out in the barrio. The research involved asking people about their sexual attitudes, including sexual positions and sexual pleasures. He said that the people of the barrio lacked the words (*sin vocabulario*) to talk about sexuality, much less had they ever heard of the word *orgasm*. His point was to tell of the problems in talking with them about health problems and having them understand health campaign messages due to their "lack of vocabulary." Through this description, they are metaphorically rendered speechless—*sin vocabulario*.

Along the same lines, Dr. Lomas related another account of a study that was done in the barrios by his daughter, a social worker. She went into homes to interview residents about televised public health messages, in order to evaluate individuals' comprehension of them. According to Dr. Lomas, the results indicated that "they could not understand even the simplest health messages displayed on the television." His assertion that the health messages were "simple" implied that the barrio residents were themselves simple. The possible inadequacy of the health messages was not questioned.

Moreover, the characterization of barrio residents included a psychosocial profile in which he described them as lacking in self-confidence and being unaffectionate. According to Dr. Lomas, "A woman can spend an entire day with her baby lying on the floor next to her and not caress or talk (cooing) to her baby with affection [*cariño*]." This leads to poor socialization because children in the barrios grow up in an environment with little outward affection.

Dr. Lomas did discuss the economic hardships and social marginalization that residents of the barrios experience, but interestingly, his observations were reduced to an articulation of the psychological deficiencies propagated by the barrio environment. Moreover, the description of poor socialization is problematized in a female-gendered way by positing the woman's role as mother and nurturer at the center of the socialization framework. These descriptions carry powerful social images and meanings that are imbued with professional medical and to some extent "scientific" legitimacy. These characteristics become medical and social pathologies. His conclusions focused on the deficits—mostly social and psychological, and to a lesser extent economic—of those living in the barrios. Moreover, these characterizations (e.g., unaffectionate, lacking vocabulary and understanding) are described as if rooted in the bodies of individuals, if not masses. There is a sense of "naturalness," almost of biological determinism, in the attributes affixed to those who live in the barrios. This description renders them not unlike the nomads that Mayhew (in his account of the laborers and of the poor of London) constructs in terms of "his desires ('passion,' 'love,' 'pleasure') and in terms of his rejections or ignorance ('repugnance,' 'want,' 'looseness,' 'absence,' 'disregard')" (as cited in Stallybrass and White 1986, 128). Or similarly, those characteristics of Australian "aboriginals" who, Povinelli (1997, 516) notes, were described by colonial writers in the following way:

> Aboriginal sexual and emotional interactions were irregular . . . because the passions, not social convention or reason, were the agent of all Aboriginal action. The passions (an emotion category inflected by class and race) snatched the Aboriginal body and were the motivating forces of Aboriginal temperament, sexuality, and other interpersonal affairs.

The residents who inhabit the margins of society, physically and figuratively, are cast as morally suspect, unclean, and potentially diseased; topography and morality converge in the configuration of this "other"—the barrio dweller.

Moreover, women, viewed as the natural caretakers and providers of affection, are marked as deviant and psychologically ill if they are perceived as not conforming to this socially acceptable norm. This perceived behavior, lacking *cariño*, which is couched in terms of psychological aberration, is ascribed in this doctor's characterization to an entire population: women who live in the barrios. Just as "the term *prostitute* always already confirms associations between class, immorality, and disease and the need for police and public health intervention," reference to the barrio equally calls to mind taken for granted associations among class, hygiene, disorder, and disease—"all of these elements are assumed to follow naturally" (Smart 1992, 31).

These discourses of public health relay a message about gender, health, and order. They produce and maintain a particular type of order: women's bodies are disciplined to engage in certain bodily practices, natural bodily practices. This is what Foucault would call "the order of things." "Order is," for Foucault (1970, xx),

> at one and the same time, that which is given in things as their inner law, the hidden network that determines the way they confront one another, and also that which has no existence except in the grid created by a glance, examination, a language; and it is only in the blank spaces of this grid that order manifests itself in depth as though already there, waiting in silence for the moment of its expression.

The "grid" that Foucault refers to in this case comes into view precisely through the medical glances and medical examinations that serve to both create and confirm that which appears to be already there: metaphorically, orderly cells ascribed to orderly (upper- and middle-class) women, and disorderly cells concomitant to disorderly (lower-class) women. Interestingly, cancerous cells are often described, popularly and medically, as cells that are out of control. That cancerous cells and subaltern populations are articulated in the same way can be seen as a trope in the medicalization of "at risk" (poor, promiscuous, unhygienic) populations.

The "lack of control," that the doctors, social workers, and public health officials spoke of is, in effect, a transgression of the "order of things": women are viewed as compromising their roles as mothers, nurturers, wives, and virgins, as a consequence of a "culture of poverty" in the deterministic vein of anthropologist Oscar Lewis (1971). Because poor women in these medical discourses are framed in terms of natural disorderliness, public health messages are consequently understood as fighting against an "inner law" or inherent state of being, not in their genes, but in their culture, which ultimately provides no better explanation than that of biological determinism (di Leonardo and Lancaster 1997; Balibar and Wallerstein 1991). These class divisions also function as cultural divisions, as references to difference by middle and upper classes are made in terms of urban culture versus rural ways, order versus disorder, socialized versus unsocialized, civilized versus uncivilized, and a host of other dichotomies that imply different, "less than" lifestyles. Ultimately, the urban middle class and elite survey and classify their own antithesis in the barrios (Stallybrass and White 1986).

Barrios in Caracas, in this context, are depicted as part of a rural landscape, although people who reside in the barrios are not strictly emigrants from rural areas. Some come from other Venezuelan cities and from cities in surrounding countries as well; the populations in the barrios are quite diverse. Nonetheless, the image, which overshadows the diversity of the population, is often that of a rural-urban peasantry with all the social, economic, cultural, and health problems that are emphasized as properties of the barrios and "its people." This portrayal is different from that in which Venezuelan peasants, rooted in a rural geography, are depicted. They are imagined as part of an "ordered" pastoral calm and folkloric past. At the same time, the nostalgia for the countryside is not erased by images that simultaneously emphasize the exploited past of peasants. Roseberry (1989) has noted that these contradictory images of the Venezuelan peasant are often expressed concurrently and unproblematically in public rallies, state occasions, and the media. Configurations of the peasant as tranquil or folkloric and exploited are further complicated by the movement from country to city, which in discourses of development and modernity may be described as a movement toward progress. As Roseberry (1989, 77) has noted:

> When these histories are written, or when the past is unfavorably compared with the present, the ideologues are touching on one aspect of the lived experiences of peasants and proletarians. The move from country to city, from peasant to proletarian or "other" from backwardness to development can be experienced as progress.

However, when this movement is seen as incomplete and marginal within the city, peasants may be reconfigured in terms of a rural-urban hybridity, conceptualized as unsuccessful modern, urban subjects. The concern of a public health official noted earlier in this work (see Chapter 1) articulates this point precisely. He is troubled by the "ruralization of the urban" and the implications for health problems resulting from people "living in their same rural ways" in the city. These concerns are also echoed in the mass media. Consider, for example, the title of a recent Venezuelan newspaper article: "From the Rural *Choza* [Hut] to the Urban *Rancho*," which depicts the latter (*rancho*) as a transplanted rural artifact.[2] Another article reminisces about the days when "Caracas, in every sense was a healthy city. The *ranchos* had not yet crept up the hillsides . . . great urban works were projected for the middle-class. That has been forgotten" (*El Universal*, October 7, 1997). The modern and civil urban is troubled in the face of the rural-like encroachment of the *ranchos*, which the article implies, has left the city sick. Metaphors of health and disease anthropomorphize the city, casting the barrios and their residents as a monolithic pathogen on the urban landscape. The *barrios*, in this sense, have supplanted the envisaged mythico-landscape, a longed-for place where self-ascribed modern citizens (a concept I explore further later) exist unencumbered by the poor, diseased, and deviant "others" who pollute the space for legitimized subjects. It is a nostalgia—not for what was—but for an imagined could-have-been cityscape, whose facade obscures the social inequities that have given rise to the barrios.

Those who reside in the barrios emerge as an example of—in the view of this dichotomizing gaze of the rural and urban—unsuccessful transitioners; they are no longer romantic and "ordered" rural folk, but they are not "urban" either. Instead, they are failed urbanites (they are a rural-urban hybrid) who have not made the transition from rural folk to modern urbanites. They are confined by the very thing that as rooted folk made them historical icons of Venezuelan culture: tradition. As long as they are located physically and metaphorically in a rural geography (i.e., not within the city but within the countryside), they are less problematic (because rurality, often marked as unmodern, is also viewed as a potential health problem due to lack of health care in the rural-urban barrio).

Moreover, this view of the barrios as somehow extraneous to the city is similar to what Leeds (1994) has pointed out regarding the literature on favelas in Brazil (poor neighborhoods in the cities like the *ranchos* and barrios of Caracas). Leeds (1994, 237) argues:

> Almost without exception, all literature on favelas treats them as enclaves having their own unique internal characteristics in all respects: They are self-maintaining, culturally autonomous outsiders; strangers to the city; in fact, they are rural migrants who have squatted in the physical confines of the city, remaining isolated in it, but not of it.

The barrios of Caracas have, at least in popular (i.e., urban) opinion, been described in a strikingly similar manner. Leeds is critical of those characterizations that do not contextualize favelas within the historical, political, and economic structures of the state. He has commented extensively on the problematics of studying the favelas of Brazil without attention to the variables that create the conditions of poverty found in them. These variables include but are not limited to:

> the interests of the social and political elites of the city; . . . the conditions of the labor market with special reference to pressures varying the rates of unemployment and underemployment and to barriers to attainment of specialized training; the structure and operation of the rent and labor laws, especially the salary structure, including differential pay rates; the structure, accessibility, and costs of the metropolitan transportation system, and so on. (Leeds 1994, 237)

These observations are generally missing in configurations of Latin American favelas and barrios, as well as *barriadas, ranchos, cortiços, callejones, vecindades*, and so on, and they are precisely the conditions that maintain these marginal areas on the outskirts of society, both physically and ideologically. As this book does not pretend to be a study of barrios in Caracas, I do not look at these issues extensively in this work. However, I have pointed out some of the political and economic conditions that have allowed for the barrios to be popularly imagined as somehow "outside of the imagined (urban) community."[3]

The barrios get much attention in the media and are often described as places that foment disease and violence, as I explore in the next section, and threaten national goals of progress, development, and modernity. There is tension between urban Caracas, a symbol of modernity, development, and progress, and the rural-like barrios of Caracas, which symbolize the so-called traditional, undeveloped, and backward elements of the city. In the anthology *Critically Modern*, Bruce Knauft (2002, 18) captures the meaning of modernity that I employ here:

> Modernity can be defined as the images and institutions associate with Western-style progress and development in a contemporary world . . . [it] is often associated with either the incitement or the threat of individual desire to improve social life by subordinating or superseding what is locally configured as backward, undeveloped, or superstitious . . . modernity is a geography of imagination that creates progress through the projection and management of alterity.

Modernity also, I would argue, implies a certain morality as it is configured positively as moving forward, as morally good, regardless of the negative affects that modernization projects, particularly under the auspices of neoliberal policies, may have on the politically and economically disenfranchised. And in Caracas the antithesis of modernity is quite literally located in the geography of the hillsides.

Barrios: Locating Lawlessness and Disorder
I have thus far presented one depiction of the barrios: that of a rural-like margin of the urban. However, the barrios have also been characterized as a place that breeds criminals and antisocials of all types: drug dealers, dark-skinned foreigners, *malandros* (thugs), and urban guerrilla groups (Coronil and Skurski 1991, 322). These characterizations have important implications for the ways in which the residents of the barrios are implicitly and explicitly defined in the Venezuelan health discourse, a point that will be emphasized throughout this chapter. However, first it is necessary to look more closely at the images of the barrios.

In times of crisis, the boundaries between the civilized order of the urban center and the chaotic mass of the marginal barrios become more clearly delineated. For example, in 1989 Caracas experienced what came to be known as El Masacrón (The Massacre), also known as El Sacudón (Tremor) and El Caracazo (Coronil and Skursky 1991; Smilde and Hellinger 2011; Ciccariello-Maher 2013).[4] The violence and civil unrest that occurred over five days, between February 27 and March 3, 1989, were largely in protest of rising prices but also were more broadly rooted in the political and economic transformations that had taken place within the country over the previous two decades. Venezuela, which had once constructed itself as a wealthy oil-producing nation and a model of Latin American progress, had suffered a drop in the price of oil, a widening crisis of the protectionist model of development, and a hardening of the political system. Pérez, in 1989, upon assuming the presidency, began a campaign of economic austerity in which the rationality of the free market and the health of the economy became the goals of the nation. The goals of the pueblo were subordinated to the demands of the economy, and the curative shot for the economy was the dismantling of protectionist structures. The idea was that people would turn to productive work with the removal of coddling protectionism. Pérez would cut tariffs, remove price controls and subsidies, and unify the exchange rate. But as Coronil and Skurski (1991, 313) have noted, "The reality that consumers faced diverged wildly from one of market rationality. Confronted with the imminent dismantling of protectionism and the rising costs of imports, manufactures cut back production and businesses hoarded products." And thus began a snowballing effect of price increases, consumer hoarding, shortages, rising gas prices (with the removal of gasoline subsidies), and increases in transportation costs.

The working classes, fearing hunger, a shrinking economy, and unemployment, took to the streets in protest and looted stores a few short weeks after the inauguration of President Pérez. The protests were put down by violent actions of the state as a means of restoring "order" to the barrios, and hundreds of people were killed and buried in the anonymity of mass graves. During this time, "the dominant discourse soon constructed these disturbances as the unleashing of this primitive mass upon the city's center. At this moment of crisis, otherness was projected onto the city's barrios, as if the residents of these socially diverse areas in their entirety constituted a threat to the civilized order" (Coronil and Skurski 1991, 323). The divide between savagery and civility against lawlessness and order had been successfully constructed by the state and internalized by the more privileged of the country. This dehumanization by the privileged classes of those residing in the barrios is starkly evident in the following quote:

> "I would have killed all those savages, as I am sure they would have killed us if they had a chance. They hate us," Sofía, a wealthy young lawyer and Harvard-trained business woman, told us as she shaped her arm into a machine gun and pointed her finger toward the slums that surround her office in a skyscraper overlooking the hills from which looters had descended. (Coronil and Skurski 1991, 330)

The Venezuelan barrios, particularly those of Caracas, have been largely configured in opposition to the urban center, whether as a rural-like invasion, a criminal threat, or a disorderly mass. Violent clashes between barrio residents and police (and the military), often expressed as necessary restorative measures of public order, have been described in other Latin American countries such as Colombia and Brazil (Levine 1993). The divisions are most particularly salient during times of crisis.

Barrios: Locating Political Mobilization

In Venezuela the barrios have long been sites of political contestation and activism in the face of government repression like the Caracazo of 1989 discussed earlier and in the introduction to this book. Indeed, to understand the rise of Hugo Chávez and his election in 1998—connected to both the Caracazo and his failed coup attempt in 1992—one has to understand the lengthier history of the barrios as collectivist political sites.[5] I discuss the Chávez presidency in relation to health reforms in more detail in the epilogue. However, a discussion of the barrios and political mobilization is relevant here, as historically entrenched activism in the barrios was tightly linked to these reforms. In fact, both George Ciccariello-Maher (2013) and Alejandro Velasco (2011) emphasize not how Chávez created the Bolivarian movement, but rather how the popular sectors, those residing in the peripheral neighborhoods of the barrios, effectively created Chávez. Velasco focuses on the political activism of the 23 de Enero (January 23) barrio, which has been a site of mobilization since the 1950s. He disabuses us of the notion that political activism in the barrios is a relatively recent phenomenon emerging in the1980s with the Caracazo and the 1992 coup attempt. Although the "amalgam of 1950s-era superblocks and densely packed squatter settlements ... has long been considered one of the staunchest bases of urban popular support for Chávez," the neighborhood, known as El 23, has been a part of the revolutionary landscape since before Chávez (Velasco 2011, 158). In order to understand the political situation in Venezuela in relation to the barrios, it is imperative that we not misconstrue the barrios and the popular sector as always willing followers of political leadership, even those promising revolutionary reform. Velasco (2011, 181) articulates this point by noting that a common thread in El 23 today remains the "sense of community built around the pursuit of a contingent autonomy, neither fully independent from nor fully beholden to the state. As such, it is a relationship marked by negotiation and conflict, drawn in turn from an experience of activism dating to well before the rise of either Hugo Chávez or economic crisis in Venezuela." What these works speak to is the lengthy history of working-class political agency in urban communities. These contestations—as Holston (2008) reminds us—are struggles for citizenship, for the rights and responsibilities accorded to those who fully participate in society.

An analysis of the political activism in the barrios also requires that we look at the role that women play in community organizing. Women, in fact, are central actors when it comes to volunteerism in community projects like health work (Cooper 2015b). As Reihana Mohideen (2005, 67) points out, "What makes Venezuela different is the political involvement of huge numbers of women, and the fact that social change in Venezuela is being driven by a process of self-organisation of the poor and the marginalized." Sujatha Fernandes (2007, 99), in her article "Barrio Women and Popular Politics in Chávez's Venezuela," provides a historical account of the "gendered aspects of popular participation in Venezuela." She notes that some have erroneously described women's political participation as a more recent phenomenon of Chavismo and participatory democracy; this is because women's activism has been reduced to feminist movements. However, the 1970s saw the development of *círculos femeninos* as a space for women's organizing, a space for women to focus on alleviating problems specific to poor women and that were also aligned with problems facing the barrios in the areas of health, education, and work. Fernandes (2007, 104) notes that barrio women also began organizing alongside men and worked with them on what she describes as one of the most important campaigns of the 1970s, the struggle against urban remodeling:

> Christian Democratic president Rafael Caldera (1969–74) promoted a housing program known as "The New San Agustin," which proposed to eliminate the *ranchos* (small dwellings) and to build houses in the lower and middle ranges of the hills . . . the movement of community resistance grew stronger and spread to other parishes, such as La Vega, El Valle, and La Pastora, where residents also formed Committees Against Displacement to challenge the government policy.

Whether we are talking about the activism of men or of women in the barrios, it is clear that Venezuela has a history of popular-sector mobilization as old as the barrios themselves. This is not to say that Chávez didn't motivate the barrios, but they already had a history of agency. As I present medical encounters in the next chapters, the question of agency resurfaces. The barrio women who are the subject of this ethnography, through their experiences in seeking treatment for cervical cancer, are not without agency as they navigate patient-doctor interactions, even if they are imagined as such.

Barrios: Locating Community

The caricatured representations of barrio women as apathetic, disorderly, out of control, backward, and the like, stand in contrast to those which emphasize their community participation and maintaining solidarity in the face of government threats (and private threats from nearby middle-class communities) to tear down the illegally constructed homes. The *ranchos*, though described by the middle and upper classes as unsanitary, unstable, unhealthy, and disorderly, have achieved rather positive meanings for those residing there (Wiesenfeld 1997a, 1997b; Blanco 1993). Pride is taken in improvements that are made, and with the successive investments in these structures, the inhabitants create homes, not merely temporary places of residence.

Francisca
I met Francisca at Padre Machaco, as she was waiting to seek treatment for an early stage of cervical cancer. She was a first-time patient, and although it was unusual given the structure of my fieldwork, I was able to interview her on more than one occasion. Eventually we met outside of the hospital setting, and we developed a friendship near the end of my fieldwork. Francisca was tall and slender, with deep brown skin and tight brown curls cascading in a shoulder-length style. She had her children with her: a girl named Carina, who was four, and a toddler boy, Cristian, who was two. Carina, being older, was slightly better at waiting, but Cristian was a whirlwind of energy, walking and running around the spacious waiting area with the patience that all toddlers possess. As we chatted, we took turns entertaining them. Going to the hospital was usually an all-day affair, and trying to corral children and keep them entertained added stress to an already-stressful situation for women who needed to bring their kids with them. Francisca and I were close to the same age; she was thirty-one and I was twenty-eight at the time. It was clear that we got along with each other beyond the conversation we had as part of the interview. Even after the formal part of the interview was over, we continued to talk, and after she saw the doctor, we went to the little stand just outside the hospital to get snacks and sodas. Francisca had to wait for another clinic to open in the hospital later in the afternoon, so we hung out with each other while she waited.

One topic in particular that I was interested in broaching with her was her experience as an immigrant from Colombia. The subject that had foregrounded my graduate work on Latinas and cervical cancer was immigration. I had studied the hardships that Mexican immigrants to the United States face with social and economic marginalization. Because I had disclosed my knowledge on this subject and we had spent the morning building a genuine rapport with each other, she told me that she and her husband were undocumented immigrants in Venezuela. She and her husband, Norberto, lived in one of the barrios with their two children. Norberto had a degree in clinical psychology but found it difficult to open up his own practice. A friend of his came to work in Venezuela in a shoe import-export business and asked Norberto to join him. Norberto has been doing well in this business, and the couple had been able to make improvements to their home as a result. She related to me that she felt discriminated at times. People could tell she was Colombian because of her accent, and if she dared to mention that she was from Cali, sometimes people would make references to her being a drug dealer because of the drug trade associated with the city. The fact that she and her husband were undocumented only strengthened the insecurity she at times felt.

I witnessed this discrimination firsthand when Francisca came to visit me at the apartment where I was renting a room with a Venezuelan family. I had already become very close with the family and spent much of my time with them playing card games and talking about everything from where to buy food to U.S. and Venezuelan politics. I was quite disheartened when, after Francisca came to the door and my "host mother," Henriqueta, led her to the living room. Henriqueta then came into my room and whispered that I shouldn't invite Francisca into my room or other parts of the house because she is Colombian and they aren't to be trusted. With that she left, and I was left dumbfounded and angered at what had transpired. I couldn't have a conversation about it with Henriqueta in that moment, but at the end of the day we did speak about the negative perceptions that Venezuelans have about Colombians. In Francisca's case, she also had "mixed" African racial features, as marked by her skin tone and hair. So I suspect Henriqueta's reaction was not only about her being Colombian. However, Henriqueta was unwilling to have a discussion about racism; she denied that racism was involved at all and kept insisting she wasn't stereotyping in characterizing Colombians as thieves, liars, and immoral, repeatedly saying, "It's just the way Colombians are." As I discussed in Chapter 1, racism was often denied by nonblack and nonindigenous Venezuelans.

On another occasion, I met Francisca with her husband and children at a park. I did not want to bring her to the apartment again after the negative experience with Henriqueta. We played with their children and spent the afternoon discussing children, marriage, their life in Venezuela, and shoes—as her husband worked in the shoe business. Norberto thought he might be able to become licensed to practice psychology in Venezuela and find better opportunities here, but that plan was not panning out so quickly. In the meantime, he was making enough money so that they could add onto the *rancho* where they were living and make improvements. An idea that middle- and upper-class Venezuelans have of all *rancho*-style homes is that they are haphazard shacks and more dwellings than homes. Although I do not wish to romanticize the often difficult landscape of the barrios in terms of sewage, electricity, telephone access, and the like, people living there invest in their homes. Francisca and her husband discussed with me at length the floor that they were adding to their house, the yellow tiles that would match with the new kitchen cabinets. They also hoped to add a phone line so they wouldn't have to go to a neighbor's to receive calls (which is how I was able to contact her so we could meet up). People who make these kinds of investments in their properties do not see them as temporary dwellings. They do not fit the stereotype, which has painted the residents of barrios as antisocials and has negated the possibility of locating a sense of community within the barrio. I focus on Francisca here because both her undocumented status and her identity as an immigrant from Colombia represent precisely what Venezuelans were fearing at the time. And yet she and her family were participating in barrio life, sharing resources with neighbors, upgrading their *rancho* home, and generally engaging with their community.

Wiesenfeld (1997b, 47), in her study of the barrios of Caracas, quotes a resident of a barrio who articulates a sense of community taking shape in a barrio:

> Now the other important part of my *rancho* is that the children that grow in a *rancho* make friends among the bunch of children that are growing there at the same time in the community. From there come the future compadres [buddies], the future boyfriends, and the families become closer, some families to others, that is the importance of having a *rancho*. (Man, age 54)

The depiction of barrios as chaotic, lawless, and disorderly eclipses the realities of community, stability, and independence that *ranchos* can represent to those who reside in them. These categories (e.g., barrio-city, rural-urban), which get framed in terms of dualities, are not fixed, stable, or natural. They are, however, treated as immutable—fetishized and reified in such a way as to negate the possibility of movement of subjects across, between, and within social spaces. I am interested in the particular uses of these categories in the configuration of disease and what they suggest about how, where, and why public health strategies are directed. Defining barrios as unhealthy, for example, legitimizes the removal of *ranchos* and the displacement of people. *Ranchos*, indeed, have been targeted for removal, and this has been done within a health and sanitation framework, emphasizing lack of proper sewage and potable water. This is not to suggest that disease, poverty, and violence are not important problems within marginalized areas such as barrios. In fact, the issue of clean water is so important in the barrios that in current-day Venezuela—with the establishment of *consejos comunales* (community councils)[6]—community water committees known as *mesas técnicas de agua* (MTAs) work on the problems of access and contamination that the barrios face (Caswell 2014). My concern rests with the ways in which categories may mask social realities, such that, for example, economic and political constraints are rewritten as attributes of a culture or a people (e.g., lack of water becomes "dirty," "unhygienic" people). The general sense of national political, social, and economic instability that was evident in Venezuela starting in the 1980s allowed for the centering of the city-barrio dichotomy in Venezuelan health discourse.

Public Health and the Creation of "Sanitary Citizens"

This policing in the production of health at the same time results in the production of insiders and outsiders—those who are configured as "citizens" of the state and those who are not—crafting citizens involves not only deciding who counts as a citizen but also who doesn't. Scholars note that the notion of citizenship is complex—it can encompass an identity; a collection of rights, responsibilities, and privileges; and a membership standing of inclusion, exclusion, or liminality, among other considerations. Here, I am not concerned with citizenship in the legal sense—those de jure rights of citizenship determined, for example, by birth or naturalization. Instead, I am interested in citizenship as a category of belonging to what Anderson (1991) calls "the imagined community." In particular, I am interested in the intersections of citizenship, disease, morality, modernity, sexuality, and gender in constructing what it means for a nation-state to cast some as insiders and others as outsiders irrespective of legal and birth claims to citizenship. Charles Briggs's (2003) concept of sanitary citizenship is useful here in that it bridges the concepts of biopower and citizenship:

108   Chapter 3

> Sanitary citizenship is one of the key mechanisms for deciding who is accorded substantive access to the civil and social rights of citizenship. Public health officials, physicians, politicians, and the press depict some individuals and communities as possessing modern medical understanding of the body, health, and illness, practicing hygiene, and depending on doctors and nurses when they are sick. These people become sanitary citizens. (10)

They are regarded as the example of moral and modern citizens. Those who are perceived as not possessing these qualities are regarded as their antithesis—that is, as "unsanitary subjects;" those "who are judged incapable of adopting this modern medical relationship to the body, hygiene, illness, and healing" or who are seen as refusing to do so (10).

However, citizenship's relationship to gender has until relatively recently been left largely underexplored. But this charge is increasingly being taken up by scholars wishing to explore the relationships among nationalism, women's bodies, sexuality, reproduction, and state policies (Patton, Schein, work in Singapore, Greenhalgh, Jolly, and a number of scholars working on these questions in India—Bhasin, Menon, Ram, the Philippines—Hilsdon, Thailand—Whittaker). A feminist perspective, in particular, for example, examines these complexities of citizenship in relation to gender—or the gendering of nationalism and citizenship—and brings a host of issues to the fore that have implications for equity and social justice, including sexuality, fertility, and reproduction. Specifically, Margaret Jolly (2004) points to some of the following questions of interest for her work on citizenship, fertility, and sexuality in Asia and the Pacific: "How are the bodies of persons, the imagined edges of their corporeal being, linked to the borders of countries, the partitioning of nation-states? And how are the flows from their bodies, their sexual desires and their children conceived as belonging within, or confined by, the borders of countries?"

In the case of women in Venezuela who have cervical cancer, their exclusion from citizenship is not formal or legal but rather is accomplished precisely through the everyday practices of configuring them as threats to the nation through their diseased fertile bodies. Importantly, the women whom I interviewed indirectly challenged and transformed these dominant discourses of morality, modernity, and citizenship. I emphasize their agency, which the medical establishment generally denies them, and I point out the ways in which they contest socio-medical perceptions about who they are and how they should be treated. However, their experiences cannot be described in terms of comfortable and unproblematic constructs of subjugation and resistance. I do not wish to romanticize resistance or leave unaddressed deeply entrenched inequalities. At the same time, it is important to recognize the ways in which these women did act and resist.

I also want to be clear that this work isn't about creating villains and victims, the good and the bad, or any other dreadful dichotomy. I am not talking about overt conspiratorial acts perpetrated by people to cause harm. The doctors and public health officials and administrators whom I spoke with did genuinely care about the health and well-being of sick women and developed public health campaigns with the goal of eradicating cervical cancer. However, I am not so much concerned with analyzing them as individual actors as with focusing on the ways in which dominant, taken-for-granted assumptions about class, race, gender, and sexuality are held collectively and permeate everyday life, including interactions between patients and doctors. That being said, I do acknowledge that in many ways power is fluid with different actors exercising varying degrees of control, collaboration, and resistance at different times and locations.

Culture, Nationalism, and Health: The Urban Civilizing Mission

In part, I argue that the role of public health can be seen as what Schein (1994, 478) has called—in a the context of the construction of the "folk" in post-Mao China—an urban elite "civilizing mission." Schein argues that China's rural peasants during the post-1979 reform period were idealized and contrasted to the hegemony of Westernization as traditional Chinese cultural products. The problematic of "backwardness" (simultaneously created in these narratives) in the face of modernization, however, would not be incorporated into the nationalist discourse, which sought to distinguish itself (as a single united China) from the West. The image of the ideal "folk," then, with the face of both tradition and backwardness, also legitimized a faintly shrouded civilizing mission, which would be the charge of urban elites—the possessors of civility and progress.

So, then, what do culture and civilization have to do with health? As pointed out in the previous chapter, culture is implicated in this mission insofar as it is seen as linked with modernity, health, and even hygiene. Let us recall the comment of a thirty-two-year-old male doctor, a *pasante*, at the private hospital:

> Generally, we speak of educational level, of formation. People of low economic status don't have the cultural level or understanding . . . or the hygienic habits, [they] lack daily genital cleanliness . . . not douching and washing themselves.

Moreover, when asked about the ways women could avoid getting cervical cancer, he said, "Better the culture of the population, avoid promiscuity, and have frequent gynecological control." In formal open-ended interviews with doctors, 35 percent referred to culture, either "low cultural level" or "lack of culture," as a risk for cervical cancer.

Culture seems to serve in this context as an umbrella for educational and class standing. Yet it is arguably a marker for a whole style of life and social position. Culture, in this sense, reminiscent of the nineteenth-century German elite notion of Kultur (Stocking 1968), is something not quite tangible, purposefully vague, an esoteric sort of essence reserved for (and owned by) the elite, and possibly the middle class, but definitely not the poor. The picture is actually a bit more complicated than that. As Martínez (2002, 258), in her study of folkloric dance and nation building in Venezuela, has noted, "'Culture,' often an undefined notion of practice and artifacts, is often used by elites as a marker of difference, identity and value." She also notes, however, that the invocation of culture is also increasingly popularized and prevalent in Venezuela. Its deployment both creates distance and unites "a people," depending upon historical circumstance and social and economic context.

What I am concerned with, in making sense of the connections among culture, nation, class, and health in Venezuela, is the uses of culture—the politics of culture. Several important questions can be addressed by understanding the strategic social and political uses of culture. We can begin by asking,

> (1) When it is that certain things get called "the culture" and other do not; (2) when it is that one sector of society invokes a cultural argument to explain a social, political, or economic reality; (3) when it is that governments make a point of developing and articulating an explicit "cultural policy," while others do not; and (4) when it is that reformist or revolutionary governments call for social, economic, and/or political change by earmarking culture as a preeminent arena for their struggle. (Dominguez 1992, 21–22)

The Venezuelan government, for instance, has increasingly looked toward popular cultural policies in (re)creating and articulating Venezuelan national identity through the implementation of committees designed to promote Venezuelan culture. As a medium through which this could be accomplished, the First National Congress of Culture took place on October 29–31, 1996, under the auspices of the National Cultural Advisory (Conac). The event was inaugurated by President Rafael Caldera and attended by various directors of cultural organizations throughout the country, members of parliament, and other local and state government representatives. Generally, the goal of the congress was to outline and define the direction of cultural politics in Venezuela. Specifically, the congress dealt with the following issues: "decentralization, democratization, and integration of the cultural administration of the state; infrastructure and conservation of the cultural patrimony; Venezuelan cultural legislation; cultural industries; artistry and diffusion of culture, and lastly, the state cultural inversion" (*El Universal*, October 28, 1996).

Moreover, in newspaper articles between 1995 and 1998, Venezuelans pointed to the need to (re)construct a Venezuelan national cultural identity, looking for "cultural roots," "a cultural revolution," and "a culture of peace," among other variants of this theme.[7] Antonio López Ortega, general director of Fundación Bigott, the Venezuelan private organization that has been most prolific in promoting Venezuelan popular culture and folklore through workshops, presentations, performances, and so on, commented on the national collective to revise Venezuelan popular culture. In an interview for the newspaper *El Universal*, he said, "We are in a period of much dispersion, a critical period in which Venezuelan society is looking to reform its entire essence, its being." When asked by the journalist if Venezuela has been able to understand its traditions and show pride in them, he responded:

> My diagnosis is, although that hasn't been achieved, we have advanced; we are in a very distinct reality than that of ten years ago. The current situation of the country moves us to try and value a bit more, what is ours, that is seen everywhere.... We don't believe that popular culture has to be something with cobwebs, we support its transformation within a certain delineation that respects the traditional. (*El Universal*, December 23, 1996)

This (re)construction was occurring at a time that many Venezuelans saw as unstable and transitory. These similar calls for a national cultural agenda were heard at the beginning of General Marcos Pérez Jiménez's dictatorship in the early 1950s. His state ideology for constructing the nation rested on the material signs that would embody progress and modernization, such as freeways and luxury hotels, but also the "spiritual" dimensions of traditional Venezuelan culture, which emphasized official folklore, religion, and national history. Both of these dimensions, material and spiritual, were managed as part of a civilizing process that would achieve the goal of modernity (Coronil 1997).

At the same time, what gets articulated as Venezuelan culture is often contested, manipulated, transformed, reworked, and politicized. As Roseberry (1989, 75) has argued, "dominant culture . . . is not a closed system, it is in a constant process of construction and reconstruction." Venezuelan newspaper articles attesting to public struggles over the meaning and assignation of culture attest to this process and to the popular invocation of culture. For example, one article stated, "The sadness that the neighbors feel in seeing how their life style has declined, has not impeded them from organizing to fight for the rescue of their parish Santa Rosalia, in the process reinforcing various areas such as culture, education, and health" (*El Universal*, September 11, 1997). The consolidation of culture, health, and education is particularly notable and is evident in another article that discusses a one-day health program in a barrio of Caracas. The program was cosponsored by the Division of Social Development and the Division of Culture. Residents received free pediatric care, dental care, general medical attention, psychological services, legal advice, haircuts, and cultural events (*El Universal*, October 21, 1996). The promotion of popular culture along with the promotion of health effectively links the two, but in a very different way than that articulated by medical and public health practitioners. For example, a 1987 Venezuelan health promotion campaign for cervical cancer identifies the target population as "those between the ages of 25 and 64 years in the most socially, economically, and culturally deprived population" (MSAS 1987). Culture was left undefined in this pamphlet, but, as I have indicated throughout, the linkages between cervical cancer risk and culture often draw on ideas about class, hygiene, and morality. Moreover, cultural "deprivation" was often described by doctors and health administrators as localized within the barrios of Caracas.

In general, the sense that Venezuela was at a time of particular vulnerability and in need of nation building, through a turn to "culture," was evident in some of the slogans played over the television during the time of this fieldwork. One, for example, extorted, "Venezuela, ours is the best!" A commercial that aired during Christmas 1994 emphasized the vulnerability of the nation by metaphorically constructing it as a child. The commercial begins with a scene in which children are working together to make *hallacas*, a food that is traditionally prepared during Christmas in Venezuela. A girl begins to speak: "Venezuela is like a child that needs to be taken care of with love, showing it the road to a better future. Venezuela is that child that we all have inside, that cries when it is sad, that laughs when it is content." All children sing together: "Venezuela is like a child that dreams of bettering itself and wakes early, a happy worker. Venezuela is like a child that doesn't stop singing, that announces with joy that Christmas has arrived." In this narrative song, the anthropomorphized nation is in need of love and guidance; it is vulnerable yet hardworking and progressive. With the proper care, it will move forward and never stop singing. Constructing the nation as a vulnerable child requires the parallel invocation of caretaker who will nurture and foster growth, and this image of nurturer is almost always reserved for women.[8]

Public Health Pamphlets: Nurturing the Family, Nurturing the Nation

Women seem to be at the core of nationalist discourses of health, focusing on their roles as mothers and wives in the maintenance of a "healthy" nation. The representation of Venezuela as childlike and vulnerable draws these connections between nurturer (taken for granted as being mother or woman) and nurtured (the nation) quite naturally.

Pamphlets are one of the sources that I used to look at the ways in which the health message about cervical cancer was presented to women. The pamphlets put out by the MSAS and the Venezuelan Cancer Society were distributed in clinics in Caracas as well as throughout Venezuela. They were distributed as a tool to inform women about the Pap exam. My purpose here is not to do an evaluative study of pamphlets but only to understand them as part of the social configuration of cervical cancer in neoliberal Venezuela. Scholars have analyzed print images, both photographic and illustrative, as a way of locating race (racism), gender (sexism), and class (classism), and framing these social phenomena within their historical and political contexts (see, for a few examples, Lutz and Collins 1997; Bordo 1997; Chávez 2001; Hill Collins 2002). The focus here is on the images of women in pamphlets on cervical cancer prevention, and in particular on gender relations and on the social disciplining of women that is implicit in these messages. Although this in no way pretends to be as extensive an analysis as those works that concentrate on the analysis of a myriad of images, it does point to the ways in which configurations of cervical cancer are embedded in socio-cultural conceptions of class, gender, risk, and responsibility.

Consider, for example, the image from a public health pamphlet distributed by the Venezuelan Ministry of Health and Social Services (MSAS). The pamphlet, entitled "Woman, A Health Message for You," explains what cervical cancer is and how the Pap exam can detect it (see figure 3.1). In this pamphlet, women are reminded of the important roles they have as mothers and wives. The first illustration is a Madonna-like image of a woman with a baby. The reader is told that her children need her (although implicitly one child is enough—as the mother-child dyad indicates[9]), and a similar message is relayed in terms of her importance to her family. The nuclear family (one mom, one dad, and one child) is presented to signify the family, and the subtext of this health message implicates the nuclear family as a health strategy for women.

The health message in this pamphlet also underscores the importance of women to the nation. The border outline of the Venezuelan nation with the centered head of a woman emphasizes this connection between woman and nation. Moreover, the face chosen to represent the nation is that of a blonde white woman. Given that 68 percent of Venezuela's population consists of brown-skinned, brown-eyed, and brown- or black-haired mestizos, it begs the question: why was this image chosen to be superimposed on the outline of the nation? If we look historically at the histories of colonization in Latin America—and the more contemporary myth of the *café con leche* society in Venezuela (discussed in Chapter 1)—we can trace colonial whiteness as it was associated with civility, "proper" (read: male) citizenship, property rights, political participation, and literacy (Appelbaum, Macpherson, and Rosemblatt 2003). Citizenship and notions of civility as a so-called cultured propriety continue to be aligned with whiteness in the current era and also with notions of what it means to be a modern subject (Bonnett 2002). Specifically, social geographer Alastair Bonnet (2002, 77–78) uses the phrase "whiteness of modernity" to describe the particular histories of Brazil and Venezuela in laying out the connections among the development of white identities, capitalist enterprise, and a so-called cultural sophistication with attention to the future:

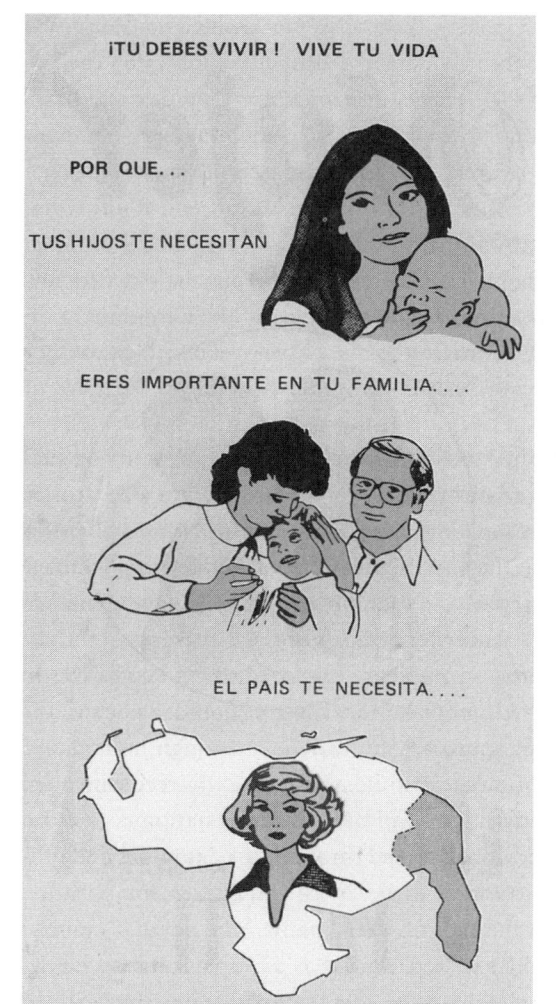

FIGURE 3.1 "Woman A Health Message for You."

SOURCE: The Ministry of Health and Social Assistance, Oncology Division.

NOTE: The inside cover reads: "You Should Live! Live Your Life / Why... / Your Children Need You / You Are Important in Your Family / The Country Needs You... / To live you should be healthy, because of that we invite you to learn what a vaginal cytology is."

To be modern, to be forward looking, demands a break with a non-European past and an immersion into the new ways and attitudes of European civilization. The range and scale of the attempt to Europeanize Venezuela and Brazil were considerable. To be culturally sophisticated, to adopt modern economic roles and practices; to build cities, roads, farms, and factories and arrange bureaucracies in an efficient manner; all these keys to advancement were symbolized by things European. And the central and cohering symbol of things European was, of course, the flesh of the European. Thus the practices and ideologies of modernity were embodied in the figure of the European, in the person of the white who offers progress as a universally obtainable project, a distributable gift, but whose own body is its defining symbol.

In this sense, a modern-identified woman in relationship to sexuality and reproduction is one who enacts a bourgeois notion of family with a controlled fertility, is an enthusiastic participant in medical technologies, and practices monogamy. She is also white in the popular imagination. The symbolic image of the white face, whether conscious and intentional or not, links whiteness to the nation, citizenship, and ideals of modernity. For these reasons—motherhood, family, and national duty—women are implored to get Pap exams in order to be healthy and to "live their lives." And even if they are not socially constructed as white, they can approximate whiteness through monogamy, control of reproduction, the nuclear family, and medically recommended monitoring. After all, the modern economically powerful nation is at stake. The message about women's health as related through this pamphlet and others like it is inextricably intertwined with capitalism, citizenship, culture, modernity, and race. Thus, in the "age of sexual panic," the popular cultural production of the ordered family is "repackaged as a prophylactic social device . . . [and] marketed as a strategic and prudential safe sex practice" (Singer 1993, 85).

The social, economic, and moral implications of such medical and public health projects are also linked to what Nikki Craske (2005) refers to as gendered citizenship in Latin American nation building. She asks us to consider the following: What expectations are placed on women as gendered citizens? And how are questions of sexuality and reproduction connected to capitalist enterprise and modernization? In analyzing gendered citizenship in Mexico, she argues that women were both promoted as modern citizens to showcase the nation as progressive and, at the same time, called upon to embody the romanticized image of the self-sacrificing mother. Relatedly, historian Raúl Necochea López, articulating the ideologically constructed connections among fertility control, capitalism, modernity and democracy in his 2014 book *A History of Family Planning in Twentieth-Century Peru*, argues that "since the 1990s, a growing body of literature connects fertility to elite projects to 'civilize' Latin Americans along Western lines. This process coincided, not by chance, with the acceleration of Latin American nation-states' insertion into transnational capitalist networks in the nineteenth century.... In this context, Latin American elites embraced science, Positivism, and European tastes as markers of high culture, and as prerequisites for national progress" (8). Moreover, public health experts and demographers in the 1970s and 1980s argued that large families could be a liability in industrial societies, as people in Latin America were increasingly moving to urban areas. Large families were seen not only as liabilities to "modern" societies but as threats to democratic stability (Necochea Lopez 2014). Analyzing this pamphlet and the ones below in the context of modernity and the intersections of gender, race, and class gives us much-needed perspective on historical projects of fertility in Latin America.

With this history in mind, I introduce another pamphlet, this time put out by the Venezuelan Cancer Society, showing a baby with the caption "Mom I need you for a long time" (*Mamá, te necesito por mucho tiempo*; see figure 3.2). In this pamphlet women are informed about and encouraged to have Pap exams and to do breast self-exams. Again, as with the previous image (figure 3.1), women are encouraged to take care of themselves for their children. The message, placed next to the picture of a baby, draws on motherhood in health promotion. As noted with the previous image, it is also a production of national identity.

The creation of an imagined community (Anderson 1991) is evident in these images that are (re)produced in the arena of public health. To be a united healthy nation, politically, economically, socially, and even culturally, requires a healthy population. Because Venezuela was economically and politically unstable, the promotion of the nation through the discourse of health is not completely surprising. The responsibility of women to take care of their health, take care of their families, and by extension take care of the nation as family requires that women control and monitor their bodies and their sexuality. Moreover, this disciplining requires that women also dutifully allow their bodies to be monitored and examined on a yearly basis (for a Pap exam), or more often, they are warned, if they have more than one sexual

FIGURE 3.2
"Mom I Need You for a Long Time."
SOURCE: The Venezuelan Cancer Society.

partner. As one doctor told me, when I asked how often it was recommended for a woman to get a Pap exam:

> There are patients that are at risk who should do it as least every three to six months, and there are patients who can have it done yearly. Every thing depends upon the circumstances in which they find themselves . . . those that don't have a boyfriend or a husband can have it done every two years, and the ones that don't change partners can have it done every year or two. It all depends.

Those who are sexually monogamous are in need of less bodily monitoring. This not only leaves unquestioned the sexual monogamy of male partners and the role that they can play in disease transmission; more importantly, the message is that as long as women are monogamous they will be safe, or at least safer. Male sexuality is not marked in the same way because it is female sexuality that materializes as naturally monogamous, and when this so-called state of nature is violated, this signals danger. This cultural configuration of gender is what Butler (1990, 33) has called "felicitous self-naturalization," where hegemonic constructs appear as natural phenomenon.

Another pamphlet, put out by the Venezuelan Cancer Society, warns of the risk factors for cervical cancer and includes lack of hygiene among them (see figure 3.3). The first paragraph of the pamphlet explains to women (the readers) that "the cervix is the part of the female reproductive system that has the most contact during sexual relations." In the second paragraph women are warned that "sexual comportment influences the potential presence of the disease." In agreement with what many of the doctors whom I interviewed mentioned as risk factors for cervical cancer, this pamphlet—under the middle section in all caps "Risk Factors for Cervical Cancer"—lists the following in order: "sexual relations at an early age, various sexual partners, multiparity, lack of hygiene and prior gynecological infections, poor postpartum attention, and smoking as risk." The last section lists "Specific Signs and Symptoms of Cervical Cancer: (1) Pelvic Pain (2) Loss of urine or fecal matter through the vagina (3) Loss of appetite and (4) Loss of Weight." What is of particular interest is the inclusion of lack of personal hygiene as a risk factor—this despite the fact that an association between lack of hygiene and cervical cancer has not been substantiated in the epidemiological literature. The meaning of this risk factor itself is vague, but when stated in conjunction with the risk of prior gynecological infections, it seems to suggest that both are related. Thus, having prior gynecological infections (given the vagueness of this statement, either some sort of sexually transmitted disease or a yeast infection) calls into question a woman's personal cleanliness. It is, however, likely that the gynecological infections alluded to are sexually transmitted in nature,[10] therefore linking hygiene and sexual comportment in this pamphlet's portrayal of cervical cancer risk. "Proper" sexual comportment is hygienic and healthy in this narrative of risk. Thus, the perception of lack of hygiene as a risk factor is not limited to doctors' cervical cancer discourse (discussed in Chapter 2), but is also present in the public health messages directed at women, emphasizing its saliency for configurations of cervical cancer in Venezuela.

The connections between sexual comportment and health are made rather explicit in another section of this pamphlet entitled "How to Control the Risk Factors." Seven suggestions are made under this section for the minimization of cervical cancer risk:

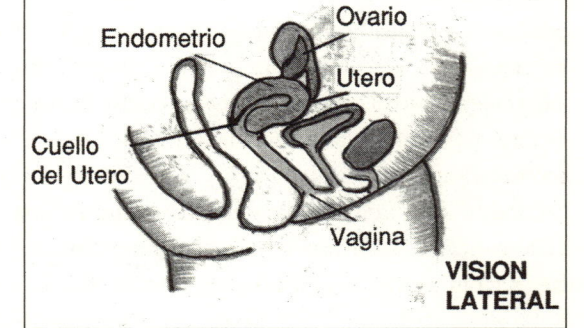

FIGURE 3.3 "Cervical Cancer."
SOURCE: Venezuelan Cancer Society.
NOTE: Title reads: *Cervical Cancer*

CANCER DE CERVIX

La Cérvix o Cuello Uterino es la parte del Aparato Reproductor Femenino con mayor roce en la relación sexual.

En el Cáncer de Cérvix, el comportamiento sexual influye en la potencial presentación de la enfermedad.

FACTORES DE RIESGO PARA EL CANCER DE CERVIX

- Inicio temprano de relaciones sexuales.
- Varios compañeros sexuales.
- Multiparidad.
- Falta de higiene personal y antecedentes de infección ginecológica.
- Mala atención post-parto.
- Hábito de fumar.

SIGNOS ESPECIFICOS PARA EL CANCER DE CERVIX

Signos y Síntomas:
1.- Dolor Pélvico.
2.- Pérdida de orina o material fecal por la vagina.
3.- Falta de apetito.
4.- Pérdida de peso.

[Diagram labeled: Ovario, Endometrio, Utero, Cuello del Utero, Vagina — VISION LATERAL]

— Having only one sexual partner is recommended
— Sexual relations should begin at an appropriate age
— Have regular medical control (checkups) after giving birth
— Avoid an excessive number of births
— Maintain good personal hygiene
— Avoid smoking
— Maintain an ideal weight

These prescriptions for a healthy lifestyle are also measures of the sexual disciplining of women's lives through the management of their bodies. Regulation takes a gender-specific form as women are targeted so as to engage in appropriate (not excessive) reproduction, monogamy, personal hygiene, and appropriate medical management of their bodies after giving birth. The image of the nuclear family presented in figure 3.1, as well as the emphasis on the role of women in relation to children and family in that pamphlet (and in figure 3.2), taken together with the advocacy of monogamy, appropriate reproduction, and the vague reference to appropriate age for sexual intercourse, constitute and are constitutive of a social, political, and historical milieu in which the social regulation of women is achieved partly through the medical regulation of their bodies. As Singer (1993, 85) has noted, in this, "the age of sexual epidemic," "the advocacy of domesticated monogamous marital sexuality geared toward reproduction take on special strategic value in an age concerned with the risks of multiple sexual contacts." Sex within the institution of marriage, therefore, is good sex; it is healthy sex. Ironically, the family, which historically has been shown to be a particularly unsafe place for women (i.e., where most violence against women occurs), is the social institution sanctioned as "healthy" for women (Singer 1993).

Cindy Patton's (1992) analysis of public health discourse surrounding AIDS in Africa at the onset of the epidemic also understands risk in the context of rigid gender and family ideologies. She argues that Western public health workers in Africa had largely been concerned with stopping the spread of AIDS through the transformation of the African family to that of the "legitimate" bourgeois family. Patton notes that media reportage about AIDS in Africa often implicitly denigrated African families "for having, besides a surfeit of children, either too many parents or too few (usually the father has died or has run off)" (234). The legitimacy of the bourgeois family as a health strategy was sanctioned above all through its association with the ideal of regulated heterosexual intercourse. The control of AIDS therefore, involved a control of family. This narrative of AIDS is suggestive of what Donzelot (1979) has referred to as "the policing of families," which in turn-of-the-century France was achieved through the use of women as vehicles for disciplining the family and by extension maintaining the well-being of society through the family. Public health legislation was in many instances directed at women, who were viewed as the monitors of health and hygiene within the family.

It is interesting that, although cervical cancer is largely portrayed as a sexually transmitted disease (focusing on correlations between certain strains of the human papilloma virus and the development of cervical cancer), the health recommendations for decreasing risk as demonstrated through these pamphlets do not include condom use (none of the health pamphlets mentioned this). The discourse on risk remains at the level of sexual and reproductive regulation of women. The concept of safe sex (or "safer" sex) had not entered in this configuration as it had in the discourse on sexually transmitted diseases such as AIDS, herpes, syphilis, and other sexually transmitted infections.[11] Given that cervical cancer has been largely configured in terms of sexual behavior, this is somewhat incongruous. However, if we view this absence in light of the public health emphasis on family, monogamy, and motherhood, it shouldn't seem that surprising that condom use would not be presented as an option. It is also important to note that Venezuela is a country that is mostly Catholic and abortion is illegal. These points should be explored at greater length in an analysis that focuses on the specific strategies of health promotion in regard to cervical cancer.

"Woman! Your Health Depends on You"

The slogan "Woman! Your Health Depends on You"—taken from a pamphlet produced by the Oncology Division of the Venezuelan Ministry of Health and Social Assistance (MSAS), ends with the phrase "Only you can prevent cervical cancer" (see figure 3.4).

Much of the health discourse directed at cervical cancer prevention in Venezuela has focused on individual behaviors (of women in particular). The pamphlets presented here emphasize individual behaviors in health promotion (and conversely individual fault for disease), whether on the level of changing sexual or reproductive behavior or in terms of encouraging women

FIGURE 3.4 "Woman! Your Health Depends on You."
SOURCE: Venezuelan Ministry of Health and Social Assistance.

to have annual Pap exams. In particular, the pamphlet distributed by the Venezuelan Cancer Society (figure 3.3) focuses on the at-risk sexual behaviors that women should not engage in. In analyzing the imagery of these pamphlets, one questions whom it is that these pamphlets are targeting. The answer is easy enough: those at risk. And those at risk have been largely defined as poor and marginalized women. Much has been made of behavioral risk factors (particularly evident in interviews with doctors and the cancer society's pamphlet "Cervical Cancer Can Be Prevented") that have been associated specifically with (and as a property of) poor women: promiscuity, lack of hygiene, and multiparity. In fact, middle- and upper-class women are attributed a higher moral standard and have been defined de facto in antithesis to these risk factors. They are what poor women are not: hygienic and monogamous. They are the unmarked subjects while subaltern women are the marked objects. Thus, in locating gendered regulation, class regulation has also been located. It is poor women, in particular who are targeted. Yes, this appears logical because they have the highest incidences of cervical cancer, but below the surface of that reasoning lies another: moral convictions about the behavior of "poor women" as a category. Under this rubric, it is poor women more than any other group of women who need to be reminded of what a family should look like (i.e., the nuclear family presented in figure 3.1), and of the danger of promiscuity, uncleanliness, and birthing too many children, because they are the ones identified with (and defined in terms of) these habits. In this case, health promotion is at the same time a civilizing mission in which poor and working-class women's behavior is perceived as both health risk and social transgression, and as such is in need of medico-moral regulation.

Where structural factors have been acknowledged as obstacles to health care, they are still largely expressed as group pathologies and only superficially make reference to problems of social inequality. Lack of education, for example, is often listed as a risk factor for cervical cancer in relation to low socioeconomic status—lack of education both in terms of the level of formal education attained by individuals and in terms of education about, in this case, cervical cancer prevention. The latter (lack of education about a disease) is largely described as a result of the first; education level, then, translates to having appropriate, proper, and true knowledge about one's body. Education is the taken-for-granted solution to combat this risk factor (lack of education), but it is not entirely unproblematic. Education can be many things all at once: empowering, disciplinary, regulatory, informative. The failure to look at education critically obscures the many ways that education can operate. The type of education described in Venezuelan health promotion is often unidirectional from top (e.g., health educator, doctor) to bottom (target population). For example, the director of Venezuela's Cancer Society expressed in an interview that lack of education is the most important obstacle to cervical cancer prevention:

> Education is the most prevalent obstacle. When a woman is informed and educated about the benefits of cervical cancer prevention, . . . the woman responds. The most fundamental obstacle is information and education . . . if this obstacle is overcome everything else will come along on its own.

The woman's role here is to absorb information and to respond appropriately (eliminating risky behaviors and/or getting an annual Pap exam). Once this is accomplished, it is assumed that other obstacles will take care of themselves. Reception of legitimate medical knowledge is taken to mean education, and response equals results. In this schema, education leads to the favorable outcome of medically managed bodies. Moreover, if there is no response, the assumption is, as the director concluded, that the message did not get across, which in turn may diminish serious attempts to confront other obstacles that are a more direct reflection of the material conditions of people's daily lives.

Cervical Cancer and National Health Policy

Cervical cancer health education in Venezuela must also be understood within the schema of the national health programs aimed at controlling the disease. In November 1987, the first national workshop for the integration and evaluation of the Program of Cervical Cancer Control took place in Caracas. The workshop was organized by the Oncology Division of the Ministry of Health and Social Assistance. Representatives from the Pan American Health Organization, the Venezuelan Institute of Social Security, the Ministry of Education Institute for Social Attention, the Sucre District Health Division from the State of Miranda, and the Venezuelan Cancer Society were in attendance. The stated goals of the program were to implement an epidemiological study over three years that would provide Pap exams to those women between the ages of twenty-five and sixty-four designated as "at risk" for cervical cancer. Interestingly, the focus at the time was not on educating women about risk factors for cervical cancer because it had been determined that "sexual comportment is difficult to modify and because of this prevention is based fundamentally and almost exclusively on the taking of vaginal cytologies" (MSAS 1987, 29). Nonetheless, in the evaluation of this program, education for health professionals and the public is cited as a priority in the future design and development of these types of programs. In terms of health professionals, the goals of education are "primary care training in the taking of cytology samples and motivating the health professional (doctors, nurses, social workers) in the area of patient follow-up and control" (MSAS 1987, 29). The following is the suggestion for educating the public: "The existing resources at the level of mass communication, conferences, talks, and workshops that inform the public about risk factors (sexual promiscuity, smoking, etc.) should be utilized. Additionally, people should be motivated to get a cytological exam as a fundamental measure in prevention and early detection" (MSAS 1987, 29). Although the proposal had originally played down the role of educating women about risk factors, the program evaluation actually stresses risk education and treats the Pap exam with only slightly less significance. Moreover, the inclusion of the education of health professionals as an important goal of this program is limited to training them to better monitor patients. There is little sense that this educational agenda, although making mention of the need to educate both health professionals and the public, is any different from simply stressing the need to educate the masses.

In 1991, however, we see the emergence of the participatory model of health education in the national agenda for cervical cancer prevention. The participatory model of health promotion focuses on the role of community and professionals in creating, disseminating, implementing, and evaluating health policy and programs. It is emphasized in the 1991 document *Strategies of Communication, Education, and Participation of the Woman for the Prevention of Cervical Cancer*, cosponsored by the Pan American Health Organization, the World Health Organization, the Venezuelan Ministry of Health and Social Assistance, and the Venezuelan Ministry of the State for the Promotion of Women. The focus on the participatory model of health education has been noted in other Latin American countries, particularly in Brazil, since the 1980s (Gastaldo 1997). This "emphasis on participation should be seen ... as part of an international network in which agencies like the WHO and UNICEF disseminate trends in the health arena that deserve recognition from countries linked to the network" (1997, 122). It should not be surprising, therefore, that Venezuela's health strategies for cervical cancer prevention, in which the WHO is directly involved (such as the 1991 campaign), should look similar to those found in Brazil. The historical particularities of each region, however, also shape the development, implementation, and evaluation of health policies.

Education discourse in this 1991 campaign looks very different from that found in the earlier 1987 version. In this latter campaign, the authors stress that "communication has to be conceived of as processual, and never as a forced action. In this sense, communication as process implies education, awareness, information, and action" (MSAS 1991, 10). Moreover, in terms of the relationship between health educator (e.g., nurse, doctor) and patient, a critical position is taken. The authors suggest that the following areas need to be examined at greater length:

a) The situation of subordination that is established between patient and doctor.

b) The situation of gynecology and obstetrics as it relates to the ideology of power.

c) The god-like image of the doctor in relation to the patient, with emphasis on the patient-doctor relationship, where one of these entities (the doctor) tends to engage with an "amorphous mass" (the patient).

However, the tenacious nature of these problems is also taken rather lightly. This section concludes with the observation, "These negative aspects, which can be easily overcome with awareness programs and information directed at health personnel, turn into obstacles at the moment when the interest and dedication of women to the care of their bodies and health is evaluated" (MSAS 1991, 10). In the end, the assertion that these negative aspects "can be easily overcome" does little to seriously engage with relationships of power in the medical setting. Moreover, this statement suggests that women may ultimately be to blame for their own objectification if it is decided that they are disinterested and not dedicated to the care of their bodies and health. Nonetheless, the attempts at participatory health promotion, which suggests a more balanced relationship between health educators and the public than the unidirectional approach, is evident in the health campaign.

It is also important to emphasize that "social policy is not a single stream of power from the federal to the local level. The process of promoting knowledge and norms occurs within a web of micro-powers of forms of control and resistance" (Gastaldo 1997:123). Thus, what is articulated in health promotion policy does not necessarily come into practice at the local level. For example, if we understand the physicians as disseminators of health information, it was evident, from observations and interviews at the hospitals, that physicians differed in the amounts of information they disclosed to patients, and the amount of "participation" elicited in most cases was mainly at the level of the patient following doctor's orders.

Furthermore, the inside of the pamphlet, "Woman! Your Health Depends on You" (see figure 3.5) makes one wonder whether, within the context of the MSAS's participatory model of health education, the subtext of the image, given the asymmetry of doctor and patient, actually suggests something other than participation. Notice, for example, the figure that is centered and whose face is visible is that of the doctor. This pamphlet was printed in 1993, almost

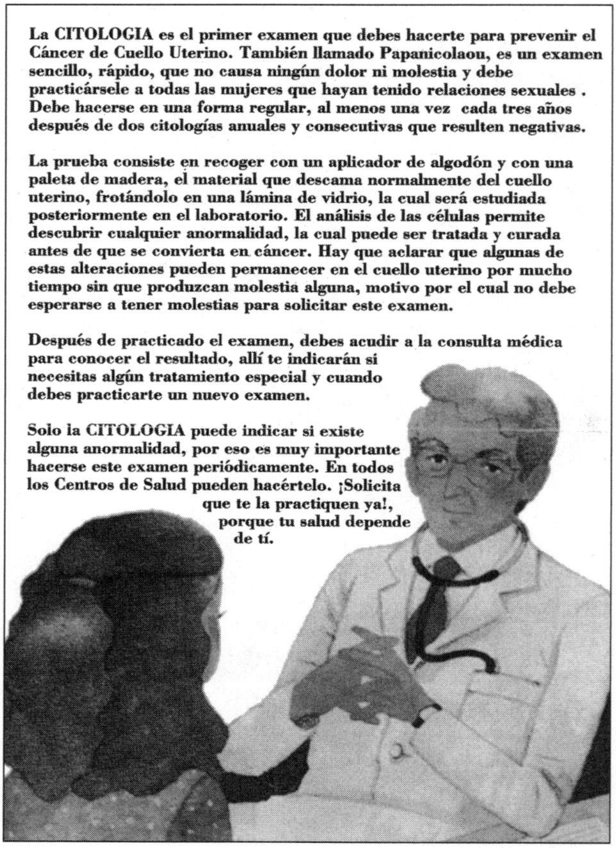

> La CITOLOGIA es el primer examen que debes hacerte para prevenir el Cáncer de Cuello Uterino. También llamado Papanicolaou, es un examen sencillo, rápido, que no causa ningún dolor ni molestia y debe practicársele a todas las mujeres que hayan tenido relaciones sexuales. Debe hacerse en una forma regular, al menos una vez cada tres años después de dos citologías anuales y consecutivas que resulten negativas.
>
> La prueba consiste en recoger con un aplicador de algodón y con una paleta de madera, el material que descama normalmente del cuello uterino, frotándolo en una lámina de vidrio, la cual será estudiada posteriormente en el laboratorio. El análisis de las células permite descubrir cualquier anormalidad, la cual puede ser tratada y curada antes de que se convierta en cáncer. Hay que aclarar que algunas de estas alteraciones pueden permanecer en el cuello uterino por mucho tiempo sin que produzcan molestia alguna, motivo por el cual no debe esperarse a tener molestias para solicitar este examen.
>
> Después de practicado el examen, debes acudir a la consulta médica para conocer el resultado, allí te indicarán si necesitas algún tratamiento especial y cuando debes practicarte un nuevo examen.
>
> Solo la CITOLOGIA puede indicar si existe alguna anormalidad, por eso es muy importante hacerse este examen periódicamente. En todos los Centros de Salud pueden hacértelo. ¡Solicita que te la practiquen ya!, porque tu salud depende de tí.

FIGURE 3.5 "Woman! Your Health Depends on You" pamphlet.
SOURCE: Ministry of Health and Social Assistance, Oncology Division.

two years after the 1991 health campaign that emphasized the important role of community participation (most particularly of women) in designing, implementing, and evaluating programs to combat cervical cancer. The translation of the pamphlet is as follows:

> The cytology is the first exam you should do to prevent Cervical Cancer. Also known as the Pap smear, it's a quick and easy exam that doesn't cause any pain or discomfort, and every woman who has had sexual relations should have this exam. It should be done on a regular basis, at least once every three years after having obtained two consecutive Pap smears with negative results.
>
> The exam consists of using a cotton applicator and a wooden palette to take a sample of the material that is discharged normally from the cervix and plac-

ing it on a slide, which will then be studied at a laboratory. The analysis of the cells allows for the discovery of any abnormality, which can be treated and cured before it turns into cancer. It should be made clear that some of these abnormalities can remain in the cervix for a long time without producing any symptoms, that is why you shouldn't wait until you feel problems to have this exam.

After the exam, you should go back to the doctor's office to find out the results. There they will tell you if you need any treatment, and tell you when you should have your next exam.

Only the Pap exam can indicate whether there is an abnormality. Because of that, it is very important that you have this exam periodically. All of the Health Centers can do it. Go and get one now!, because your health depends on you.

There are two points in particular in the pamphlet that I draw attention to. First, although the goal is to target the population of women who have had sexual relations, by not focusing, instead, on having a base-line Pap exam regardless of sexual activity, younger women, who may not wish to disclose their sexual activity, may be dissuaded from having the exam. Given that patient privacy at the time of this publication wasn't exactly a faithfully followed doctrine in the patient-doctor interactions and exams I witnessed, I can imagine some young women fearing information being disclosed to parents and others. Second, notice also that the pamphlet ends with the slogan "Your health depends on you." While this urges women to take responsibility for their health, it is also potentially disempowering. The underlying message is that if a woman gets cervical cancer she is at fault because, after all, her health depends on her.

As of 1995, when I finished my first fieldwork in Venezuela, the Ministry of Health and Social Assistance and the Venezuelan Cancer Society were just beginning to implement a health campaign designed to decrease cervical cancer morbidity. The pilot study for the campaign was to be implemented in various health centers in four Venezuelan states: Aragua, Táchira, Trujillo, and Anzoátegui. They were chosen on the basis of having the infrastructure necessary to carry out such a program, which provided Pap exams and low-cost treatments in the case of positive results. In addition, these states registered the highest incidence of cervical cancer–related morbidity. It appears, then, that Venezuelan national health policy was actively developing strategies aimed at combating cervical cancer. However, large-scale changes in cervical cancer campaigns and the health sector in general wouldn't arrive until 1999, after the election of Hugo Chávez and the development of Misión Barrio Adentro (Inside the Barrio), which I discuss in the epilogue.

As I have argued throughout this chapter, configurations of cervical cancer that are conveyed in public health are embedded in cultural assumptions about class and gender, which in turn are manifested in ideas about hygiene, culture, urban versus rural, risk, and blame. Consequently, as I have shown here, it becomes important to trace and understand the ways in which these concepts can translate into the regulation of (certain) women's bodies. Indeed, as Smart has commented,

> The construction of women's bodies as unruly and as a continual source of potential disruption to the social order has given rise to more sophisticated and flexible mechanisms for imposing restraint and achieving docility (1992:31).

She also warns, however, that, "we must be cautious of recreating a conspiracy theory of history or assuming an unwavering chain of developments further to subjugate women" (1992:31). Health education can be viewed as both empowering and subjugating depending on how it is developed, implemented, and received (Gastaldo 1997). After all, we would probably like to believe that most (if not all) public health programs are genuinely set up to reduce morbidity and mortality. Yet it is difficult to ignore the ways in which they also control and manage social and individual bodies (Lupton 1995). Rapp put this paradox of medicine quite well when she said, "The practices of biomedicine are at once emancipatory and socially controlling, essential for healthy survival, yet essentializing of women's lives." (1990:29). The same can be said of the area of public health. However, public health programs and materials developed within a framework of Latin American social medicine (as I described in Chapter 1) can be an antidote to the problems of power and representation in public health messages described above.

As scholarship in critical medical anthropology, feminist studies, and postcolonialism (to name a few) can attest, docility is not always achieved; nor is it necessarily an all-or-nothing phenomenon. Individuals manipulate, resist, negotiate, and transform meanings at various levels. We must not overlook the ways in which women express agency. For this particular survey of public health configurations of cervical cancer in Venezuela, I did not look at the ways women may resist, interpret, and/or (re)construct the images used in health promotion. However, concepts of negotiation and resistance in the face of disciplinary and regulatory mechanisms in the hospital setting will be discussed in Chapters 4 and 5, and it is likely that public health messages and images are similarly reworked in ways that are made meaningful to people's lives. Unfortunately, I did not present the women I interviewed with these pamphlets and ask them to interpret the words and images. Had I thought to do that, I might have discovered the ways in which the women engage with the materials that were meant to be purveyors of health education and much more: culture, modernity, civility, and citizenship that encapsulate notions of bourgeois motherhood, monogamy, and ultimately an imagined racialized whiteness of middle-class or elite propriety. I suspect a number of women may have offered critically insightful readings of these messages given that when asked about how they thought they might have developed cervical cancer, as noted in Chapter 2, some offered straightforward theories about the infidelity of their male partners. While the pamphlets suggested regulation of their own sexuality and reproduction, the women troubled these analyses and recommendations by insisting on including the sexual practices of their partners in searching for explanations as to how they developed cancer.

4 The Hospital Encounter
Bodies Marked, Mended, and Manipulated

Be Patient: The Medical Encounter as Disciplinary Practice

Medical anthropologists, sociologists, and scholars from diverse disciplines have investigated the medical encounter from various perspectives (Kleinman 1980; Zola 1985; Young 1989; Lazarus 1988). Work has been done, for example, in the area of linguistics, where the focus has been on the verbal interactions between patients and doctors, and the power to control and direct verbal communication resides mainly with the latter (Fisher and Todd 1983; Fisher 1986; Waitzkin 1991). What has also been of particular interest for the analysis of the medical encounter is Foucault's (1975, 1979) work on the disciplinary power of modern institutions such as prisons and hospitals. For example, Foucault's "docile body," "regulated by the norms of cultural life," and Bourdieu's (1984) "made body" molded through trivial cultural practices of various "routines, rules, and practices" are the result of practical, banal, and direct social control (Bordo 1997) such as that found in the hospital.

The process of treating patients in the hospital setting also involves converting people into patients. From the moment individuals enter the hospital, the disciplinary process that transforms them into patients begins (Young 1989). The focus of much of this disciplining is on the body. This process is evident in both hospitals where I conducted research. From the time they entered the hospital to make their first appointment in admissions (at Razetti) or triage (at Padre Machado), the women were being disciplined into the role of patient. At Razetti, for example, in the gynecology department each patient must form a line in the morning (at seven in the morning), turn in her appointment card, and wait while her chart was pulled. She then waited until she was called in to see the doctor (usually one or two more hours depending on the number of patients seen that day). She needed to be physically present to turn in her appointment card or she risked being refused the consultation with the doctor. Gastaldo (1997) has written about a similar procedure in clinics in Brazil, where patients must stand in line to obtain one of a limited number of tokens to get in to see a doctor. The result is that "the body has to be present for the existence of the person to be acknowledged and patient status to be given as a reward. This prerequisite creates the opportunity to make the national health system an experience of disciplining bodies" (Gastaldo 1997, 126).

Patients who do not follow the rules are not rewarded with patient status. The department secretary at Razetti, Minerva, commented that patients who come late to their appointments cannot be seen. Otherwise, "they will learn that it is OK to be late and take advantage by coming late all of the time." As a patient, she is required to follow hospital rules. The punishment for transgressing the rules is removal of her patient status. She would be required to make another appointment and return at a later date, having learned that she must not be late.

Similar disciplining procedures for becoming a patient were also in place at Padre Machado. Physical presence was required to make appointments and turn in appointment cards. On a few occasions, I accompanied a couple of the women whom I had interviewed as they navigated the hospital to make appointments at the various departments where they were required to have tests. One of the women, thirty-year-old Patricia, needed to make appointments at three separate hospital departments. As the hospital procedures would not allow her to make the appointments by phone, Patricia needed to go to each department in person. She first went to radiology, as she had to have X-rays taken, but there she was told that she should first have her blood drawn. However, she was told that that department was closed until the next day. She also had to make another appointment at the gynecology department but was told that she would need to make the appointments at the other departments first. In the end, Patricia was left very frustrated, but she resolved that she would return the next day to make her appointments. To be granted patient status, she had no other choice; her physical presence was required to be in compliance with the hospital rules. In this way, the hospitals function as institutions of bodily discipline.

On Seeing the Doctor

I have already discussed the process of appointment making (including physical presence) that is necessary for patients to see a doctor. As I continue with the descriptions of patient-doctor interactions in the offices and examination rooms, I focus on the relations of power inherent in these interactions. At the same time, the political economy serves as another theoretical thread that runs throughout, contextualizing these interactions. Although medical encounters are micro-level processes between (or among) individuals, it is important to recognize that these interpersonal processes occur in a social context, which is formed by macro-level societal structures (Waitzkin 1991).

One element of the doctor-patient interaction is the time doctors might spend talking to patients about their medical conditions and courses of treatment. I recorded the time that patients spent in the office upon initially meeting with the doctor, the time spent in the examination room, and the time spent with the doctor in the office before leaving the hospital. Because the length of time spent during the examination was contingent upon the procedure being performed (e.g., Pap exam, biopsy, treatment), I do not present information about the length of the examination, but only some of my observations about what went on during the examination. In the initial office meeting, doctors first met patients and had an opportunity to ask them about symptoms, problems, and so on. Because most of the women were first-time patients (only two of the women at Razetti and three of the women at Padre Machado were patients on their second visit), this first meeting was an important time for the doctor to interact with the patient and ask the patient to discuss her medical history. In addition, I present data on the length of time that the patient spent with the doctor in the office after she was examined. This is the time where the doctor can potentially explain something about her medical condition and options for treatment if that information was available, and for patients to ask questions of the doctor.

Differences were found in the amount of time that doctors spent with patients in office interactions at the hospitals. Doctors spent more time with patients at the private hospital than the public hospital. The mean time that patients and doctors spent together in the initial office interaction (before the patient was examined) at the public hospital, Razetti, was 2.6 minutes.[1] Seventy-one percent of these interactions lasted two minutes or less. In contrast, the mean time of this first interaction at the private hospital, Padre Machado, was 6.4 minutes, with only 12 percent of interactions lasting two minutes or less. This first meeting between patient and doctor was about two and a half times as long at the private hospital compared to the public hospital. The second office interaction (after the patient was examined) showed a similar pattern. At Razetti the mean time of this interaction lasted 4.3 minutes; 39 percent were two minutes or less. Again, the interactions lasted longer at Padre Machado: the mean time that patients and doctors spent together was 8.7 minutes (twice that of the public hospital), and all of the interactions were longer than two minutes. What do these time differences mean in terms of the qualitative makeup of these interactions?

Office Interactions

The first office interactions at Razetti followed a general pattern that included a length of approximately two minutes or less, little verbal communication between doctor and patient, and the doctor speaking first. Moreover, the doctor would rarely introduce him- or herself when the patient entered the office—in fact, I cannot recall a time when a doctor introduced him- or herself to a patient. Below, I present ethnographic vignettes from some first-time office interactions, which are indicative of the typical encounters observed between first-time patients and doctors at Razetti.

Thirty-two-year-old Carina came to the hospital on February 9, 1995, for her first appointment in the department of gynecology. She was called into see Dr. Velásquez at 9:15 a.m. Dr. Velásquez and Dr. Cortez were both in the office. Dr. Velásquez spoke first: "Go to the exam room and undress." Carina did not speak but went directly into the exam room to undress. The doctor did not spend time with Carina to introduce himself, to explain what procedures would be done, or to ask her questions about how she might be feeling. I observed that doctors would review their patients' medical histories beforehand, gathering information from the chart—it is possible that they did not believe it was necessary to speak directly with patients.

When I interviewed Angela, it was actually her second visit to the department of gynecology. She was a forty-eight-year-old woman with NIC III. She told me: "It's the beginning of cancer. I think that's what it is." Angela did not actually have an office visit with a doctor (Carina did not have much of one either). While I was interviewing her, Dr. Cortez knocked on the door to the small room where I was talking with Angela. He directed his attention to me, asking when I would be done with my interview. He looked down at her chart and said that she had seen Dr. Velásquez at her last appointment and that her results were in. I told Dr. Cortez that I would stop the interview so that he could talk with her. He insisted that that was not necessary. Instead, he looked over to Angela and told her that she should go to the hospitalization desk and get an appointment for surgery for the following week. He left almost immediately. The entire interaction lasted only about a minute. Angela began to cry when he left. She said she just knew it would turn out that she would have to have an operation.

However, the time spent with a patient does not necessarily tell you much about the interaction between the two. Although a doctor may spend fifteen minutes with a patient in the office after having examined her, that time may be spent dictating information, writing in a chart, and consulting with other doctors. In fact, few or none of those fifteen minutes may actually be spent talking with the patient.

For example, Lourdes, a thirty-nine-year-old patient at Razetti, who worked out of her home as a seamstress and who traveled two and a half hours from a rural area outside of the city to get to the hospital, was told that she had to have a *cono* (cone biopsy) and would need to come back to the hospital in the following week to have an operation. Although Lourdes spent twelve minutes in the office with Dr. Valdez after he had examined her, most of this time she sat across from the doctor and did not say anything while Dr. Valdez taped his observations about her case into a recorder. The cone biopsy procedure, for example, was never explained to Lourdes, and she never asked about it. Later, when I interviewed her again before she left the hospital, she indicated that she did not know what a *cono* was, and she was not even sure what she had or why she needed to have an operation. She appeared confused and repeated more than once: "I practically don't even know what I have." Before Lourdes left, however, I offered to go with her to ask Dr. Valdez what the procedure entailed and also about her medical condition. This decision to intervene was not straightforward. As I stated in the introduction of this book, my ethnographic training did little to prepare me for the ethical considerations I would face working in oncology hospitals, where I was faced with constant emotional pulls to help the women whose suffering I witnessed. I could not let Lourdes leave in such a confused state. It did cross my mind that I might antagonize Dr. Valdez, but that was a fleeting concern compared to Lourdes's need for information.

Similarly, Doña Estela, who spent sixteen minutes with Dr. Valdez and Dr. Sanchez in the first office interaction, was asked only one question by Dr. Valdez: "Where are you from?" She replied, "From Maturín." These were the only words exchanged between herself and either doctor. This interaction with Doña Estela is presented in greater detail in a later section, where her examination is analyzed in terms of her experience of pain. The experiences of Lourdes and Doña Estela were not unique. As will be discussed later in the chapter, because of the often short or limited dialogue between patients and doctors, women often left the medical encounter with many questions and in some cases, as with Lourdes, unsure of procedures that were to be performed on them.

The second office interactions at Razetti, after the examination was completed, and where women and doctors could potentially dialogue about test results and treatments, followed similar patterns: little time and little dialogue. The usual pattern of these interactions consisted of the doctor leaving the examination room and returning to the office to enter information on the patient's chart and to dictate the patient's medical information into a tape recorder. The patient would routinely enter the office after getting dressed and wait while the doctor recorded this information. Usually the patient was told when she would need to come back for another appointment, and if necessary, she was also given a prescription for medication at this time. Sometimes, this time was also used for the patient to ask questions and for the doctor to explain the medical condition and treatment. However, it was not necessarily routine for the doctor to spend time discussing the medical condition or for the patient to ask questions—in fact, this did not occur very often.

For example, thirty-one-year-old Alma had the following interaction with Dr. Cortez, one of the attending physicians at Razetti, after she was examined. There were six people in the office: Dr. Cortez, Alma, myself, nurse Mercedes, and two doctors who were interns. After her examination, Alma entered the office and sat down across from Dr. Cortez. It was 9:24 a.m. He was dictating notes about her case into the recorder. After he was finished, he spoke to Alma: "Ask for another appointment for next month." Alma did not respond verbally but nodded her head in agreement. She got up and left;

it was 9:26 a.m. This interaction lasted about two minutes, and there was no discussion about her medical condition. Even her first interaction with him, before she was examined, did not involve a discussion about her medical condition. During that time, the only verbal interaction between the two was Dr. Cortez's instruction to her to enter the office and his inquiry about her last menstrual period. He said, "Come here." He then motioned for her to sit down and asked, "When was your last period?" Alma responded, "On Friday." This was the only verbal interaction during the first office encounter. I interviewed Alma again before she went home, and I asked her if she had any questions she would have liked to ask the doctor but felt she couldn't. She responded yes, that she wanted to ask, "Where did it come from . . . what are the consequences?" and "Did the NIC advance, or is it still a level II." When I asked why she felt she couldn't ask, she said, "I felt that there were too many people. One always wants to have one's privacy." The cramped space at the hospital and the large number of patients made this request for privacy almost an impossibility.

For thirty-two-year-old Carina, the second office interaction was similar. She was examined by both Dr. Velásquez and Dr. Cortez. They were in the office seated behind the desk, along with myself, Carina, and another patient, who was seated across from the two doctors. After her examination Carina entered the office at 9:20 a.m. She did not sit down but remained standing close to the examination room. Dr. Velásquez spoke first. He handed her a paper and said, "Make an appointment for two weeks from today." Carina took the piece of paper and asked where she should make her next appointment. Dr. Velásquez responded that she should make her appointment at the desk across from the department. She left at 9:22 a.m.; the entire interaction lasted 1.5 minutes.

To a large degree the problem is, of course, the crowded conditions at the hospitals, which make it difficult for doctors to spend time doing more than simply examining patients. However, Padre Machado, which at the time functioned as a hybrid public-private domain, also had many of the same constraints and obstacles as Razetti; Padre Machado was also overcrowded, understaffed, and experienced medical supply shortages. In fact, because Razetti did not have a functioning radiation machine for treatments, Padre Machado often appeared more crowded in comparison as women who needed this type of treatment and had little economic resources would likely be transferred here or to the public university hospital (Universidad Central de Venezuela), where radiation treatments were available. According to the director of the Venezuelan Cancer Society (Padre Machado functioned under their auspices), it was their policy to admit even those patients who could not afford the treatments. There was at least one woman who I interviewed at Razetti who was transferred to Padre Machado to receive radiation treatments. In spite of these similar problems, however, some differences were noticed in the quality (and quantity) of time that doctors at Padre Machado spent with patients.

Having acknowledged earlier that lengthy time spent with the patient does not necessarily translate into a quality interaction, I did notice that the greater length of time spent with patients at Padre Machado did translate into what I would describe as somewhat better rapport between patients and doctors. At Padre Machado, for example, during the first office interactions, I observed doctors ask questions of their patients, such as how they were feeling and whether they were experiencing pain. Also, rather than immediately asking the patient about her medical condition, doctors were more likely to greet the women with a hello or some other salutation. This did not occur every time, but I did observe this type of interaction on a more regular basis at Padre Machado than Razetti.

One main drawback at Padre Machado, however, was the physical setting of the office space. At Padre Machado there was one main office divided into six sections, each with a desk and two chairs (one for the doctor and one for the patient). The sections, however, were not separated by curtains or walls. Instead, they were spaced apart by approximately eight feet. Therefore, if these seats and desks were taken up by doctors and patients all at once, the office could get rather noisy, making it difficult to hear, which was, at times, a problem. In addition, similar to the situation at the Razetti, privacy was also compromised by this setup. Nonetheless, office interactions at Padre Machado did seem to include more dialogue between patients and doctors compared to that at Razetti.

Josefina, age sixty-five, was accompanied at Padre Machado by her daughter, a woman who appeared to be in her midthirties. She and her daughter entered the office along with myself, and the nurse directed us to Dr. Portes's usual desk. At 10:30 a.m., he greeted Josefina by saying, "Good morning, *señora*. Have a seat." She replied, "Good morning." From then on, Dr. Portes directed his inquiries to Josefina's daughter, asking for her address, telephone, and other details. Dr. Portes was then going to send Josefina into the examination room at 10:34, but it was occupied, and she was not able to enter until 10:45. Although this interaction was also short and not much attention was directed to Josefina (but instead to her daughter), he did at least greet her when she approached the desk. Again, the greeting is a small detail that was noted at Padre Machado and more rarely at Razetti.

Similarly, forty-five-year-old Margarita was also greeted by the doctor when she met him during the first office interaction, at 3:12 p.m. Dr. López spoke first and said, "How are you?" He immediately followed that by asking, "Are you here for pain or hemorrhaging or something like that?" She responded, "Yes, I always have pain here in my womb." Another doctor, an intern, approached Dr. López to ask about a patient of his. They conversed and then at 3:14 p.m. Dr. López told Margarita to enter the exam room. This interaction lasted only two minutes, but again, there was a greeting and at least one question about how she was feeling.

The second office interaction, after Margarita was examined, was lengthier and involved more dialogue and information giving, at least by Dr. López. Dr. López sat at his desk and Margarita sat in the chair in front of him. He spoke first and told her, "I will explain what you have, Señora, in just a minute." He then left and Margarita did not say anything. Dr. López returned shortly and explained that she had an enlarged uterus and that the condition was called fibromatosis. He emphasized that "it has nothing to do with cancer," but he also told her that the condition had to be treated with surgery. He then began to write out an order and told Margarita he was writing an order for exams. At that point she spoke and asked if the exams could be done at the hospital or if she would have to go to another place. Dr. López told her that she could have them done at the hospital. Margarita then asked how much the surgery would cost. The doctor replied that he did not know but that she could find out that information at the reception desk. Dr. López then asked, "Do you have any questions?" Margarita did not respond. He asked her if she was worried, and this time she responded that she was worried about the anesthesia. Almost immediately after she said, "That is just a silly concern of mine." Dr. López did not respond. He gave her the examination orders. Margarita thanked him and left. Compared to the second office interactions at Razetti, this interaction between Margarita and Dr. López included the doctor's explanation about Margarita's condition, questioning by Margarita about the exams and the cost of surgery, the doctor's direct question as to whether Margarita had any questions she wanted to ask, and also Dr. López's recognition that Margarita seemed troubled when she did not respond to his inquiry. Although by no means did this type of interaction occur every time, I did observe these types of lengthier dialogues and exchanges between patients and doctors more often at Padre Machado than at Razetti. This is also reflected in the fact that the second office interactions, as mentioned earlier, lasted, on average, twice as long at Padre Machado (8.7 minutes) as they did at Razetti (4.3 minutes).

Examination Interactions
The interactions among patients, doctors, and nurses during examinations were similar at both hospitals: both were teaching hospitals, and it was common for *pasantes* (interns) to be in the examination room with residents and attending physicians to learn about medical cases. At both hospitals it was common for doctors to interact with each other and to interact very little with the patient. However, as with the office interactions, there were some subtle differences between the two hospitals. At the private hospital (Padre Machado), for example, doctors were more likely to explain what procedures were about to be performed, or at least when they were about to insert the speculum. Doctors did not always inform patients in this way, but I observed this type of communication more often at Padre Machado than at Razetti.

Josefina's examination with Dr. Portes at Padre Machado is illustrative of an interaction where the patient is informed about the insertion of the speculum. During the examination, two nurses, Dr. Portes, Josefina, and myself were present. Before inserting the speculum, Dr. Portes told Josefina, "I am going to insert a speculum." She did not respond. After looking at her cervix, he turned to me and said, "It looks like she has a lesion." Nothing was said directly to Josefina. During the biopsy, he asked Josefina if she was experiencing pain. She nodded affirmatively, and he assured her that he would soon be finished. However, he did not tell her specifically that he was performing a biopsy. At one point during the biopsy, Josefina asked Dr. Portes, "What is it that I have?" He did not respond to that question, but a few seconds later he told her she should calm down. A few minutes later, Josefina asked Dr. Portes again, "What is it that I have?" He responded, "Just a minute, *abuela*"—*abuela* means "grandmother" in Spanish, and he was using it as a term of endearment. He then let her know that he was going to do a rectal exam. Dr. López entered the exam room shortly after that and examined Josefina as well. During this time the female Dr. Moya, an intern, entered the exam room to ask Dr. López a question about her patient. The entire examination lasted approximately fifteen minutes. Although Dr. Portes did let Josefina know when he was going to insert the speculum and when he was going to do a rectal exam, he ignored her repeated questions about her medical condition (what is it that I have?). Rather than direct his attention toward her, Dr. Portes told me about Josefina's lesion. In addition, doctors entered and exited the exam room at various times, something that was also common at the public hospital (Razetti). So, while there were positive characteristics to this interaction (e.g., giving Josefina notice about the procedures), there were also aspects that were problematic, such as Josefina's questions being ignored.

Similarly, Delia, a thirty-six-year-old patient at Padre Machado, had a somewhat mixed interaction with Dr. Ibañez. While he did inform her about the speculum being inserted before it actually was, he did not communicate much else to her. In fact, when he was done examining her, he left the room without letting her know that the examination was over. After he left, Delia turned to the nurse and asked, "Can I get dressed now?" He also did not inform her that he had performed a Pap exam. This became evident when, in the office after the examination, Delia asked Dr. Ibañez, "When can I get the results of the biopsy?" He responded, "I did a Pap exam not a biopsy." Thus, this interaction also consisted of both desirable and troublesome elements.

The characteristic of the examination interactions at Razetti were similar to those at Padre Machado except that patients at Razetti were less likely to be told what procedures were going to be performed. For example, at Razetti it was less common for women to be told that a speculum was going to be inserted. The reason for this is not clear, but I can only propose that because Padre Machado was a somewhat private institution at the time of my first fieldwork, and had a better reputation for cancer treatment than Razetti, doctors may have been trained to pay more attention to bedside manner and patient-doctor communication. As stated earlier, both hospitals had similar problems of overcrowding, lack of supplies, and understaffing, so this is not necessarily a powerful measure of distinction between the two. In the following sections, I explain in more detail the examination experiences of two women at Razetti, which provide greater insight into the kinds of interactions that occur between patients and doctors during this time.

Once patients maneuver through the mechanisms of bodily discipline in the administrative procedures of the hospital, they then experience the office interactions and the examination, which have been outlined already. In the next section, through an observation of one woman's examination, I describe the ways in which docile bodies are created, managed, and manipulated. I look specifically at the way in which women's pain during the medical examination is perceived by physicians and their configuration of women's bodies that is a part of this understanding. Women's narrative experiences about their pain and the relationship this has to their own understandings of their bodies is also analyzed.

The Examination: The Body on Display

But to look in order to know, to show in order to teach, is not this a tacit form of violence, all the more abusive for its silence, upon a sick body that demands to be comforted, not displayed?
Michel Foucault (1973, 84), The Birth of the Clinic

Most mornings at the hospitals were similar: many women waiting, nurses moving from room to room, and doctors with piles of charts at the corners of their desks. This particular morning in March was different in one respect. When I arrived at the public hospital I noticed that there were three young women who appeared to be around the ages of fifteen or sixteen peering over Dr. Cortez's shoulder as he was examining a woman. They were in the back examination room, farthest from the department door, and also the largest. It was the exam room that was preferred for doctors' meetings because it could accommodate the most doctors at one time for patient viewing. The teenagers were wearing their school uniforms: white shirts with navy pleated skirts and black shoes. I learned from one of the nurses that they were at the hospital interviewing women who were diagnosed with cervical cancer to find out if the afflicted women knew of the risk factors for this cancer. This was to be a school research project.

From the office I could see Dr. Cortez sitting on his stool with the three young women behind him, gazing in the direction of the patient who was lying on the exam table. From the vantage point of the office, I could not actually see the patient who was lying on the table—the exam room was set up this way so that the patient could have some modicum of privacy. She was most likely in the usual position, lying on her back with feet in stirrups. However, I could see the doctors and the other individuals who were on the side of the exam room opposite the patient. I could see Dr. Cortez pointing to what

I assume was the woman's cervix, her vagina having been opened with the speculum. He was pointing and explaining the particular maladies of this cervix. Dr. Cortez saw me sitting in the office and invited me into the exam room so that I could also witness this interesting case. I declined. Nothing was said to the patient, and she was silent as well. An occasional laugh or snicker would escape from the mouths of the young women with a corresponding chuckle from the doctor.

I could hear the doctor explain that he was going to give the woman a treatment known as electrofulguration, which would use a pointy, needle-shaped electrode to burn off the bad tissue with high-frequency electric currents. Nurse Mónica went in to help set up the procedure. My sense of sound, by then disciplined to the various sounds of my hospital surroundings, was keen to the buzzing and crackling noise emitted by this piece of equipment that burns away tissue. It did not, however, drown out the occasional moans of the patient. Dr. Cortez began the treatment, only a few zaps at a time, intermittently gazing at his progress and pointing out his work to the three teenage schoolgirls who stood behind him. After the final zaps of the electrical currents that would sear the malignant flesh, nurse Mónica cried out, "It smells like *chicharrón* [pork rinds]." I could hear the nurses and doctors laughing at the description.

After the treatment, everyone cleared out of the exam room and office area, leaving the patient and myself alone in the office area. I took the opportunity of this rare occurrence of an empty office to speak with her about her treatment. She was not someone who I had formally interviewed, but I was compelled to find out what she had thought about her experience in the exam room. Was she annoyed? Was she embarrassed? Were my reactions to this scene dissimilar from her own? "It was fine," she said after I introduced myself and asked her generally about how her examination had gone. "What was your feeling of the girls being in the exam room?" I asked. At first, she glanced at me cautiously and tentatively, and she didn't speak right away, but I waited for her response, and in a sudden gesture she sat up straighter in her chair and declared, "It feels uncomfortable. It's fine if it's a doctor, but not strangers, young girls, who don't know about this sort of thing." She emphasized that she was embarrassed by having the teens watching her examination because they were "schoolgirls, not doctors." However, in terms of the joking and laughter, she said it didn't bother her at all. In fact, she said: "It actually helps when the doctors joke. It helps one feel more comfortable. Like when I had the biopsy, the doctor was joking with me, and that was the only thing that made it bearable." The joking in both of these situations (the biopsy and electrofulguration) put her at ease and made her feel less nervous. As an outsider I had a visceral uncomfortable reaction to the joking about her tissue smelling like pork rinds, but I would be remiss to assume her reaction was similar to mine whether that be because of personality or cultural differences.

Later, I wondered out loud to Dr. Cortez what the young women's' interview had to do with watching a woman being examined. He explained that one of the teenagers was interested in becoming a doctor someday. Viewing the examination was an introductory lesson. The patient was simply a body on display, a teaching tool, one might say, for a future generation of physicians.

As a working-class woman seeking care in a public hospital, a concern for her privacy or how she might feel about having the schoolgirls view her in this way was not a concern, or rather, because it was not even at the level of conscious consideration, perhaps *concern* is not the best choice of terms. It makes more sense to understand this type of interaction as a part of the hegemonic system of biomedicine, whereby taken-for-granted assumptions are made as to the roles of patients and doctors, which concomitantly engage with social understandings of gender and class relations. Specifically, as defined by Antonio Gramsci (1971, 12), social hegemony is "the spontaneous" consent given by the great masses of the population to the general direction imposed on social life by the dominant fundamental group; this consent is "historically" caused by the prestige (and consequent confidence) which the dominant group enjoys because of its position and function in the world of production." If we understand the objectifying gaze of doctors as hegemonic practice, then we are better able to explain why it is that people can be treated like body parts, where questions concerning the feelings, attitudes, fears, wants, and dislikes of patients do not enter into the consciousness of medical practice. I am referring to the "commonsense" treatment of poor and working-class patients that is garnered through the "consent" of the dominant group.

Within the framework of the political economy of health care, where the level of medical access, opportunity, and attention depends on socioeconomic status, all (e.g., patients, doctors, medical personnel) understand that public health care translates to docility on the part of the patient. Patients are quite aware of how they should behave at a public health-care institution: not asking questions, not questioning authority, and allowing oneself to be viewed, touched, and positioned in any number of ways by any number of people. However, as is discussed in the following chapter, patients also actively challenge and resist these restrictions to varying degrees and in a number of ways. The sentiment that poor and working-class patients are lucky to receive treatment is also a part of this commonsense way of thinking and is expressed by doctors and patients alike.

Bodies in Pain

As I observed what went on during the medical examinations of the women I interviewed, the issue of pain emerged as a significant area of analysis. The ways in which women expressed their pain and also the ways in which doctors reacted to it is an important aspect of the medical encounter. The subject of pain can be an overwhelming problem to confront. It has been addressed in numerous fields, including history, philosophy, anthropology, sociology, medicine, and psychology, and accordingly, it has been approached from various perspectives. Scholars have been concerned with such problems as the infliction of pain in practices of torture and violence (Foucault 1979; Scarry 1985), the experience of pain as recounted in narratives and testimonials (Finkler 1994), and a number of studies in the fields of psychology and medicine have studied the perception of pain and levels of tolerance. Physical pain is universal and, at the same time, arguably something quite individual. As Scarry (1985, 4) notes:

> For the person in pain, so incontestably and unnegotiably present is it that "having pain" may come to be thought of as the most vibrant example of what it is to "have certainty," while for the other person it is so elusive that "hearing about pain" may exist as the primary model of what it is "to have doubt." Thus pain comes unsharably into our midst as at once that which cannot be denied and that which cannot be confirmed.

Moreover, I quote Scarry at length as she argues for the importance, nonetheless, of attempts to recount narratives of pain:

> To witness the moment when pain causes a reversion to the pre-language of cries and groans is to witness the destruction of language; but conversely, to be present when a person moves up out of that pre-language and projects the facts of sentience into speech is almost to have been permitted to be present at

the birth of language itself. Because the person in pain is ordinarily so bereft of the resources of speech, it is not surprising that the language for pain should sometimes be brought into being by those who are not themselves in pain but who speak *on behalf* of those who are. Though there are very great impediments to expressing another's sentient distress, so are there also very great reasons why one might want to do so, and thus there come to be avenues by which this most radically private of experiences begins to enter the realm of public discourse. (6)

In this section, I am concerned with patients' experiences of pain during the gynecological examination. I include their narrative experiences as well as my observations during the examination. The pain and discomfort of the examination was not a topic of frequent discussion among the doctors, and when it did come up, they repeatedly reiterated to me and to the patients that gynecological exams do not cause pain. This contrasts with patients' frequent statements that the exam had caused them some amount of discomfort or pain. In some cases, the women screamed during their exams. This, despite doctors' assurances that the Pap exam if anything "feels like a pinch" and a biopsy feels like a "stronger pinch." Most of the women who underwent gynecological examinations were given Pap exams and/or biopsies (some were also given rectal exams). Of the thirty-nine women that were interviewed, most indicated that they had experienced some pain during their gynecological examinations (see table 4.1). Seventy-five percent responded that the exam had caused pain, and 26 percent of those women qualified their response by indicating that they felt only a little pain or discomfort. Twenty-six percent had indicated that the exam had caused no pain.

The following section focuses on the pain experience of one of the women at the public hospital whom I interviewed. Although this account describes the experience of one particular woman—albeit only in the partial, fractured

TABLE 4.1 Response to Question at Both Hospitals: Was the Examination Painful?

Response	Frequency (N=45)	Percentage (100%)
Yes—unqualified	19/39	49%
Yes—a little bit/somewhat	10/39	26%
No	10/39	26%
Missing (patient not examined)	6	X

way that it is possible to write about another person's pain—it touches on similar aspects of pain in the examination that I witnessed and that were discussed by other patients.

Doña Estela, Day 1

I met Doña Estela on February 1, 1995. She came to Razetti from the city of Maturín in the Venezuelan state of Monagas. She had taken a seven-hour bus ride to get to the hospital, and I spoke with her while she waited to see the doctor. She was sixty years old, and as we spoke, she told me that she had been referred to the hospital because of a "cancerous lesion." She added: "I don't know what they are going to do with me, if they are going to operate ... but I am sure that the disease, whatever it may be, that I will be cured of it. I have a lot of faith, I am entirely sure." (Later that day, I spoke with one of the doctors who had examined her, and he said she had invasive cervical cancer and "would probably die within the year.") She was very positive and upbeat during our conversation, but it was obvious that she had been through a lot with her health.

Doña Estela was referred to the hospital by a private doctor she had gone to in her home city. She had first gone to a public hospital in Maturín, where she was displeased with her treatment. She said they had told her nothing of her condition. Subsequently, she went to a private doctor, paid for by her son's social security. However, he lost his job, and she wasn't able to continue seeing that doctor. When I asked her what this doctor had told her about her condition, she replied:

> Well, he didn't tell me anything ... he didn't say anything to me directly. I heard him commenting about it to the nurse who was with him. He didn't tell me directly: "Ma'am, you have this." No, it wasn't like that. I heard him say to the nurse: "There is a cancerous lesion." ... He gave me a treatment, but he didn't tell me that he wanted to refer me to somewhere else or anything like that. So then I went with a private *doctora* [female doctor]. I made a sacrifice, you know how things are these days and all of my children are out of work. So, I paid 2,000 bolivares [US$11.76] for a consultation and the *doctora* gave me a referral [to come here].

I asked Doña Estela what the *doctora* had told her about her condition, and she replied:

Well, she told me that I had an ulcer [ulcerous lesion] . . . well, quite honestly, I will be sincere in telling you that she didn't tell me that I had an ulcer. She told my daughter that I had something called *coliflor*, which is the first time in my life that I have heard of this . . . my daughter was there when she was examining me. In the end she couldn't explain what I have, whether it is cancer after all or this thing called coliflor.

As with all the women whom I interviewed, I asked Doña Estela if I could enter with her into the office and exam room. She said yes, and at 9:17 a.m. we entered into the office (myself, Doña Estela, and her cousin). Doña Estela's daughter remained in the waiting area. Dr. Valdez and Dr. Sánchez sat behind the desk, and there were four other doctors and a nurse with another patient in the exam room that is attached to this office. Dr. Valdez spoke with Doña Estela's cousin about the fact that because Doña Estela was seen in admissions the previous day, they didn't have any of the results from the tests she had taken, in particular the Pap exam. At that moment, the woman who was being examined in the attached room walked through the office and out the door. They spoke among themselves (both doctors and the cousin), and it wasn't until 9:28 a.m. that Dr. Valdez uttered his first words to Doña Estela before sending her to the exam room. As noted earlier, it was only to ask her where she was from.

I entered the exam room with the doctors a few minutes later and stood at the head of the exam table. Three doctors (Dr. Andrade and two interns), nurse Lila, Doña Estela, and myself were in the examination room. I asked her whether she was doing OK, and Doña Estela nodded affirmatively, but she was noticeably uncomfortable as Dr. Andrade began the examination. She closed her eyes and winced as the speculum was inserted, and he began to feel around. Dr. Sánchez entered the exam room and began to examine her after Dr. Andrade was finished. Shortly after that Dr. Valdez entered with Dr. Santana. (Both Dr. Andrade and Dr. Santana were doing three-year residencies at the hospital. Dr. Andrade was in his last year, and Dr. Santana in his second year.) In that moment Dr. Andrade was serving as a teacher to the interns, and Doña Estela was the embodied teaching tool. After Dr. Santana examined Doña Estela the interns took turns feeling inside of her. Dr. Andrade was explaining to them what to look for, and during this time Doña Estela was crying. None of the doctors spoke to her, and the nurse who was assisting them told her, "Everything will be fine." I lightly touched Doña Estela's arm and she reached for my hand. I held her hand and felt her grip tighten and relax with what I assume was the intensity of the pain. I remember wondering whether I was witnessing a medical examination or a torture session, or both. It's odd how these ostensibly incongruous acts, one linked to healing and the other to punishment, can be easily confounded as the boundaries between examination and torture or healing and punishment come into question.

The doctors remained fixed on her lower half, as if her body were divided in two. They didn't cross over this imaginary line at her waist, which effectively separated her lower half from her upper half. Nurse Lila stayed mostly in this center zone, assisting the doctors with gauze and instruments and occasionally directing her attention to Doña Estela. I also did not cross this line and remained at the head of the table holding her hand. Dr. Santana returned to the stool that was positioned at the proper level for viewing Doña Estela's vagina and cervix. He asked nurse Lila for the pincers, which I recognized as the biopsy pincers. He didn't tell Doña Estela what he was about to do; he told her only to cough and then he extracted the tissue. I felt her hand tighten around mine as she moaned and sobbed lightly. Shortly after, a nurse's assistant walked into the exam room and exclaimed rhetorically, "What is going on in here?!" and remarked on the amount of blood that was flowing from Doña Estela's body. She added, "I've never seen so much blood like this during an exam." She left and later came back after the exam was over to clean up the blood.

When the exam was over and Doña Estela got up, I saw the pool of blood on the table and watched as it dripped onto the floor. Doña Estela was still crying lightly after the exam. At 9:59 a.m. she left the exam room and went into the adjoining office but remained there for less than a minute before she was escorted out into the hallway by one of the doctors. Her exam had lasted twenty-six minutes (the next day she told me she thought it had lasted about an hour). Doña Estela's daughter and cousin were asked into the office, where Dr. Andrade explained her condition. Doña Estela was never asked to join them in the office, and I remained in the hallway with her. Normally, I conduct another short interview at this point (at the end of the exam), but Doña Estela was in no shape to talk. I explained the interview process earlier, but after her experience, I doubt that she remembered me saying that I wanted to interview her again after the exam, and I didn't remind her. She asked if I would be there again the next day, because Dr. Santana told her she would have to return to have some gauze removed that he had inserted all the way up by her cervix to control the bleeding. I let her know that I would be glad to go in with her the next day if she wanted me to. She replied that she would like it very much if I could do that.

Doña Estela, Day 2
When Doña Estela returned the next day, I conducted the second part of the interview (that I normally would have done the day before) to find out how she felt about her examination experience. I began by asking her if she knew what exams they had performed on her and she replied, "I don't know what it is called—cytology, I think." She was not aware that she had had a biopsy, which isn't surprising given that she was never told what was being done to her during the examination. When I asked if the examination had bothered her in any way, she said, "Yes, it was very painful." In response to the question of what her condition is or what it is called, she told me that she had cancer and that the doctor had told this to her daughter. I asked her what the doctor had explained to her, and she replied, "He didn't explain anything to me." The following exchange took place when I asked Doña Estela if she had any questions that she wanted to ask the doctor. It touches upon her experience of pain, but more than anything illustrates the embarrassment that she endured—similar to that experienced by the woman who was "examined" by the three schoolgirls:

> DOÑA ESTELA: No, I didn't want to ask him anything.
>
> R.M.: *Why?*
>
> DOÑA ESTELA: Well, maybe because of *pena* [embarrassment], because one doesn't know anything about those things. They do so many things to you. They even stick their finger in you and shake you around in there. It is embarrassing. . . . I am embarrassed to see the faces of the doctors today. They already did everything they wanted with me and again they are going to stick who knows how many things in me.
>
> R.M.: You're embarrassed to see the doctors?
>
> DOÑA ESTELA: I am very embarrassed. When one comes alone [to examine] that is fine, but when various doctors come—five, six, or seven . . .
>
> R.M.: How did you feel?
>
> DOÑA ESTELA: Very embarrassed.

R.M.: How did you feel with me being in there?

DOÑA ESTELA: Well, that gave a little more bravery, certainly because you were there.

R.M.: Then, it didn't make you feel uncomfortable my being there?

DOÑA ESTELA: *No.*

R.M.: With all confidence, please let me know if it bothered you at all.

DOÑA ESTELA: No. I felt wonderful. I felt as if it gave me strength, I don't know. I was able to withstand the embarrassment more because you were there. I felt like you were supporting me.

R.M.: And when you saw all of the doctors what did you feel?

DOÑA ESTELA: Well, I felt much embarrassment—embarrassment and fear because the whole world arrives and starts poking around and the next one comes and inserts [something], and oh God. I repeat, I felt more tranquil because I saw you there, and I felt that you were giving me strength.

R.M.: Would you have liked there to have been only one doctor there?

DOÑA ESTELA: Yes, correct, just one. Look, that is fine, but that bunch no. One [doctor] arrives and pokes around, the next one arrives and pokes around and sticks a finger there. *¡Cónchale!* What I was was nervous. It makes one nervous.

R.M.: Did you feel like telling them all to leave?

DOÑA ESTELA: Yes. I felt like saying, "That is enough already. How long are you going to have me here?" But at least I felt the support from you, as you touched me I felt more tranquil.

R.M.: Why do you think there were so many doctors there?

DOÑA ESTELA: Well, I think it's because of the disease that I have . . . they all have to be there to—what do you call it?—find out the results of the disease. What can one do?

It is quite clear that Doña Estela was bothered by the number of doctors who examined her. The experience was painful and embarrassing as each one took turns, as she states, "poking around." The experience was embarrassing to her because she found herself in a situation where her genitalia were on display in, for all practical purposes, a public environment in which many mostly male doctors touched and looked at her. I say "public" because, although only doctors were in the examination room viewing her cervix, the sheer number of doctors (about six or so in total) and her embarrassment at the situation effectively blur the boundaries between public and private spaces. To Doña Estela this private examination, in fact, seemed rather public. She felt as if she were being viewed by "the whole world."

Moreover, as Doña Estela said, she was also embarrassed to "see their faces" the next day, as "they did everything they wanted with me," reminiscent of the sexualized discourse of having one's way with a woman, whereby the patient or woman is the object of the man's desire. Her embarrassment and shame, suggested by her comment of not wanting to "see their faces" and her remark that they had done "everything they wanted" with her, could arguably be interpreted as suggestive of the discourse of a rape account. Although this is a rather harsh statement and in no way meant to minimize rape, the tone in Doña Estela's voice as she strung those words together was that of powerlessness, as her body was manipulated and "everything" allowed to be done with "it." The only other appropriately sanctioned place for a woman to reveal her genitals is during sexual intercourse with her husband or during childbirth. The gynecological examination required that she allow her genitals to be viewed at a time that is neither during childbirth nor during sexual intercourse, thus violating this norm. In addition, she experienced many doctors examining her at once, which also felt discomfiting.

I cannot say for sure whether or not Doña Estela's comment—that my being there helped her—was because she felt she had to say this, but she did seem sincere, and when I asked her if she wanted me to go into the exam room with her again to have her gauze removed, she said yes. Doña Estela was seen by Dr. Velásquez this time. Unlike the situation the day earlier, only he, nurse Lila, Doña Estela, and myself were in the room. As he began to examine her, she winced and closed her eyes as she had done the day before. I took her hand in mine and she squeezed it tightly. At that moment Dr. Velásquez looked at me with a puzzled expression as if to say that this interaction between "the patient" and myself was unusual. I cannot know what he was thinking, but his expression did convey a certain bewilderment at the moment that I began to stroke Doña Estela's arm and offer her my hand. That was one of those moments that felt oddly divisive. Why would my comforting handholding of Doña Estela be at odds with the medical examination? It shouldn't be. But once Dr. Velásquez had removed the gauze, he walked out of the room, followed by nurse Lila. Doña Estela asked me if she could put on her clothes, but I did not know if the exam was over or not, as Dr. Velásquez left without saying anything. He was in the corresponding office taping notes about her case. I asked him if she was done. He nodded affirmatively, so I told Doña Estela that she could get dressed. The ending to this exam was ambiguous, as nothing was communicated to Doña Estela to let her know that it was over and that she could put on her clothes. This is but one of the ways that Doña Estela was objectified; on this second day at the hospital her body was once again examined, and the proper manipulations performed to remove the gauze from her cervix. Once this was accomplished, further interaction was no longer necessary, as was evident by Dr. Velásquez's retreat to the office without saying a word to Doña Estela letting her know that the exam was over (for that matter, neither did the nurse). At the same time, my role was tacitly questioned with the doctor's body language, which seemed to question my presumed objectivity: as a researcher, why was I offering comfort in the form of handholding?

This focus on the body, which is notable during both of Doña Estela's examinations, is due in part to contemporary medicine's commitment to a positivist model, whereby science is divorced from (and defined in opposition to) humanistic inquiries such as those of religion and culture. This process is rooted, at least partly, in the Cartesian dualism in which mind is treated as separate from body and spirit from matter (Scheper-Hughes and Lock 1987). In this paradigm characteristic of biomedicine, "most physicians, . . . irrespective of their professional activities and philosophical views on the nature of the mind, behave in practice as if they were still Cartesian dualists" (Dubos 1984, 56). Moreover, the common biomedical metaphor of the body as machine and the increasingly narrow focus from the whole body to the cellular level, attests to the prominence of the mind/body distinction within the framework of an objective biomedicine (Martin 1987).

In analyzing Doña Estela's first examination, it is apparent that she was viewed through an objectifying gaze. She expressed to me that she had experienced much pain during this examination, which, given her cries as each doctor felt around inside of her, is not surprising. Shortly after this experience, I asked Dr. Valdez (one of the attending physicians who had been examining Doña Estela that day) about the painfulness of the biopsy, using Doña Estela's experience as an example. He responded that many women cry during examinations because of "nerves," meaning that they get nervous and frightened and do not "really" experience pain.

During the examination, Doña Estela's cries went unacknowledged by the doctors; they were taken to be routine and therefore were not regarded as needing any special attention. Her cries were, for the most part, regarded as nothing out of the ordinary. As Scarry (1985, 7–8) notes:

If the only external sign of the felt-experience of pain (for which there is no alteration in the blood count, no shadow on the X-ray, no pattern on the CAT scan) is the patient's verbal report (however itself inadequate), then to bypass the voice is to bypass the bodily event, to bypass the patient, to bypass the person in pain. Thus the reality of a patient's X-rayable cancer may be believed-in but the accompanying pain disbelieved.

Not only was Doña Estela's pain bypassed; *she* was bypassed in the process. The discourse and practice surrounding this event was so effectively disembodying that to describe what took place as Doña Estela's examination, or even as the examination of a woman, or a patient, does not accurately convey that it was actually the disembodied object, the cervix, that was being examined. Like the picture of the pink, fleshy, and "clean" cervix that hangs on the wall in the office adjacent to the exam room, so too can one imagine Doña Estela's cervix created through the medical gaze—a snapshot framed by the matter of her body.[2] She "is transformed from a full person into an object, into a 'person-possessing-a-pelvis' and even into a 'pelvis-that-incidentally-belongs-to-a-person'" (Henslin and Biggs 1971, as cited in Kapsalis 1997, 11). As the feeling and emotional being is rendered nonexistent through this form of disembodiment—where a person becomes simply the matter (i.e., Doña Estela) surrounding the object (i.e., Doña Estela's cervix)—it is not surprising that a patient's pain can be easily bypassed.

Moreover, I asked myself whether it was necessary for all of those doctors to have a turn poking inside her? Given her strong cries each time a doctor would examine her, it is certainly questionable that they continued to probe her in this way. Because her prior tests and the attending physicians had already confirmed a diagnosis, the fact that many doctors examined Doña Estela's cervix was clearly not for diagnostic purposes, as Doña Estela had assumed. When I asked her why she thought there had been a number of doctors examining her, she replied, "To find out the results of the disease." The response to my own naïve question lies in the "case" of Doña Estela. This is a teaching hospital and, as one might expect, the interns were especially eager to see what a cancerous cervix—the interesting particularities of this cervix—looks like. As physicians learn to differentiate normal from pathological, "cases" become important sources of information—of "firsthand" knowledge. Doña Estela's case also provided something out of the ordinary; she (or rather her cervix) was "interesting" and gave the interns a chance to view the distinct characteristics of this malignant body part, thereby providing the storehouse of knowledge to recognize something similar when and if a comparable case should present itself. Therefore, the examination of Doña Estela's cervix was a mode of power, whereby she was (re)created as a case—surveyed and cataloged—and coming into existence by virtue of her (or more precisely her cervix's) features and markings. As Foucault (1979, 192) reminds us in writing on the history of the medical examination:

> The examination as the fixing, at once ritual and "scientific," of individual differences, as the pinning down of each individual in his own particularity . . . clearly indicates the appearance of a new modality of power in which each individual receives as his status his own individuality, and in which he is linked by his status to the features, the measurements, the gaps, the "marks" that characterize him and make him a "case."

Thus her value as a teaching tool is reflected in the individual particularities of her cervix. Her features make her up as a case, whereby she is identified not by name, but by her "marks" (e.g., the NIC III). She materializes through modes of medical power as a case with a medical history that contains a recording of her measurements, features, markings, and risk behaviors and is at the same time a reflection of cultural productions of female and womanhood. As Butler (1993, 251) notes, "Materiality is the dissimulated effect of power." In the realm of biomedicine, the ways in which bodies materialize, that is, the power to define "normal" female body parts, and behavior (e.g., such cervical cancer risk factors for women as sex at an early age, multiple sexual partners, and multiparity), is a medical mode of power in which "female" and "woman," although cultural, historical, and political products, appear as timeless, spaceless, and ahistorical properties of nature.

Talking Back

In crying out in pain during an examination, women are expressing on one level, of course, the physical manifestation of their hurt, but on another level, they are contesting their position as object. For the doctors, this can be uncomfortable, as the patient is not behaving as an ideal docile body, one that is quiet and motionless.[3] Indeed, talking during the examination is reserved mainly for the doctors, who are teaching, diagnosing, questioning, and responding among themselves. The proper time for a patient to speak is in the office, prior to entering the exam room, where she is questioned about her medical history. The dynamics of proper gynecological "patient performance" in these Venezuelan hospital settings is similar to what Kapsalis (1997) has described in the United States; the patients should remain still and with muscles relaxed (for speculum insertion and proper viewing). Hortencia, a thirty-three-year-old woman whom I interviewed, learned this lesson. She explains how she was treated by the doctor who had examined her: "During the exam he was fine, except that he reprimanded me because I was moving up when he was trying to examine me. But it was because of the pain that I was behaving so badly." Hortencia learned that moving around during the examination is inappropriate or, as she interpreted it due to the reprimand she received, "bad" behavior, even if one does so due to pain.

The cries, not only of Doña Estela but also of other women whose cries I was privy to, are a way of talking back in a situation that is otherwise quite disempowering—lying on one's back with knees separated and feet resting in stirrups—while being viewed, poked, and prodded by a seemingly endless number of doctors. I suggest that their cries remind the doctors that they are not machines; doctors are dealing with conscious people who are capable of feeling pain.

It was not uncommon for doctors to dismiss pain. Moreover, in some cases the women were reprimanded by the doctors for expressing pain: "It's not that bad," "You would think I was killing you," and "Why are you crying?" I observed and heard stories of these occurrences. For example, one day at Padre Machado, while sitting out in the room near the front desk writing in my notebook, I noticed a young woman who was crying. I began talking with her, and she said she had been waiting to see a particular doctor for a long time. I asked her if she felt sick or frustrated. She replied, "*Both.*" A woman who was sitting next to her chimed in, "That's what happens when you come to see a doctor, frustration." I went to the restroom and brought her some toilet tissue so she could wipe her eyes. I continued talking with the young woman. She turned to me and said, "That Dr. Molina scares me." I looked in the direction that she was gazing and noticed that Dr. Molina had stepped out of one of the examination rooms. I asked her why he scared her and she replied, "I don't know, maybe because his voice is so deep and strong." Then she related an interaction that she had had with him. She said, "One time he was examining me and I was crying because I was in pain. So then he told me, 'You certainly are a cryer.' He reprimanded me and it made me want to cry even more. I don't like to be reprimanded like that. I would rather be hit."

Thus not only can ignoring women's pain be alienating; by telling women that it is not acceptable to express this pain doctors are also silencing them. This silencing can extend into the office setting, making women less likely to want to ask questions of the doctor, even though they may have questions and concerns. This point about patients having but not asking questions will be discussed in the next chapter.

It is important to analyze the two major points illuminated by this vignette: women's silence is expressed through the "talking back" of crying, and waiting is a common theme in the bureaucracy of health care. From a psychological perspective, crying can be misread as sadness, when, in fact, it can be an expression of anger. For women, the process of gender socialization in most parts of the world means that they can access few socially legitimate emotional outlets. Expressing anger often goes against the grain of feminine expression.

Waiting is a common theme that emerged in informal discussions with patients; the chairs and benches found throughout both hospitals were more plentiful than basic necessities like disposable gloves. Waiting is built into the fabric of bureaucracy and has been creatively articulated as such in the Latin American context by Javier Auyero (2012) in his book *Patients of the State: The Politics of Waiting in Argentina*. I quote from some of his important insights at length:

> Poor people's actions, feelings, and thoughts while they wait for a welfare benefit or for a court ruling may look unimportant, but they are highly consequential for the production of compliance. These processes are thus an integral part of the daily and silent recreation of political domination, which masks itself as an exercise of power and secures poor people's subjugation by constraining their use of time and by preventing conflict from arising. (34–35)

He goes on to state:

> Poor people learn that they have to remain temporarily neglected, unattended to, or postponed. The poor comply because they do not have an alternative; . . . they comply silently, if begrudgingly, because they also learn that there is no use in protesting publicly. My comparative ethnographic work in three different "waiting sites" portrays poor people who *know* through repeated encounters that if they are to obtain the much needed "aid" (i.e., a welfare benefit, a service, or some other good), they have to show that they are worthy of it by dutifully

waiting. They *know* that they have to avoid making trouble, and they *know*, as many people told me, that they have to "keep coming and wait, wait, wait." (9)

Although to some this might appear to be acquiescing to the hegemonic power of the state in disciplining its population, we can also understand waiting, as Auyero suggests, an exercise in patience and resilience without a romanticization of the frustration of waiting. But waiting to see a doctor about a (potential) cancer diagnosis is something altogether different. This type of waiting in the public health setting needs further exploration. It is also why I inserted myself into the waiting experience when I noticed that waiting to make appointments in a series of other clinics (e.g., radiology, hematology) before one could see the gynecological oncologist was a tremendous obstacle to health care. I would take their appointment cards and offer to wait for the women who I met whether I interviewed them or just chatted informally with them in the waiting areas. As a woman anthropologist studying a gynecological cancer, the empathy for the women I spoke with was, at times, overwhelming. Unlike what doctors sometimes experience, I never grew desensitized to the experiences of the women who I met in the oncology hospitals. I do not attach a value to this realization; I simply think that in terms of career choice, I am better off as an anthropologist than an oncologist.

Virginity, Reproduction, and Pain

Interestingly, physicians also measured pain against women's sexual and childbirth experiences. On more than one occasion, I heard doctors tell their patients who have given birth that they should not be nervous about experiencing pain, and the implicit reasoning behind such a statement is that a woman who has endured the pain of childbirth should in comparison not find the gynecological exam, Pap, or biopsy painful.

Consider, for example, an examination interaction that I observed. It involved Rosario, a thirty-four-year-old woman whom I interviewed at Razetti, and Dr. Valdez, one of the attending physicians. On February 8, 1995, Rosario came to the gynecology department at Razetti for the first time. After interviewing her, I asked her if I could enter the exam room with her. She agreed, and after she was lying on the table, I entered with Dr. Valdez, the nurse Marcela, and Dr. Carillo (an intern, or *pasante*). During the exam Rosario became visibly upset. She began crying softly. Dr. Valdez asked her rhetorically and with a slight edge to his voice, "Are you that way when you give birth?" He then asked Rosario if she was nervous. Rosario began to explain that her last pregnancy, which was only about five months prior to this examination, was very "difficult." She said that she had delivered her baby in the breech position and had experienced much pain during this delivery. Dr. Valdez was busy examining her cervix and pointing out things to Dr. Carillo; neither responded. At one point, Rosario said that she was experiencing pain and that she "hurt inside." Dr. Valdez responded by saying, "We aren't doing anything inside. We weren't even touching you there." Rosario remained silent after that, tears still streaming from her eyes. I tried to comfort her by holding her hand.

When the exam was over and Rosario entered the office, where Dr. Valdez was sitting behind the desk, the first thing that Dr. Valdez said to Rosario was, "It's as if we hit you in there or something." Rosario responded by telling the doctor that she was nervous. Before leaving, Rosario apologized to both doctors for having cried in the exam room. She said, "I'm sorry for . . . " and then she pointed to her eyes to signal the tears that she had shed during the examination. Dr. Valdez responded by saying, "It's all right. You shouldn't worry about it. It's normal."

Later, when I asked Rosario if the exam had caused her any pain or discomfort, she said that it had been painful and elaborated on why she had felt uncomfortable and nervous during the exam:

ROSARIO: It's just that I felt nervous. I told you before and I told the doctor that when I gave birth to my baby girl she was coming out with her bottom first. So, I was very nervous because she was coming out this way. I suffered a lot because I gave birth that way. You know, the logical thing is to have a cesarean section and they didn't do that. They let me give birth like that. I had a sonogram at seven months and the doctors said the baby was cephalic [head down], and I kept saying that she was feet first, that she was in a sitting position and they thought she was in the encephalic position. Well, when I got labor pains, I just felt that she was feet first, one can just tell these things. But the doctor kept saying she was in the right position, that she was encephalic and who is going to argue with him? . . . I got nervous now when the doctor was in there doing all that poking around [*hurgando*]. He did a rectal exam and that made me nervous. That hurts. One isn't used to that.

R.M.: Did you feel pain when they were examining you?

ROSARIO: Yes, it was bothersome. . . . I think more than anything it was "nerves." I was nervous that they were going to, well, you don't know how much I suffered giving birth, that they were going to touch something and that it was going to hurt a lot. You see, it is the "nerves" that are attacking me.

A number of points can be made about Rosario's experience and her narrative about the examination. First, Dr. Valdez assumed a lot about Rosario's gynecologically related experiences of pain. His question "Are you that way when you give birth?" was clearly to let Rosario know that she should not be crying under these circumstances. Interestingly, he linked the birthing experience with the gynecological exam, as did Rosario, but each had differing ideas as to what that might mean in terms of the gynecological exam and biopsy. Because she had given birth, Dr. Valdez expected that she should be able endure without complaint what he considered the comparatively minor pain of the biopsy. He did not listen carefully to her narrative experience about having relatively recently delivered a breech baby, which was obviously very traumatic and painful for her. Rosario, however, having this experience in the forefront of her mind, feared that Dr. Valdez might touch her in a way that would cause her pain. Had he taken this into consideration, he might have been better able to understand her distress and to console her.

Alternatively, it is perfectly reasonable to suggest that giving birth and having a gynecological exam need not be connected experiences, such that it would make little sense to compare a priori the pain of one experience to the pain of another, as they are contextually different experiences. Therefore, it is misguided to assume that the pain of childbirth should necessarily preclude the pain that one might experience during a gynecological exam and biopsy. Women are indirectly told that if they have experienced childbirth, they do not have the right to feel pain, that they should find gynecological procedures bearable. If not, they may be made to feel embarrassment and guilty for, as Hortencia said, having "behaved badly." In Rosario's situation, she felt like she had to apologize for crying, as she learned through the comments of Dr. Valdez that her behavior was inappropriate.

In addition, Rosario expressed ideas about her own body, about how she felt her baby was in the breech position before she was going to give birth, ideas that differed from how her doctor had described the baby's position. In the end, however, she declared that she couldn't question the doctor ("who is going to argue with him?") because her knowledge of her body was secondary to the authoritative knowledge held by the medical practitioner. With this statement, Rosario expressed her awareness of the disparate relationship of power between doctor and patient. In both medical encounters, Rosario comes away with the lesson that her bodily knowledge and experiences count for little in the face of medical knowledge, which even tells her when she should and should not be experiencing pain. As Jordan (1997, 57–58) notes, through her extensive work on authoritative knowledge in medical encounters, "People not only accept authoritative knowledge (which is thereby validated and reinforced) but also are actively and unselfconsciously engaged in its routine production and reproduction."

Both Rosario and Dr. Valdez accepted the assumptions inherent in the medical knowledge regarding the experience of pain—that the exam should not hurt. Rosario even participated in the lessening of her experience of pain by attributing it to "nervousness." Often what occurs in the evaluation of one way of knowing as authoritative is the simultaneous dismissal of alternate ways of knowing, which are trivialized, seen as backward or simply seen as irrelevant if not completely ignored (Jordan 1989). In this situation, what Rosario could say about her body and her experience, as we have seen, was altogether ignored during the examination. Nonetheless, as we will see in later sections of this chapter, women do contest and resist authoritative knowledge to varying degrees, particularly when medical knowledge challenges their morality.

In contrast to Rosario, who was expected to be able to endure the examination with no problem because she had given birth, Doña Carmen, a patient at Padre Machado whom I interviewed, was examined with special care because the doctors felt that the exam might be painful for her, given that she had had sexual relations only a few times, many years ago. The doctors said because she was "virgin-like," they would not be able to use the regular-sized speculum. A narrower instrument would have to be used so as not to cause her pain. In addition, they decided that to do a cervical biopsy, they would need to give her a local anesthetic. This is not normally done, but because of Doña Carmen's "virgin-like" status, the doctors were concerned that the biopsy would be particularly painful. When I asked why Doña Carmen required anesthesia compared to all the other women who come in and are not anesthetized, one of the doctors replied, "Because she is a virgin and she'll scream."

The doctors were certainly concerned with not causing Doña Carmen pain; however, it is unclear why a woman who is not a virgin would experience any less pain with a biopsy than a virginal woman (or virgin-like woman). In this procedure, the tissue is extracted from the cervix with biopsy pincers, and for any woman this could be painful or at least uncomfortable (as noted earlier, the majority of women interviewed expressed having felt pain when they were being examined and biopsied).

I am not arguing, of course, that Doña Carmen should not have been treated delicately. On the contrary, the point is that Rosario, or any other woman, might have also benefited from similar considerations. When a woman's sexual history is taken as the principal indicator of what she should or should not experience during the examination, she may have to endure unnecessary pain. When Rosario indicated that she was experiencing pain, this was not taken seriously by the doctors because, as she was sexually active and had had children, she was expected to be able to endure the examination without pain. Perhaps if Dr. Valdez had paid attention to Rosario's narrative of her childbirth experience, he could have made the examination less traumatic and more comfortable for her. Moreover, by focusing on a woman's sexual history, the discourse surrounding the speculum, virginity, and pain implicitly draws on a sexual analogy, whereby the penetrating penis becomes synonymous with the penetrating speculum. The implicit medical determination is made that a woman who has experienced a penis (and in some cases childbirth) should have no qualms about experiencing a gynecological examination (including a speculum). This configuration is indicative of the way in which gynecological examinations are sexualized, revealing strong cultural attitudes about women, their bodies, and their sexualities (Kapsalis 1997). At the same time, such taken-for-granted assumptions about sexual intercourse, childbirth, pain, and the gynecological examination are also a convenient way to make quick judgments about medical procedures in an environment that is not conducive to time-consuming dialogues between patients and doctors (e.g., overcrowded, understaffed).

Disease, Not Dis-ease!

The patients' experiences of pain, grief, fear, and anxiety, as described through the narrative vignettes that have thus far been presented, are not merely a direct reflection of the hospital, disease, and/or illness experience. These feelings and emotions also are generated from prior experiences and the social and economic circumstances in which the women find themselves. For example, as discussed by the women that I interviewed, fears about one's health may resonate with fears about how one will be able to afford treatments or with the often low quality of care and treatment one has learned to expect from public institutions. These circumstances, which are often seen as secondary to the biological functioning of the body, are largely ignored by medical practitioners. Once again returning to the predominance of the Cartesian perspective in medicine, the biological body is divorced from the social body. The focal point for physicians remains at the level of the body. As Waitzkin (1991) has argued, doctors do not deal with the social problems that people face in relation to illness. Because socioeconomic factors are seen as outside of the domain of medicine, their focus is seen as necessarily on the body. Kleinman (1988, 5), for example, points out:

> Disease is the problem from the practitioner's perspective. In the narrow biological terms of the biomedical model, this means that disease is reconfigured only as an alteration in biological structure or functioning . . . the body is a discrete entity, a thing, an "it," machinelike an objective, separate from thought and emotion.

Although health problems are also embedded in larger political, economic, and social circumstances, these areas are seen as too vast and removed from the specific task of medicine, which is to focus on healing the body—in other words, to treat disease, not dis-ease (problems external to the actual biological manifestation of disease). This perspective is exemplified by the comments of Dr. Núñez, a radiologist at Razetti in her late thirties with whom I became friendly. Late one afternoon I found Dr. Núñez in the hospital's social services department. She looked slightly agitated with arms folded as she paced the floor a bit. She said she was waiting for a patient with whom she had made special arrangements to see, but the patient, who couldn't come at another time, was late. Dr. Núñez spoke about this patient, saying she has many difficulties in her life besides her disease. She is very poor and has many familial problems. Dr. Núñez guessed that that is what may have caused her to not show for her appointment. But, she added, "I can't help her with all of those other difficulties, that is not my problem." By this Dr. Núñez meant, of course, that she could attend to her patient's bodily problems, but not to the broader social and economic milieu in which this "body" is situated. The body is necessarily her focus of attention within the neoliberal contraints facing the public health system. I could tell that she felt frustrated by her own inability to help. A superficial reading of her comment as "not my problem" would miss her internal struggle, as the broader obstacles of medical structural violence rendered her helpless.

Patients are also aware of the medical focus on their bodies and cautious against sharing their personal problems with the doctors. The comments of Rosario, whose experience of pain was discussed in the previous section, shows this hesitancy to share problems that are seemingly not directly related to the medical condition for which diagnosis and treatment are sought. Below, I continue recounting Rosario's narrative, which exemplify the way medical and social problems are inextricably linked and cannot be circumscribed as separate domains.

Rosario

Rosario came from a small town in the state of Lara, approximately eight hours from Caracas. She was in a marriage-like relationship with her partner of fourteen years. Rosario didn't work outside of the home and had four children. Her most recent was born just five months before I first interviewed her. In addition to her medical problem of in situ cervical cancer, Rosario related many difficulties that she faced in her personal life, which cannot be divorced from her disease. She spoke about these problems at length when I asked if there were questions she would have liked to ask the doctor but felt that she couldn't:

> ROSARIO: No, well, it's just that I'm scared. He asked, "Could it be that you are pregnant?" Because I haven't had my period and that makes me more nervous. Because in reality I'm going to be sincere, my husband and I haven't had a good relationship and I am afraid. That is why I feel attacked by nerves.
>
> R.M.: You are afraid that you could be pregnant?
>
> ROSARIO: Yes, because then the process will be much longer, just imagine. That really has me nervous. It's just that he [her husband] isn't a reasonable person. In that aspect we just don't understand each other. If I say no, he says yes, and he puts a lot of pressure on me to have [sexual] relations. It's just not good.
>
> R.M.: He pressures you to have [sexual] relations when you don't want to?
>
> ROSARIO: Yes. I have to satisfy him, because what else can I do? I don't have a house. He is not my husband. He is married. When he got involved with me he was separated, but he is not divorced. So I am living in his mother's home. They are four brothers and each has their area and I am there. I have to accept

that even though I don't like it because he gives me [money] for the children, the house, well . . . things that I need, and this isn't just now, but has been going on for fourteen years. Where do I go, *mi niña* ["my child," a term of endearment]? I don't have a family. My problem is that between my husband and me there is no love, we get along fine and that, but there are just certain things where we just don't understand each other. Like if he wants to [have sexual relations] and I don't, he can be somewhat of a brute. It's that he is fifty-one and he still hasn't grown up.

R.M.: Has he become violent? Has he hit you?

ROSARIO: Yes. I've had to put up with a lot of things from him for my children too. Where can I take them? You tell me. This problem of mine is so great that it won't be over with today and I am very nervous. If I am pregnant . . . that is my desperation now. The doctor said, "Could it be that you are pregnant?" That made me even more nervous. It's just that since they did that thing [biopsy] my period hasn't come [normally]. It lasted three days and just stopped. I'd like to ask the doctors to write down on a piece of paper telling him [her husband] not to touch me to respect my illness because if not, he becomes an ogre. He becomes an ogre.

R.M.: How come you feel like you can't speak with the doctors about this?

ROSARIO: Yes. That is something that I don't know. What will they say to me? "*Sinvergüenza* [shameless one], then why do you live with him?" Then I would have to explain why it is that I live with him, that I don't have a family, right. They will categorize me in that way; they will think that a woman who puts up with being beaten by a man and puts up with all of his needs does so because she is a *sinvergüenza*. A lot of people are mistaken that way. They have that type of mentality, but they just don't understand. For example, I don't have a family, my family is my children, and if I begin to think about where I can go with them, well, what else . . . ? I have my cross to bear, what else can I do? God gave each and every one of us a cross to bear and to carry it along little by little. The only thing I can ask God to do is to give me the strength to put up with it, lots of strength.

She was crying softly during most of this narrative. The possibility of being pregnant was an extremely upsetting thought, not only for health reasons but also because of her family life at home. The prospect of taking care of another child with a loveless partner who is abusive while also contemplating the threat of a disease that she knew little about was extremely anxiety provoking. She was visibly upset as the problems she was facing mounted with few options for material, social, and emotional support. Her experience of pain discussed earlier in this chapter, which was related to a prior experience of a difficult birth, her anxiety at possibly being pregnant, and her difficult family life, are all relevant to her health. However, she was careful not to talk with the doctors about these issues for fear that she would be judged negatively.

I missed Rosario's second visit to the hospital, and when I saw her on her third visit to the hospital, she told me that her precancerous lesion (NIC III) and pregnancy had both been confirmed. She was, unsurprisingly, distraught when she was called to see the doctor, I asked her if she wanted me to go in with her, and she said she would appreciate it if I did. Shortly after we entered the office, Dr. Valdez (one of the attending physicians) and Dr. Casas (an intern doing a rotation at the hospital) began questioning her as to why she did not protect herself from pregnancy. She explained that at another clinic she was told that she could not take the birth-control pill. In response, Dr. Valdez told her that there were other ways to prevent pregnancy. Rosario remained quiet after that, and in a half-joking tone, Dr. Valdez told her, "We are going to have to take out your ovaries so you can't get pregnant again." She replied that the situation did not please her either—all the while with tears running down her face. Dr. Valdez informed her that they would just have to wait until the baby was born, that there was no other choice (abortion is illegal in Venezuela). He told her to return in a month. The consultation was over.

Because in our first interview Rosario had mentioned getting some pills from a friend that would make her "period come" if indeed she was pregnant, after her interaction with the doctors, I asked her if she would have an abortion if she could. She replied that she would and that it should be an option for women in similar circumstances. She added, however, that she is a very nervous person and would be afraid to do it.

In analyzing the office interaction, it is obvious that the main discussion was about her pregnancy and why she didn't "protect herself." Virtually nothing was said about her condition in terms of her precancerous lesion. Instead, the doctors reprimanded her for becoming pregnant, something that she obviously was distraught about as well. When she tried to offer an explanation as to why she couldn't take birth-control pills, she was immediately interrupted with the comment from Dr. Valdez that "there are other ways." This leads me to believe that when Rosario was questioned about her method of birth control, the purpose of such questioning was not really meant to elicit information on this matter, but to castigate her for becoming pregnant again. It did nothing to help Rosario deal with a situation that she herself was extremely distraught about. She was only made to feel worse.

Dr. Valdez's comment about removing her ovaries, though said in a joking manner, was nonetheless a threat to regulate her reproduction. Of course, no mention was made of her partner's role and (even in a joking tone) the possibility of giving him a vasectomy. This would hardly be considered a way of regulating reproduction.[4] The regulation of reproduction is almost naturally directed at the woman, and in this case, a poor woman. Multiparity was one of the risk factors for cervical cancer that was mentioned by the doctors I interviewed, including Dr. Valdez. Often this was described as a problem of lower-class women. Reproduction that is marked by class in this way (as a product of the lower classes) is viewed as a pathology of excess and is configured as "a domain susceptible to pathological processes, and hence one calling for therapeutic or normalizing interventions" (Foucault 1978, 68). In this case, the surgical removal of ovaries was suggested as the therapeutic intervention for reproduction.

Some patients learn not to share too much, not to ask too many questions, and generally not to take up too much of the doctor's time. In fact, when Rosario did try to explain that she was nervous about the examination because she had had a difficult birth, her concerns were largely ignored. The doctors examining her remained fixed on the problem at hand—her cervix. Lack of physician response to and/or a curt response to questions clue the patient into the "proper" patient role. But patients are not objects, and the subaltern can speak (Chibber 2013). In the next chapter I focus on the ways in which the patients who I interviewed demonstrated agency and resilience in the medical setting. If we insist on defining agency narrowly as overt behaviors and words, we will likely miss the many ways in which silences, gestures, and utterances enact meaningful oppositional agency to the situational medical apathy and/or power they may experience.

Regulating Hospital Women

Thus far I have focused on the disciplinary practices of patients in the medical setting, but this leaves unexamined the experiences of other hospital women who are not patients. Although patients are the focus of much regulation by doctors, nurses, secretaries, and other hospital personnel, they are not the only women who experienced this in the hospital setting. Indeed, *doctoras* (women doctors), women nurses, secretaries, technicians, and myself shared some form of regulation directed at us because of our gender. At one time or another, then, we held a common position of subalternity. "Countering essentialist taxonomies of the subaltern," Coronil (1997, 16) views "subalternity as a relational and a relative concept that refers to heterogeneous social actors that share a common condition of subordination." I find this definition of the subaltern useful in analyzing how "heterogeneous social actors" can share experiences of subordination.

In this section I explore forms of regulatory and disciplinary power that were experienced by women at both hospitals. The "disciplining of hospital women" that I refer to focuses specifically on the construct of gender and discipline. Foucault's theories on discipline and the creation of docile bodies provide much explanatory power in analyzing the hospital as institution. To this end, we must understand power as residing not in the hands of one group that oppresses another, but in the "network of practices, institutions, and technologies that sustain positions of dominance and subordination in a particular domain" (Bordo 1997, 92). In addition, it is necessary to view power as productive or constitutive power, which emphasizes the construction, and not the repression, of desires, beliefs, and behaviors (Foucault 1978). Drawing on these points, Foucault's theories have been reexamined within a feminist framework, which take into account the particular ways in which women are disciplined (Diamond and Quinby 1988; Ramazanoglu 1993; Bordo 1997). For example, Bordo (1997, 91) argues:

> Through the exacting and normalizing disciplines of diet, makeup, and dress—organizing principles of time and space in the day of many women—we are rendered less socially oriented and more centripetally focused on self-modification. Through these disciplines, we continue to memorize on our bodies the feel and conviction of lack, of insufficiency, of never being good enough.

Bordo's analysis focuses on the gender-related disorders of hysteria, anorexia nervosa, and agoraphobia. She looks at how women engage in self-disciplining that reinforces the social norms of what it means to be a woman.

This gender-directed disciplining can also be seen in the everyday functioning of the hospital with women doctors, patients, nurses, secretaries, technicians, and myself, the anthropologist. Despite class divisions and relationships of power that dictate a hierarchy within the institution (physicians being at the top and patients at the bottom), it is still possible to see the saliency of women's social roles within this order and the ways in which women doctors, secretaries, patients, and nurses experience regulation and discipline. Without essentializing difference, it is still possible to discuss the ways in which gender remains central to the structuring of relationships in the hospital setting. As Cassell (1996, 49) argues:

> What we must reject . . . are ideologies that maintain that difference is innately deep—or epiphenomenally shallow. Difference may be deep, difficult to eradicate, and yet not essential. Gender is done, negotiated, socially produced, but it is real, as real as any other social phenomenon that structures our experience, our bodies, our behavior, our values, and our lives.

In addition to the tenacity of gender difference and what that means for the disciplining of women, I also look at negotiation and compliance in the disciplinary process and the ways in which women create it, partake in it, and contest it. I include my own experiences of gender and identity disciplining and negotiation in the hospitals.

Locating a Hospital Woman: Chicana, Anthropologist, Woman

In thinking about how or where (or even whether) to write about my personal experiences in the field, I am both drawn to and skeptical of the common experiences that I shared with other women at the hospital, including secretaries, nurses, patients, physicians, and technicians. My concern resonates with the work of many feminist scholars who have sought to problematize the essentializing category of "woman" (Haraway 1997; Butler 1990; Spivak 1990; Zavella 1996; Fraser and Nicholson 1990; Scott 1995). One of the main concerns has been the erasing of difference with this totalizing category. For example, black, Chicana, and lesbian feminists in particular have questioned the absence of class, race and sexuality in scholarship about "women." On the other hand, there have also been reservations about the emphasis on difference to the exclusion of common experiences that serve to unite women and to create a social, political, and economic force.

I am aware of these arguments, and align myself with those feminist scholars who in their work explore difference between and within gender(s), taking into account the intersections of race, class, history and sexuality (Crenshaw 1991). In this section I focus on common disciplining experiences that are shared by the women at the hospitals. This is not to say that I choose to ignore the many differences that separate us, nor do I uncritically accept essentialist and universal categories. Rather, I argue that this dichotomy needs contextualization; it can both illuminate and obfuscate the moments and places where and when it is possible to talk about both difference and sameness, within and across categories. Placing this argument within the framework of anthropological concerns about the relationship between researcher and informant in feminist fieldwork, one might discuss these issues of sameness and difference in terms of insider and outsider status, and "rather than assume some type of panfemale solidarity . . . or a lack of shared experience between researchers and subjects, we should realize that we are almost always simultaneously insiders and outsiders" (Zavella 1996, 141). This unmasking of the objective anthropological observer is meant to situate us in "self-reflexive analysis of our own experience [that] will push us to provide "provisional" analyses that are always incomplete, but which make clear whose viewpoint is being represented" (Rosaldo 1989, as cited in Zavella 1996). This self-reflection helps us to understand how it is that we interpret, understand, and write about the things that we observe, and also how it is that we are situated within our own fieldwork—for example, recognizing our positions of power as we conduct research. This type of self-reflection has been central to the research agendas of those of us who conduct feminist fieldwork (Wolf 1996).

I obviously cannot ignore that my location or position in the hospital was at some level a relationship of power in relation to the women patients that I interviewed. I experienced similar dilemmas as those articulated by Zavella (1996) in her account of ethnographic research among Mexican American women cannery workers. She grappled with the problem of being both an insider and an outsider among those she was researching. In her experience, she notes that her ethnic identity, being a Chicana, allowed her to make connections as an insider and at the same time, although coming from a working-class family, her status as a graduate student set her apart as the women whom she interviewed were keenly aware of her privileges as an educated woman, thus making her an outsider.

Because the research presented here involved interviewing those in positions of power (e.g., doctors) as well as those in relatively powerless positions (e.g., patients), my relationships to those I interviewed was in constant flux moving between insider and outsider status (and sustaining both simultaneously). Relationships of power also shifted depending on whom I interacted with and according to gender and class. For example, the fact that I was required to wear a white physician's coat at the hospital served as a visual marker, a sign, of the power differential that I held in relationship to the women that I interviewed, even though I attempted to negotiate and lessen this distinction by taking off the coat during the interview or whenever the head nurse, who required me to wear it, was not around. That was my own "weapon of the weak" (Scott 1985) in the face of hospital regulations.

I was also an outsider in terms of education, even though I too came from a working-class background. At the same time, however, my identity as a Latina, my ability to speak with them in Spanish fluently, also gave me insider status. Although not a Venezuelan, my Mexican background provided me with connection to doctors and patients alike. I also exchanged stories with the women I interviewed, telling them about my family, and as is exemplified later in this chapter, I also shared my feelings of what it was like to be newly married and separated from my husband while conducting research. Since they were responding to personal questions that I had for them, I felt the desire to reciprocate with them about my life. Thus I could relate as a woman, and particularly as a married woman, as most of the women whom I interviewed were either married or living in "married-like" relationships.

Some feminist scholarship, particularly that of Stacey (1988), has suggested that there are traditionally female strengths such as empathy and human concern that allow for a relationship between researcher and subject that is nonexploitative and mutual. She states that ironically and unfortunately, however, this situation masks a deeper form of exploitation as a result of the inevitable abandonment by the researcher, who in the course of conducting a feminist ethnography has developed close relationships with those whom she studies (Zavella 1996). This "ultimate betrayal" described by Stacey assumes a panfemale identity, described elsewhere as "cultural feminism" (di Leonardo 1991, as cited in Zavella 1996), where "women" share a common and "natural" bond in term of empathy, concern, and mutuality irrespective of class, race, ethnicity or sexual preference (Zavella 1996). To assume, however, that women share the same interests based on some essentialist characteristics is rather naïve. This glossing of difference does not take seriously the ways in which feminist fieldworkers and those they study differ in identity markers other than gender, and therefore it ignores the extent to which power marks this relationship. Both extremes, assuming "pan-female" common interests and experiences among female researchers and informants and assuming no common interests and experiences, are equally misleading.

Power is a messy and elusive subject to contend with and cannot be easily attributed in fixed terms as always the hegemonic property of a person or group over another or others. As Zavella (1996) points out in her critique of Strathern's (1987) assumption that power always lies with the researcher, it is not always necessarily the case that the researcher has more power over and no common interests with those whom she studies. Consider those researchers who find themselves in both positions of relative power and powerlessness. This is seen, for example, in the work of Hsuing (1996), where she was "between bosses and workers," and found herself exploited and also sexually harassed as a factory worker during participatory research in China. Her gender and Chinese identity made this possible and also gave her insider status with the other female factory workers whom she interviewed. At the same time, she was an outsider in terms of her U.S. education. While bosses were a part of her study, she did not necessarily hold power over them, and in fact she found herself in a relatively powerless position.

In my fieldwork experience, for example, my simultaneous status as insider and outsider was quite evident as I moved in and out of different levels of access to power. My relationship to both doctors and patients placed me in a precarious position as I struggled to find my place among both, realizing, of course, that getting close to one might distance me from the other. Recall, for example, in the previous chapter where I described having been given a strange look, and what I interpreted as disapproving look, from Dr. Velásquez as I tried to comfort Doña Estela, who cried in pain during an examination. While getting close to Doña Estela, I felt like an outsider among the doctors, which was unavoidable because I could not and would not be emotionally unattached in that situation. I also learned, however, how to use the white lab coat, a definite symbol of power, to mark my insider status within the hospital setting, and the ways in which it was possible to be insider and outsider at the same time and to negotiate power accordingly. The following account illustrates this point well.

At both hospitals (Razetti and Padre Machado), patients were required to make appointments in person or to have someone make an appointment for them in person; in other words, someone needed to be physically present. They could not make an appointment by telephone. This is part of the disciplining procedure of turning people into patients through control of bodies described previously. Because the appointment desk at the private hospital, in particular, would sometimes close before the women were finished seeing the doctor, the women would sometimes have to return another day to stand in line to make their next appointment. For some women this meant a one-, two-, three-hour or longer trip back to the city just to make an appointment. So, whenever possible I began making the appointments for the women whom I interviewed who were in this situation. I would have the women leave their appointment cards with me, and I would make the appointments for them. I would then call them and tell them when their next appointment was scheduled and bring their card with me that day. In this way we were able to circumvent the problem of appointment making when the appointment desk was closed by the time they were finished being examined. One might also describe this as a way of negotiating hospital rules by replacing my body with their body, even though the end result is that a body (mine, theirs, or someone else's) is disciplined to engage in the practices (e.g., waiting, forming lines, arriving on time) required for admission and attendance by the institution.

This arrangement worked well, after initially feeling the frustration that patients do in terms of the administrative procedures of appointment making. The first time that I tried to make an appointment for Sandra, a woman who I interviewed at Padre Machado, I was told by the young man at the appointment desk that the next appointment available was three months later. I mentioned the doctor had written down on the appointment card that her appointment should be in another month. He refused to grant the appointment and said that he would have to have a special note from the doctor to be able to make the appointment for the next month. I felt completely powerless and frustrated, as were many of the women in the same situation. But imagine being in that situation with your health on the line. I was determined that Sandra should have her appointment and kept thinking about how I would feel in this situation. I observed the anxiety created by this situation as well on occasions where I just sat and watched women in line as they made appointments and overheard the worries of some at having to wait two, three, or four months for their next appointments.

I returned to the office and approached the head physician of the gynecology department and told her of the difficulty in making an appointment for Sandra. I asked if she would write a note indicating that the woman should be given her appointment for the following month. In doing this, I was aware that my role as an outsider looking at their medical system provided me with a certain amount of power in terms of a host-guest relationship such that my request would likely be accommodated.

The doctor wrote me the note and I returned to the appointment desk. Before doing so, however, I slipped on the white lab coat, which I had not worn in my earlier interaction at the appointment desk. Yes, I did so knowing that this would be a symbol of power and provide me with a level of authority that I did not have without the coat. I was normally very careful to try and lessen the disparate relationship of power between myself and those I interviewed, but in this case the alliance that I felt with the women that I interviewed and the frustration that I felt with appointment making led me to use the power available to me to try and ensure success in this endeavor, even though I did have the doctor's note (yet another mechanism of power). I should also mention at this point that I had been privy to a conversation with the doctors in this department a month earlier in which Dr. Molina had mentioned his belief that a woman, who had erroneously been given an appointment six months after her first visit to the hospital, had returned with a more advanced stage of cancer. This, I am sure, fueled my desire to help Sandra get her appointment by wielding whatever power I could, and knowing full well that this power was not available to Sandra herself or any of the other women I interviewed.

With note in hand and lab coat on, I returned to the appointment desk and presented the young man with the note. Sandra was given an appointment for one month later. I don't know if the note alone would have gotten the same results, but in making every effort to get this appointment for Sandra, I knew that the coat would symbolize power and authority, which, when dealing with the administrative procedures of the hospital, was helpful to get anything done. Just as some of the patients whom I interviewed and observed used whatever means (e.g., persistence, pleading) they could to access care,[5] I too used available resources to help them receive the care that most so desperately sought. I knew that my role in the hospital would not be that of neutral observer and that I would want to help the women whom I interviewed in any way that I could; it would be impossible and unconscionable to pretend otherwise. At the same time, however, I did not want to alienate myself from doctors, nurses, secretaries, and other hospital personnel who were also a focus of my research project. These groups, of course, are not neatly diametrically opposed, as my lumping of them together might suggest, but, for the most part, the generally less powerful position of patients does foster distinctions of power between the "two" groups. My main concern in the hospitals, nonetheless, remained that of minimizing the relationship of power between myself and the patients by positioning myself as an insider among them, while still recognizing that on some level I was still an outsider (and still in a position of power).

I was simultaneously an insider and an outsider not only among the patients that I interviewed but also among the hospital personnel. However, the extent to which I was an insider, or outsider for that matter, was always limited. The very fact that I could be both at the same time attests to this partial positioning. It may be fruitful, then, to talk insider and outsider status in terms of partial positionings. By this, I mean that my location was always partially that of insider and outsider. My various roles and partial positionings within the two hospitals, required me to constantly evaluate my situation and to consciously manipulate my own presentation of self in the negotiation of power.

Interestingly, as I became more of an insider with hospital personnel, such as becoming friendly with secretaries, it was difficult for me to be as effective in helping patients make appointments as I had when I was more of an outsider among the personnel. For example, I became friendly with one of the women (María) who worked at the appointment desk at Padre Machado. María worked with the young man who I dealt with when making Sandra's appointment. María, Verónica (the administrative assistant for the gynecology department), and I would sometimes chat when they or I had breaks and would eat lunch together.

One day, after I had finished interviewing Hortencia, a patient at Padre Machado, I went with her to go make her next appointment with María, who was on duty at the appointment desk. She told Hortencia that she was missing an important piece of paper that the nurse should have given her to be able to make the appointment. I went back with Hortencia to get this paper, and a few minutes later María walked into the gynecology department. After we got the appropriate paperwork, we walked out to the appointment desk to see if anyone had taken María's place, but no one had. The appointment desk was closed. I returned to the gynecology department to see if María would make the appointment. I explained what had happened, that Hortencia went to get the paper from the nurse and that when she went back the appointment room was closed. María responded that it was the nurse's fault for forgetting to give her the paper in the first place. She stated, "I'm not going to open that room again." She looked down at her watch and said, "I close at four o'clock" (my watch read 3:50). She wouldn't make the appointment for Hortencia. María looked at me and reiterated that it was the nurse's fault that Hortencia would be unable to make an appointment that day. However, that wasn't going to help Hortencia. Fortunately, Hortencia had an aunt who lived by the hospital, and she said she would ask this aunt to come by and make the appointment for her. I also volunteered to make the appointment if she needed me to. Otherwise, Hortencia would have had to take a ninety-minute bus ride each way just to make an appointment.

Although it appears counterintuitive, I suggest that as I became more of an insider among hospital staff, it was likely easier to say no to me. As an outsider, I held a certain amount of authority, as hospital staff were uncertain of my role within the hospital. As an insider, I was another hospital worker. I was constantly negotiating not only my location within this setting but also relationships of power with doctors, patients, and hospital staff.

However, to frame this interaction with María more completely, it is important to explain what happened next. Wanting me to understand her perspective as to why she would not reopen the appointment desk, María approached me when I returned to the office. She explained that in the previous year, the hospital had appointed a new administrative board and that many changes had taken place, many of which had not been agreeable to the staff. María was particularly annoyed that now they all had to punch time cards, and, as she put it, "In the past we would stay late and we didn't care because we didn't mind working for the hospital, but now that they monitor us like this, we are no longer like a family. Like the way it used to be." During this time, the hospital employees were also facing problems with the hospital union. The workers accused the union of stealing from them, and they were organizing a petition to bring in a new union to replace the old one. The morale among the hospital employees was, understandably, at a low. Therefore, to better understand María's response to my request, it is important to also contextualize her actions within the milieu of hospital politics. As I became more of an insider, María felt more comfortable in denying my request and in discussing hospital politics with me.

The roles of Hortencia (and other patients) as "waitee" and staff like Maria as the ones in charge of directing waiting, also brings them into a relationship of power. In his book *A Lover's Discourse: Fragments*, Barthes (1978, 40) discusses the idea of transference as an actionable exchange between those who are required to wait and those who make them wait. He states:

> In transference, one always waits—at the doctor's, the professor's, the analyst's. Further, if I am waiting at a bank window, an airport ticket counter, I immediately establish an aggressive link with the teller, the stewardess, whose indifference unmasks and irritates my subjection; so that one might say that wherever there is waiting there is transference: I depend on a presence which is shared and requires time to be bestowed—as if it were a question of lowering my desire, lessening my need. To make some wait: the constant prerogative of all power, "age-old pastime of humanity."

"You Should Have Told Her to Stay"

The negotiation of power that I've discussed throughout can best be underscored by relating an event that happened at the public hospital, which ended with one of the doctors saying about a woman whom I had interviewed, "You should have told her to stay. . . . We do her a favor by seeing her." As will become evident, the very idea that my partial positioning as hospital insider gave me the potential power to make someone "stay" caused considerable self-reflection as I, in the role of feminist anthropologist, critically engaged with relations of power in the field.

Fieldnotes, April 20, 1995
Today I probably should have stayed in bed. I've been feeling emotionally down, and I woke up with a splitting headache. By the time I got to the hospital, Margarita (the secretary) told me that the one first-time patient of the day had already been seen. I was talking to Dr. Velásquez and asked him if he was done seeing patients because I wanted to interview him if he wouldn't mind. He said, "OK, but not now, on Monday, but you will have to invite me out to lunch." Smiling broadly, he added, "And you have to give me a kiss, you can't forget the kiss." I said I would invite him to lunch, and I ignored the comment about the kiss. I had no patience for his harassment today.

A few minutes later Margarita handed me a chart and told me it belonged to a first-time patient. I introduced myself as usual and asked her (her name is Carmen) if I could interview her while she waited to be called in to see the doctor. She agreed and when the first part of the interview was nearly complete, she was called into see the doctor, so we stopped, and I figured I would finish the last few questions after her examination, as I've done before on similar occasions.

After she was examined, I escorted her to the side room where I conduct my interviews. She asked if it would take long because she had to get back to work. With this question I could tell that she was rushed and likely in no mood to continue with the interview. Her eyes roamed the room and she clasped her hands and twiddled her fingers nervously. I reminded her that she didn't have to stay if she didn't want to and that I understood that she needed to get back to work. However, as she got up to leave, my eyes began to tear up. All I could think of was that I had a splitting headache, I missed my husband, and that I really wanted to complete "the interview." As soon as this thought came to my mind, I realized that my objectification of her as "the interview" was no better and probably worse than that which I had been witnessing in the hospital all along. After all, I did not want to be a hindrance to the women whom I interviewed; my goal was to be able to hear their stories, and make them known. I understood the economic hardship that she faced with her minimum wage salary of 15,000 bs. [US$88] a month, and her desperate need to get back to work. At the same time, I was feeling depressed and guilty for feeling this way and wondering—what kind of a failure of an anthropologist am I? Here was Carmen, who must have been worried and scared about having to come to the hospital (not to mention the fact that she was probably thinking about the added economic strain caused by having to miss work), and all I could think about was my own emotional turmoil.

Carmen looked at me as my eyes watered and asked me what was wrong. Then her eyes began to well up with tears as well. I told her nothing was wrong and she said, "But you weren't like this before. Did the doctor tell you something that I didn't understand? Do I have something serious and he didn't want to tell me?" The situation was getting worse. I was now causing her distress as she attributed my emotion to her medical condition, which selfishly had nothing to do with her illness at all. I told her that it was nothing like that. I explained that I was feeling homesick, that I missed my husband, and that I was feeling physically ill. (I also think that almost a half a year of being in the oncology hospital setting has begun to wear on me emotionally as well.) Carmen seemed relieved that my state of being had nothing to do with her medical condition. I apologized for my emotional outburst and for making her more anxious as well, and she said it wasn't a problem and that she understood why I was out of sorts. I told her that finishing the interview was not important and so she left I returned to the back office where Dr. Velásquez and Dr. Cortez were chatting. Dr. Velásquez looked up and asked me why I wasn't interviewing Carmen, whom he had examined only shortly before. I replied that she needed to return to work. Dr. Velásquez shook his head disagreeingly and Dr. Cortez said, "You should have told her to stay and finish the interview. We do her a favor by seeing her."

There are many different levels at which this interaction needs to be analyzed. There is of course Carmen, whose anxieties about her health and economic situation are drawn out by, on another level, my own anxieties, physical state, and objectifying treatment of her as an interview. Then, there are the doctors who, based on Carmen's working-class status, interpret their relationship with her (and the other patients who seek treatment there) as one in which a favor is performed, and by implication, something is owed in return (as is extrapolated from the statement: "We do her a favor by seeing her"). This situation places the doctor and patient in a relationship of creditor and debtor, whereby the latter can never extricate herself from that position. The doctors implicitly included me as an insider in the "we" of their statement, and subtly reprimanded me for not exercising the power that they felt I (or "we") should have had in my interaction with Carmen.

In reflecting on my own state of mind in particular on the day that I met Carmen, it is clear that aspects of my own personal history shaped the interaction, as I am sure it did every day in various ways and to different extents. My anxieties and physical state brought to the forefront the unequal power relation between us, and the real possibility of my exerting power over her should I have tried to convince her to stay when she really did not want to. Power is always present at some level between researcher and subject, but it is important to try and diminish this unequal relation. These emotionally laden moments are the ones that no one talks about in fieldwork. However, as I mentioned in the introduction of this book, power was also exerted over me as my notes for this day also make reference to the ongoing sexual harassment of a particular doctor that had become a part of my almost daily routine at the hospital, which is discussed in greater detail in the next section.

Sexual Harassment in the Field

While my attention here is to the regulatory experiences that women—a category that Haraway has pointed out is itself complex, elusive and lacking innocence (1995, 95–96)—shared as we navigated the hospital settings, it is impossible to fetter out our identities; all are interwoven and become salient in different contexts. Despite our differences, however, our gender marked us in such a way that as female doctors, secretaries, patients, nurses, and researcher, we were varyingly subject to social, professional, sexual, and reproductive disciplining based on our social location as women within the society.

In both hospitals, I was among a mostly all-male department of physicians, particularly at Razetti where all of the attending physicians in the gynecology department were male. In these environments I experienced sexual innuendoes directed at me by a few of the doctors. They also told sexually explicit jokes about women, and in some cases within earshot of patients. One physician in particular, an attending physician at Razetti, routinely made sexual advances toward me and each morning would greet me with a kiss on the forehead (he did not do this with any other person at the hospital). I dreaded seeing him in the mornings and would try to avoid him by stepping out for coffee or engaging in a conversation with another one of the doctors in the hopes that he would not approach me. He was often at the hospital, and I tried to ignore his comments rather than confront him because I feared that he might make it difficult for me to conduct my research.

In one of my early interactions with this doctor, he challenged my identity when I declined his offer to buy me a gift. A group of doctors (including him) and myself had gone out to lunch, and when a couple of the doctors said they had to leave, this doctor, who would later make sexual innuendoes toward me, asked me to stay and tell him about my project. I agreed. However, he did not ask much about my research, and instead began commenting on my physical appearance. He then said that he wanted to buy me a Christmas gift and wanted to know what I would like. When I politely thanked him and said that I did not want anything and that I could not accept a gift from him, he replied, "Now you are being a *gringa*." (As I had spoken about my background with the doctors and nurses in the department, they knew that my mother is Mexican, my father was Mexican American, and that I had grown up speaking both Spanish and English. I identified myself as a Chicana.) The comment was meant as a challenge to my identity in the hopes of getting me to prove my "Latin" heritage by leaving behind the so-called cold and unfriendly behavior of a "gringa," and engaging in the "proper" behavior for a Latin woman, which for him seemed to include accepting gifts from men that one hardly knows. By constructing my identity in that moment as a "gringa," he was also designating me as an outsider. He played upon my Chicana identity, my identity as a woman, and my role as an anthropologist, warning me that I was not fitting into Venezuelan society. The manipulation of my identity in this way was an attempt to control my behavior by getting me to respond positively to his advances.

To dissuade him without jeopardizing my own position within the hospital, I spoke often about my husband and let him know that I was happily married. However, his comments continued. Some comments included asking me, "How's your husband? Is he better than me?" and "If you think he is being faithful while you are away, you must be crazy." On one occasion when I was wearing sandals he told me, "I want to suck on your big beautiful toe." After that, I regulated my dress by no longer wearing sandals to the hospital because I did not want to subject myself to further remarks, even though many days it was very hot, and I probably would have been more comfortable wearing sandals. He monitored my dress in other ways as well. One day I wore a baggy linen shirt, and he said that it made me look like a *malandra,* a female thug. He suggested I wear dresses—more feminine garments. When my glasses broke and I started wearing contact lenses, he expressed his disapproval by telling me he liked the way I looked in glasses much better. As with most of his comments, I ignored him, but I felt extremely uncomfortable when he was around.

The almost-daily sexual innuendoes that I experienced were mainly from this doctor, but other male doctors on occasion participated in the telling of sexually explicit jokes as well. For the most part, however, this one doctor was the only one who had consistently made sexual comments toward me. I felt powerless in this situation, as I did not want to jeopardize my research by confronting him directly. Although, as pointed out earlier, it is often assumed that the anthropologist is always in a position of power in relationship to those we study. In the context of the almost-all male surgeons at both hospitals, I was not in a position of power as a woman in these environments. I felt I simply had to put up with the unwanted sexual advances of this doctor and the sexually demeaning jokes about women from many of the others. As I discuss below, female doctors were also subject to sexually demeaning comments and regulatory practices from their male counterparts.

Doctoras

In spite of their social positioning as professionals, women doctors may experience marginalization in relationship to the elite or core group of male doctors. Thus, distinctions may not solely be drawn between the doctors and their patients but may be drawn on the basis of gender between the doctors themselves. As Bourdieu (1984, 103) notes:

> The common image of the professions, which is no doubt one of the real determinants of "vocations," is less abstract and unreal than that presented by statisticians; it takes into account not only the nature of the job and the income, but those secondary characteristics which are often the basis of their social value (prestige or discredit) and which, though absent from the official job description, function as tacit requirements, such as age, sex, social or ethnic origin, overtly or implicitly guiding co-option choices, . . . so that members of the corps who lack these traits are excluded or marginalized (women doctors and lawyers tending to be restricted to a female clientele and black doctors and lawyers to black clients or research).

This marginalization of women doctors can especially be seen in the case of surgery, which has been historically exclusionary of and antagonistic toward women surgeons. As Cassell (1996, 42) notes, surgery is an "embodied occupation" (like those of "firefighting, waging war, and race car driving where") where "we find ritualized ordeals for initiates, active male bonding, and profound distrust and exclusion of female participation." This exclusion of female participation manifested itself in the comments of some male surgeons who expressed the belief that women make bad surgeons. This opinion was first brought up by Dr. Velásquez at the Razetti during a conversation we had about the increasing numbers of women doctors. When I asked him why he thought this, he didn't expand on his response, but only emphasized that that is "just the way things are." When I asked Dr. Cortez, "What do you think about what I've heard, that women make bad surgeons?" he replied, "That's true." Unlike Dr. Velásquez, he elaborated on his response by saying that "to be a surgeon requires much dedication and women always have other obligations with family and children and can't dedicate the necessary attention [to surgery]." He added that women also don't have the necessary ability with their hands. As he put it, "They don't have dexterity."[6] His reasoning as to why women make bad surgeons is framed in terms of both biological and social phenomenon—not only are women physically handicapped for this profession; their familial responsibilities impede their ability to fully dedicate themselves to surgery.

I would bring up this belief that women make bad surgeons in the casual conversations and interviews I had with doctors to gauge the extent to which this was a commonly circulated view among Venezuelan surgeons. While most doctors had admitted to hearing this, the younger interns and residents mostly agreed that it was a product of the old vanguard of "*machista* surgeons." And one male intern at Razetti suggested that this negative attitude toward women surgeons actually works to their advantage. He said that he has seen the rough treatment that the women get by the senior male surgeons; they are worked harder and asked tougher questions compared to their male counterparts, but because of this, he believes that they are ultimately better trained. I asked Dr. Méndez, a female obstetrician and gynecologist and surgical intern who did rotations at both Razetti and Machado about whether she had heard that women make bad surgeons. She recounted her experience with one of her male professors, who would regularly discourage her from going into surgery because, as he told her, "Women just don't belong in surgery."

Bourdieu's concept of habitus is useful for understanding this perception about female surgeons. As Cassell (1996, 43) has pointed out, it permits one to move beyond the abstraction and disembodiment of sexism to an understanding of gender and power relations that is a "visceral rejection of the wrong body in the wrong place." Habitus illuminates the differences that exist between members of various social groups and classes as well as gender differences between those belonging to the same group. Thus, habitus functions, in this case, to make marked distinctions between male and female bodies and between members of different social classes. In other words, the ontology of the body is itself a "bodily technique" that gives way to distinction, division, and domination, in terms of gender and class. Articulated in this way, her analysis of the subordinate position of women in the practice of surgery is that of a social process that is thoroughly embodied. Similarly, we can understand the negative view of women surgeons in Venezuela in this embodied form.

5 Women's Agency and Resilience

"The Way I Want to Be Treated"

THE WOMEN I INTERVIEWED, and who were described by some doctors and public health workers as fatalistic and apathetic about their own health, were largely the economically marginalized women living in the barrios. These are the same women, as I pointed out in Chapter 3, who have a long history of community engagement and activism that goes back decades before the popular sector mobilization that helped elect Hugo Chávez in 1998 (Fernandes 2007). Women's political activism has also been at the heart of the Bolivarian Revolution (Fernandes 2007, 2010; and Motta 2013). A number of factors have contributed to the centrality of women's political subjectivities in the movement, which has also challenged patriarchal scripts of political participation and social transformation (Motta 2013). Namely, we can point to neoliberal policies leading to economic restructuring, the reduced power of organized labor, and both an increase in women's labor force participation and the feminization of poverty as important influences in women's popular activism (Motta 2013).

So as I am speaking of the women I interviewed, I am also speaking about women who have been central to political struggles not only in Venezuela but throughout Latin America. But when we look at much of the public health literature in Latin America (and in the United States about women of Latin American ancestry), we often find the word *fatalistic* attached to descriptions of medical encounters and advice. Women are regarded as not doing what is "logical" in terms of their health care and instead leaving things "up to

God" (Chavez et al. 1995). How could these women with vibrant histories of political mobilization be reduced to caricatures of the all-too-pervasive "Latina fatalist" who lacks agency (see Espinosa de los Monteros and Gallo 2010)? We need not ahistorically decontextualize and romanticize social movements and individual actors; nor should we see agency as necessarily connected to actionable outcomes of well-being. People can be agentive without necessarily seeing immediate outcomes of well-being or even social and political transformation. In the case of the latter, sometimes those actions need historical hindsight, and even with the passage of time they may never rise to the level of expectation that was intended. Even in the case of individuals in a medical encounter, acts of agency and resistance need not be evaluated based on an outcome of well-being. I use the term *well-being* following the work of philosopher Amartya Sen (1985). A little over three decades ago, Sen articulated a definition of agency as follows:

> What a person is free to do and achieve in pursuit of whatever goals or values he or she regards as important. Agency invokes an ability to overcome barriers, to question or confront situations of oppression and deprivation, and, as individuals or together with others, to have influence and be heard in society. Agency has intrinsic value; it is important in its own right regardless of whether its exercise leads to increased well-being. (Sen, as cited in Hanmer and Klugman 2016, 238)

Thus, agency can lead to empowerment, but questions of well-being need not be tied to agency itself. In fact, Sen argues that "some types of agency roles e.g., those related to fulfilling obligations, can quite possibly have a negative impact on the person's well-being. Even when the impact is positive, the importance of the *agency aspect* has to be distinguished from the importance of *the impact of agency on well-being*" (Sen 1985, 187). Agency can, of course, lead to empowerment, as discussed by Naila Kabeer (2008): "women's agency leads to empowerment when it exercises questions, challenges, or changes regressive norms and institutions that perpetuate the subordination of women" (as cited in Hanmer and Klugman 2016, 238). In some ways it may even be more conceivable to bring about agentic well-being collectively, as in the case of political movements, than it can be to bring about well-being (e.g., leaving the clinic feeling informed) in microencounters, even as one engages personal agency through subtle acts of questioning and seeing. This is what I explore below in drawing upon my interviews with women after they were seen by a doctor(s). Women didn't necessarily leave the medical encounter feeling that they had acted in a way that empowered them in regard to their health and well-being, but they were agentive actors in ways that would be missed if we solely understand agency as engaging in overt actions.

Questions, Concerns, and Other Ways of Knowing

Despite the fact that the women are disciplined to be "good" patients, which includes having learned to read doctors' faces (e.g., is the doctor approachable, friendly, or hurried), not to ask too many questions, not to share personal problems, to be still when being examined, and so on, does not mean that they do not in fact have many questions and concerns that are left unexpressed during the medical encounter. Many women asserted these concerns when I asked them, after they had been examined by the doctor(s), whether they had any questions that they would have liked to ask the doctor but felt they couldn't for some reason or other. Taking both hospitals together, the majority of women (69 percent) said that they did have questions they would have liked to ask the doctor but felt that they couldn't (see table 5.1). Results for each hospital taken separately are also given below (see tables 5.2 and 5.3). As one can see, the percentage of patients who responded affirmatively to this question at Razetti and Padre Machado were each quite high, at 69 percent and 70 percent, respectively.

Interestingly, this pattern holds true for both hospitals despite the fact that, as was stated earlier, doctors at Padre Machado spent more time with patients explaining procedures, treatments, and medical conditions. Thus, it appears that despite the increase in time that doctors spent with patients, patients still left with questions regarding their medical conditions and treatments. There are a number of possible explanations for this incongruous

TABLE 5.1 Both Hospitals Combined, Responses to Question: Was There Something You Wanted to Ask the Doctor but Felt You Couldn't?

Response	Frequency N=45	Percentage 100%
Yes	31	69
No	12	27
Missing	2	4

TABLE 5.2 Razetti, Responses to Question: Was There Something You Wanted to Ask the Doctor but Felt You Couldn't?

Response	Frequency N=25	Percentage 100%
Yes	17	69
No	6	24
Missing	2	8

TABLE 5.3 Padre Machado, Responses to Question: Was There Something You Wanted to Ask the Doctor but Felt You Couldn't?

Response	Frequency N=20	Percentage 100%
Yes	14	70
No	6	30
Missing	0	0

finding: (1) patients have a difficult time absorbing this information at a time that is filled with much anxiety; (2) explanations that are given by doctors are inaccessible to the patient (i.e., medical terminology is used that the patient does not understand); and (3) although doctors spend more time explaining at Padre Machado, the information is still not thoroughly explained.

Given my observations, some combination of these three explanations is likely. For example, doctors at both hospitals often used the term *malignancy* as opposed to cancer because, according to them, there is a negative connotation associated with the latter, such that patients may see it as a death sentence and react with depression and hopelessness and not seek further treatment. However, it was not at all clear that patients understood the meaning of the term *malignancy*. So, in their desire to decrease anxiety, doctors likely ended up providing incomprehensible information and in the process did nothing to decrease anxiety and probably increased it. Also, as will be discussed in the next section, the medical encounter at an oncology hospital of all places creates much anxiety and makes it understandably difficult for patients to concentrate on what is being said to them. Finally, even though doctors at Padre Machado spent, on average, twice as much time with patients than the

Razetti doctors did after the examination, all of the patients concerns may still have not been addressed. Moreover, as will be discussed later, unless doctors directly asked patients whether they had any questions (which only happened on a few occasions at Padre Machado and was not observed at Razetti), patients were not likely to ask questions of the doctors. The result was that patients at both hospitals left the medical encounter still having questions that they would have liked to have asked of the physicians.

When patients at both hospitals were asked what questions they would have liked to ask, responses were varied, but most had to do with wanting to know about their condition: Is it serious? Curable? How might it affect their lives? Other questions centered on wanting to know about the treatment procedures that they were scheduled to have. Sadly, it was not uncommon for women to be told that they were going to have a particular procedure performed without having the procedure clearly explained to them. Because women were often given very little information, some developed techniques for gathering whatever information they could by listening in, reading body language, and paying close attention to the instruments being used to examine them. Most women expressed that they wanted information about their conditions, and some suggested ways that they felt the doctor should treat them. The following vignettes illustrate these points—unless otherwise stated, all are in response to the question "Was there something you wanted to ask the doctor but felt you couldn't?"

What Is Wrong with Me?

Because both hospitals are referral hospitals, most of the women whom I spoke with were already at a stage in which they had been previously examined, gotten a Pap exam, and obtained abnormal results before arriving at the hospital. However, many women were still unclear as to what was wrong with them and seemed to have been given little information along the way. Even after seeing the doctor(s) at the hospitals, women were left with questions that they hadn't asked. Many of those simply had to do with what was wrong with them. Take, for example, the concerns of Claudia, a forty-eight-year-old patient at Razetti:

> CLAUDIA: Yes, of course, I wanted to ask what it means that I feel so bad. I wanted him to explain why I feel so bad, but I didn't ask.
>
> R.M.: Why not?

> CLAUDIA: Well, maybe because I just became shy with embarrassment. I was also going to ask him about the [sexual] relation too, but I was embarrassed. I think I should have asked, but I just didn't.
>
> R.M.: What about the [sexual] relation did you want to ask?
>
> CLAUDIA: That I feel bad when I have relations, but I was embarrassed. That is why I told you that it is better to have a woman [doctor] than a man [doctor].
>
> R.M.: Would you have told a woman doctor?
>
> CLAUDIA: Yes. Well, I guess a man [doctor] too, but I was just embarrassed to ask him at that moment.

In addition to wanting to know what was wrong with her, Claudia also had a question concerning sexual relations causing her discomfort, which seemed rather important to her well-being. For Claudia, her reason for not asking questions of the doctor—embarrassment—had to do with the fact that the physician was male and not female. Earlier in the interview she stated that she would feel more comfortable being examined by a female than a male.

Lucia, a twenty-seven-year-old woman, was concerned about how she contracted cervical cancer:

> LUCIA: Yes. How did I get this? How was it transmitted to me?
>
> R.M.: How come you felt you couldn't ask this question?
>
> LUCIA: The consultation is just so quick. Everything is so quick.

Several women brought up the concern that the consultation went by too quickly.

Forty-one-year-old Ana, a patient at Padre Machado, echoed the same sentiments about disease transmittal and rushed consultations:

> ANA: Yes. I wanted to ask about why in 1994 I had a cytology exam and nothing was wrong and now in December [of 1994] I came out with a positive biopsy and cytology exam. I wanted to know why? Why? How did I get it? How was it transmitted? What virus is it? I don't know.
>
> R.M.: Why did you feel like you couldn't ask about these things?
>
> ANA: Many times because—how do you say?—you don't because the consultation is so fast, everything is like so fast.

Nineteen-year-old Anita also lamented that the doctor examining her appeared rushed, and this was also the main reason she didn't ask questions either:

ANITA: Yes. I wanted to ask why it is that why my period is so heavy. Why does it come down so heavy? And also about some pains that I have in my waist.

R.M.: Why did you feel like you couldn't ask?

ANITA: Because I felt shy to ask these questions to the doctor. Everything was just so fast. I saw him really rushed I guess you just have to ask right at that moment.

Forty-six-year-old Beatriz, a patient at the Razetti remarked similarly about her doctor:

BEATRIZ: I would have liked to ask where this uterine lesion came from.

R.M.: Why do you feel like you couldn't ask?

BEATRIZ: I saw that he was very rushed.

Consider also forty-two-year-old Tivisay's response:

TIVISAY: OK, well, I don't know why I didn't ask about what that was, what I was asking you about. He said that depending upon what comes out on this second biopsy they are going to have to do a *cono*. That is why I asked you. I was going to ask him but I didn't. [A *cono* is short for "conization" or "cone biopsy" and is a type of cervical biopsy that removes abnormal tissue in a cone-shaped wedge far up into the cervical canal. An advantage of a cone biopsy is that it may remove the abnormal cervical tissue without further treatment necessary.]

R.M.: How come you felt you couldn't ask him?

TIVISAY: I don't know. He seemed very rushed, or maybe I was the one who was rushed. I don't know.

Tivisay considered the idea that perhaps she did not take the time to ask questions of the doctor and that he was in a hurry as well. The combination of these factors made it likely that information would not be communicated between patient and doctor.

For Delia, age thirty-six, the reluctance to question her doctor, who appeared rushed, was compounded by her own fatigue:

DELIA: Oh yes, I at least wanted to ask why that liquid that he applied to me produced such a stinging sensation. But no, I didn't ask because I saw that he was very rushed and well, maybe I am a little tired too.

In the end, both reasons, but probably the former to a greater degree, contributed to her feeling like she couldn't ask the doctor about the liquid that had been applied to her.

Similarly, twenty-year-old Olga's experience of being rushed and her disinclination to ask questions of her doctor was complicated by her nervousness and pain:

> OLGA: Yes. I wanted to ask about the NI . . . [referring to the diagnostic label of NIC] If it was necessary to do the NIC or not.
>
> R.M.: The NIC?
>
> OLGA: Yes
>
> R.M.: And why did you feel like you couldn't ask?
>
> OLGA: Well, because he was all rushed.
>
> R.M.: He was rushed?
>
> OLGA: Well, yes I saw him that way, and also I am a nervous person.
>
> R.M.: What do you mean?
>
> OLGA: Because of the nerves I forgot to ask him too and also because of the pain that I had and all of that.

Thirty-four-year-old Teresa also commented about feeling rushed in the medical encounter, but she articulated this experience as a product of the public health system, distinguishing it from private medical care.

> TERESA: I'll tell you something. My doctor in Altagracia is what they call a gentleman. Everything he does is with affection [*cariño*], and I will tell you that is the difference between a private consultation and this type of consultation. You have to understand that.
>
> R.M.: How did you feel here?
>
> TERESA: Rushed, very rushed. The doctor, as a doctor, I thought was an excellent person, a nice doctor and who I imagine is very knowledgeable, but rushed, yes. You see, I understand that I am in a hospital where the whole world has to pass through the same room, and that the doctor can't spend three hours with each patient.

For Teresa, feeling rushed was a part of the expectation she had for the public hospital. She wanted to get across to me that this is simply the way things are. I suggest that this expectation about the kind of attention that one will receive at a public institution also figures into the way one behaves, including not taking up the doctor's time with questions.

In addition to refraining from question asking because of feeling rushed or sensing that their doctor was rushed, some patients, like twenty-year-old Perla, felt that in asking questions, they would be interrupting the doctor:

> PERLA: Well, I wanted him to explain to me what it is that I have.
>
> R.M.: Why do you feel like you couldn't ask him?
>
> PERLA: Because he was busy doing the exam. He was busy examining me. Maybe next time when I get the results back he will tell me.

Perla recognized that the doctor's focus was on the examination of her body, and although she wanted to ask him a question, she decided to hold out until her results were back in hopes that he would then give her information about what it is she has.

For thirty-three-year-old Elsa, the anxiety of finding out "something [is] wrong" led her to forget about asking for a clear explanation as to the meaning of her diagnosis:

> ELSA: I wanted him to explain to me what exactly is NIC I and II, and how grave what I have is.
>
> R.M.: And how come you felt you couldn't ask him?
>
> ELSA: I just forgot. I was so disillusioned to find out that I have something wrong that I just forgot to ask him.

Most of these women wanted to have a basic understanding of what it is that they have. Some women may not have been told anything or some, like Elsa, may have been given terms (*NIC I* and *NIC II*) that were not explained clearly. Various reasons, including embarrassment, feeling rushed, and anxiety, contributed to why the women felt that they could not ask questions of their doctors.

For other women, some questions that didn't get asked were directly related to invasive procedures that they were to have done but knew little about. For example, Lourdes, a thirty-nine-year-old patient at Razetti, was told that she needed to have an operation. She, however, left the medical encounter with no knowledge as to why the surgery was going to be performed. Even though she was evaluated by the hospital's social services department, the overworked staff concluded in her profile: "The patient demonstrates herself to be tranquil and conscious of her diagnosis." The poor hospital conditions provide the environment in which the staff cannot thoroughly evaluate each patient. As is evident in Lourdes's narrative, she was not "conscious of her diagnosis":

> LOURDES: I wanted to ask what it is that I have, and why are they going to hospitalize me? What are they going to operate on me for?
>
> R.M.: Why didn't you ask?
>
> LOURDES: Because I just forgot, or maybe because I am a bit frightened as well. I got scared because I didn't think that I had anything really wrong with me. Because I've never gotten a bad result [on a cytology test or Pap], I thought the result would be fine, and that I wouldn't have to have another cytology exam. I just don't understand the result.

Earlier in our discussion, however, Lourdes had mentioned the possibility of having cancer, and when I asked who had told her that, she said the doctor whom she had seen at the university hospital (Universidad Central de Venezuela). As we talked, however, the story changed, and Lourdes said that she herself had come to this conclusion because of something she saw on her results and because she was sent here to the oncology hospital. She said the doctor hadn't actually told her she had cancer. The doctor simply told her that "something" that had come out in the cytology exam done in her hometown also had come up in the biopsy that they had taken. Lourdes said, however, that the "something" was never explained. It wasn't until she was referred to this hospital (Razetti) and went to admissions to be examined that she was told she had "NIC III." I asked Lourdes what this meant, and she replied, *"I really don't know."*

As demonstrated by her response, Lourdes was not clear about her diagnosis, about why she needed an operation, and this news was clearly a shock to her, as she had expected that there would be nothing wrong with her, even though she herself had contemplated the possibility of cancer. Because I could not imagine her leaving with such little information about such a major procedure, I told her that I would accompany her to ask the doctor these questions if she felt up to it (as I did with many of the women whom I interviewed). She agreed, and I told the doctor who had examined her that Lourdes had some questions and concerns that she needed to ask him. I left her with him, and after she met with him, I was able to ask her if she found out more information. She said that she understood more now, but she understandably was still nervous about the operation.

Catalina, a thirty-four-year-old patient at Padre Machado, had an uncommon experience in that she was told that they were going to perform a Pap exam, a biopsy, and a *cono* (cone biopsy) on her before being examined. The doctor explained what the cone biopsy was and said that depending upon the results of the procedure, a hysterectomy might have to be performed. After his explanation, he asked Catalina, "Are you conscious of this?" She responded, "Yes." Despite the doctor's explanation and her affirmative response, however, Catalina still came away wondering what a *cono* was:

CATALINA: Yes, but I didn't ask because of my nerves.

R.M.: What questions were those?

CATALINA: I wanted to know what a cone is.

R.M.: Why did you feel like you couldn't ask him?

CATALINA: In the moment that you are about to speak you just keep quiet. You get nervous and you just keep quiet.

Catalina's question regarding the cone biopsy procedure suggests that, even though she told the doctor that she had understood what he told her, she did not fully grasp his explanation. This could be due to a combination of factors, including those suggested by some of the patients themselves: technical terminology, nervousness, and anxiety. Catalina may have felt compelled to respond that she understood what he had explained, knowing that she was expected to respond that way. Additionally, patients are not given enough time to think about the questions that they might have. As pointed out earlier, for many patients the consultation seems to go by very fast, and they have little time to digest information. So, even when information is shared, the patient might still come away with little knowledge about her medical condition. It would be quite traumatic to be told that one has cancer and needs to have surgery.

For Mercedes, a forty-three-year-old patient at the Razetti, the lack of information shared with her led her to wonder why she was even referred to the gynecology department in the first place:

MERCEDES: No, no I didn't want to ask him any questions.

R.M.: Did you have a question in mind but felt you couldn't ask it or did you not have any questions at all?

MERCEDES: Well, because what I wanted to tell him was that I came here for a consultation for my ear not for a Pap exam, and I asked him that question. That was the only thing I wanted to ask.

R.M.: So, the question was why did they send you over here to gynecology?

MERCEDES: Yes.

R.M.: And how did he respond to your question?

MERCEDES: I don't know. I didn't hear. I think he told her. [Mercedes pointed toward the waiting area, where her aunt was sitting.]

Mercedes had been referred to the hospital because of a problem with her ear, which was secreting a foul-smelling liquid. However, when I asked her why she was being seen in the gynecology department she replied that she didn't know. As I spoke with her, she related to me that on her first visit to the hospital her aunt had come with her to admissions, and when her aunt went to get the next appointment, she was told that she (Mercedes) needed to be seen in the gynecology department. She added that she believed that type of thorough exam was a matter of preoperative routine because of the problem in her ear. However, she was never directly told why she had been sent to the gynecology department.

Reading Bodies

Some of the women who remarked that they felt unable to ask questions—because they felt rushed, anxious, or nervous—looked for clues as to the gravity of their condition in the facial gestures and mannerisms of their doctor(s). These women were not unaware of their surroundings, and in fact, even as "docile bodies," they actively searched for small hints in the form of body language as to the status of their health. In contrast, two of the women that I interviewed read the body language of their doctors and felt intimidated to ask questions of them because they "read" their doctors as unfriendly.

I begin with those women who read their doctors as being unfriendly. For example, thirty-three-year-old Hortencia, a patient at Padre Machado, said that although she did have questions she would have liked to ask the doctor, she felt intimidated by him and was therefore reluctant to approach him:

HORTENCIA: Yes. I wanted him to tell me concretely what it is that I have, and if I have the possibility of overcoming it.

R.M.: And why did you feel like you couldn't ask him?

HORTENCIA: I felt shy and inhibited. I saw his face and I felt afraid that he wouldn't answer me. He had the face of someone who is not so friendly. During the examination he reprimanded me because I kept scooting up when he was examining me, but I think it was because of the pain why I was behaving so badly. The doctor also looked pretty concentrated on the papers that were in front of him, and I didn't want to ask him so as not to disturb his concentration.

Similarly, thirty-two-year-old Carina said this of her experience:

CARINA: I really didn't have any questions because he still doesn't have any results in yet. I imagine that after he has all the results in and after he has done all the exams on me, he'll see what the solution should be.

R.M.: But so far you don't have any questions?

CARINA: No. Not so far, but what I did want to ask him was why he was sending me to gastro [referring to gastroenterology]. But because I didn't see that he was going to talk to me, I didn't ask. He told me to go and get an appointment, that they were going to see me in gastro, but I don't know why. I don't know what motivates this.

R.M.: Why didn't you ask him?

CARINA: I saw that he was occupied with the other woman, the other patient, I didn't ask. I had asked him where I should go to make the appointment for gastro and he said, "the central appointment desk," and I felt that he said it in a mean tone.

At first she said she did not ask a question because the doctor didn't speak to her first or didn't direct his attention to her ("no vi que me hablara"). The interaction seems to be more conducive to the patient if the doctor speaks first and asks the patient if she has questions rather than leaving that up to the patient herself. In fact, other patients had the expectation of the doctor speaking first and asking them, "do you have any questions?" In Carina's case, when she did ask a question (where should she make her next appointment), she felt that the doctor answered her in a "mean tone" and was bothered by her inquiry. As a result, she did not want to ask him anything else even though in the end she did not understand why she was being sent to gastroenterology.

Carla, age forty-three, also suggested, like Carina, that in the patient-doctor interaction, it is the responsibility of the latter to ask the patient if she has any questions:

CARLA: Of course. I wanted to ask about the closed cervix. What does that mean?

R.M.: Why did you feel like you couldn't ask?

CARLA: He didn't give me the opportunity. He didn't ask me anything.

For Carla, the fact that the doctor didn't ask her "anything" meant that she didn't have the opportunity to respond with her inquiries. It is not the case that Carla—and patients like her—were disinterested or apathetic about their health care. They were attentively observing, processing, and interpreting their environments and responding accordingly.

Other women, bypassing the verbal interaction altogether, searched for signs of bad or good news on the expressions of their doctors. Take, for example, the conclusion María, a seventy-year-old patient at Padre Machado, drew from the lack of preoccupation on the face of her doctor:

MARÍA: Yes. I wanted to ask him how I looked—if there was any danger.

R.M.: Why did you feel like you couldn't ask him?

MARÍA: Well, I saw that he examined me, and I didn't see that he had an expression like there was anything wrong.

Patricia, age thirty, used both visual and verbal clues to gather information about the gravity of her condition. She tried to gain knowledge by listening to the conversations that the doctors had among themselves, by reading their body language, by asking some questions, and generally by being aware of her surroundings:

R.M.: What did the doctors here tell you about your condition?

PATRICIA: They said so many things that I really don't know what they said.

R.M.: Did they tell you directly?

PATRICIA: They were speaking among themselves.

R.M.: Do you know the name of what you have?

PATRICIA: No.

R.M.: What did they explain to you?

PATRICIA: They gave me a lot of hope.

R.M.: Why? What did they say?

PATRICIA: Because I didn't see them alarmed. I saw that they were calm. They were reassuring. They didn't see me as being really sick because they gave me my next appointment for far in the future. They would look at me and say that I was strong.

R.M.: What did they say verbally to you?

PATRICIA: I saw that they were tranquil and that made me tranquil. They said that what I have isn't serious. It is something that could be serious, but it has a solution.

R.M.: Was there something that the doctor told you that you didn't understand?

PATRICIA: Well, because they speak in code or they call things by other names—well, it's difficult to comprehend. But I asked them if it was something serious, and they told me that I should remain tranquil, that it wasn't very serious. I feel tranquil because they don't have to do anything out of this world [for treatment]. It's normal, but because one doesn't know one thinks that it is something bad I thought they were going to give me some sort of treatment without putting me to sleep or anything, that they were going to go ahead and start my treatment, that would have been horrible. I was looking at the apparatuses to see if I noticed any strange looking apparatus; I do that when I go to other medical appointments too.

R.M.: You pay attention to the apparatuses?

PATRICIA: Yes. I pay attention to the biopsy pincers. My other doctor has those, but they are bigger. There weren't any large machines though, like for X-rays.

Patricia paid close attention to her surroundings in order to try to figure out for herself the status of her condition and the medical procedures that were going to be performed on her. She studied the medical instruments to see if there was something she didn't recognize, indicating whether an unfamiliar procedure or treatment was going to be done.

Like Patricia, Rocío, a forty-five-year-old patient at Razetti, tried to gather information by overhearing the doctors' conversations:

ROCÍO: Well, I would have liked to find out what it is that I have and to have had him explain it to me. But I imagine he wants to have all of the results in so that he can tell me, so that he can explain it to me.

R.M.: Why didn't you ask him?

ROCÍO: Because I think he can't say anything yet. He says he needs to have all of the results in. He said that the other cytology exam had come back normal. When you were writing some things down, I heard him say that the cytology exam was normal.

She overheard this information; he did not directly tell this to her, again relying on ways of knowing other than direct questioning. She, like many of the women, did not ask many questions of the doctors, not because she was disinterested, fatalistic, or apathetic, but because she (like other women) was disciplined to not ask questions in an environment that is often rushed and in which doctors are most often explaining diagnosis, procedures, and treatments to other doctors, not to patients. Still, they creatively searched for ways to find out information.

The Way I Want to Be Treated: *Háblame en cristiano*

In addition to eliciting responses that reflect concerns over diagnosis and treatment, my inquiry as to whether the women had questions that they would have liked to ask their doctor but felt they couldn't also led some to volunteer suggestions as to how they would like their doctors to treat them. Some of these suggestions included having the doctor(s) explain the procedures that would be performed on them and having them explain their medical conditions.

Consider, for example, the questions, concerns, and suggestions of Elena, a thirty-six-year-old patient at Razetti:

> ELENA: Yes. Yes there were questions I wanted to ask. I didn't ask because I thought I would interrupt.
>
> R.M.: And what did you want to ask?
>
> ELENA: I wanted to know how I was. He was looking at my internal part and I, being the "great inquisitor" want him to tell me what can be done, how it can be cured.
>
> R.M.: When did you want to ask these questions? During the examination or in the office?
>
> ELENA: In both places. As he was doing the exam, he told the other doctor, "She has some little white spots" and "How would you take this sample?" Well, what does that mean? I don't know. You see I am the "great inquisitor."
>
> R.M.: You said earlier that you felt like you would be interrupting?
>
> ELENA: Yes.
>
> R.M.: What made you feel that way?
>
> ELENA: They are talking that way and it creates a certain doubt in you, but I didn't want to interrupt the teaching that the doctor was doing. He was ex-

plaining something to the other doctor. But he should explain more to me, not using terminology or technical language, but in plain language. Like they say, "Speak to me in Christian" [*háblame en cristiano*].

R.M.: What did you want them to explain?

ELENA: Like, we are going to do such and such. We are going to take a sample of this, like that. They are missing that more natural explanation. You see?

Elena mentioned that she did not want to ask questions so as not to interrupt the pedagogic conversation between the two doctors, although she emphasized that they were looking inside of her at her body. Likely having had previous experiences at public teaching hospitals and clinics, Elena recognized the interaction between the doctors as one between student and teacher—one in which she was excluded. This allusion to feeling alienated from the discussion of her own body was also evident in her assertion that she would like to be given explanations without the use of technical medical terms. In addition, she said she would like to be told which procedures would be performed ahead of time.

Some of these same sentiments were echoed by thirty-one-year-old Petra:

R.M.: How do you feel that the doctor treated you?

PETRA: Well, look, like any other patient. He arrived without explaining what I might feel at that moment.

R.M.: At what moment? During the examination?

PETRA: Well, of course. This is the first time that I find myself in this situation. So I would say that the doctor, before taking me to a cubicle, should say, "Look we are going to do this to you, we are going to do the other." Right? At no time did he say anything.

For Alicia, age forty, the inquiry as to whether she had any questions she would have liked to ask the doctor elicited her opinion on the appropriate question-asking interaction in the medical encounter:

ALICIA: Yes. Well, why were they doing that exam. What was he trying to observe—a lot of questions.

R.M.: Why do you feel like you couldn't ask him?

ALICIA: Because they just barely even see you and it's over. They don't ask you anything. They simply tell you when you should make your next appointment and that's it.

R.M.: So then it was because he didn't ask you anything first?

ALICIA: Yes. He should have been the one to ask me if I wanted to know anything or to tell me why he did that exam. I would have asked him a lot of questions, right? But since he didn't say anything to me, I didn't say anything to him either. Anyway, I'm just that way. If someone doesn't talk to me I remain quiet. But I want to know, he should have explained more to me.

Alicia felt that it was up to the doctor to first approach her and ask her whether she had any questions. According to Alicia, this would have given her the chance to ask the numerous questions she had. As we have seen in some of the narratives presented thus far, this point was made by other women as well. Thus, rather than this comment simply being due to Alicia's personality as she stated ("I'm just that way. If someone doesn't talk to me I remain quiet"), it also reflects the way in which patients, particularly those seeking care at public institutions, are taught to behave in the medical setting. As pointed out by Teresa earlier, women know that the doctor can't spend a lot of time with them, so there is the expectation that public health care will be rushed. This expectation, which is likely shared by many of the women whom I interviewed, places the power to ask questions in the hands of the doctor(s), not the patients, who are discouraged from speaking—because they feel rushed, the doctor(s) appears to be too busy, there are too many people around, and so on. Many times patients left the medical consultation feeling as if things were not explained to them well enough, which is how Alicia expressed her situation.

Lourdes, the thirty-nine-year-old patient at Razetti who was told she needed a *cono* but did not understand what that meant, raised the similar sentiment that procedures and treatments were not explained to her:

R.M.: And how do you feel like the doctor treated you?

LOURDES: Good, except that he didn't explain things to me well. They should explain what it is that I have, what they were going to do with me, so I can be more sure of what is going on. Because now I'm coming on Tuesday, and I don't know what it is that they are going to do.

R.M.: You don't know what they are going to do that day?

LOURDES: I am going to ask again. I'm not sure what they are going to do. I'm going to ask because that is bad, but it's just that so many patients came in and out.

R.M.: He didn't explain?

LOURDES: He didn't tell me. He practically didn't tell me anything, anything about what they were going to do with me.

Julia, twenty-five, also expressed some concern about her treatment. However, the issue was not with a lack of information about her medical condition but about not being alerted to the fact that three male doctors were going to examine her. She was embarrassed by the number of doctors who examined her, and by the fact that they were men:

R.M.: How do you feel like the doctor treated you?

JULIA: He treated me good. All three of them treated me good. [She said this with slight sarcasm and emphasized the word *three*.]

R.M.: Yes. How did you feel about having three of them there?

JULIA: It bothered me a bit. They really bothered my left side, where I have the inflammation.

R.M.: In what sense did it bother you having the three of them there?

JULIA: Well, the embarrassment. You are there, open, in front of three men. That's the way I felt. I think that the opinion of the sick person counts too. I know they are doing their exam, looking for something . . . but they should ask you, like, "Is this fine?"

R.M.: They should ask your opinion?

JULIA: Of course. That would be great. But no, they just all entered at once, and it was cold in there.

R.M.: Did you notice when the three of them entered?

JULIA: Yes.

R.M.: What were you thinking?

JULIA: That I wanted to die.

It was the number of doctors, and also their gender, that made this a particularly embarrassing situation for Julia, as she expressed that she was "open in front of three men." (Recall that for Doña Estela, discussed in Chapter 4, the many doctors who had entered to examine her was also a source of embarrassment to her.) Julia emphasized that they were "men," not doctors. Julia also asserted that the opinion of the sick person should count and would have preferred to have been asked if it was all right for the three of them to enter and examine her. This is how she would have wanted to be treated.

The subject of the physician's gender also came up in the conversation I had with thirty-year-old Patricia. She was not happy with the way she was treated by the doctor who had seen her in triage on her first appointment at Padre Machado, and she attributed her poor treatment to the doctor's gender:

R.M.: How do you think the doctor treated you?

PATRICIA: He treated me very well, even though he is a man. [She is speaking about the doctor that she just saw in the gynecology department.] When I came here for the first time, the doctor who treated me didn't inspire my confidence. [She is speaking about the doctor that she saw on her first appointment in triage.]

R.M.: Why? What happened?

PATRICIA: He treated me in a brusque manner, and I was in pain. He was, *tun-tun-tun* [makes a twisting motion with her hand]. Darn! [*¡Cónchale!*]. That part is delicate, injured, sick, and they treat one like that.

R.M.: Brusquely?

PATRICIA: Yes. I thought it would be that way.

R.M.: Why?

PATRICIA: I came out and I told my husband that the doctor was a man and that he had treated me badly. If the doctor would have been a woman, maybe she wouldn't have treated me so badly. When I saw that it was a man, I told myself, "He is going to treat me badly." And because there are always references made that they treat patients badly—I mean I haven't had that bad luck; they have treated me well—but there are always people who say that they have been treated badly. They are complainers; they say that the doctor is just ordinary, nothing special, that he is this or that.

R.M.: People that you know have had this experience?

PATRICIA: Yes. People who have said that it has gone badly for them at the hospital, that they have been treated badly, but I know that he treated me badly. Well, he must have just said to himself, "Just another patient" . . . because one is not paying like one should be, like in a private consultation. My female doctor back home is wonderful. I've been lucky. Patients have told me that when you pay, you are attended to better.

R.M.: So when you pay, you get better medical attention?

PATRICIA: Yes, for the love of money. I do think it is that way. My female doctor has treated me well. I can't say anything. She has even cried with me, because she has given me much support. She has given me a lot of confidence. I wouldn't change her for another doctor.

R.M.: Do you have to pay here?

PATRICIA: Well, the two times that I have come I have paid. Last time I paid 500 or 600 bolivares [US$2.95 or $3.53]. I can't exactly remember and now I paid 750 [$4.41], but the doctor treated me well. He treated me very well, even though it is a hospital. I thought they were going to treat me the same, and that had me nervous.

R.M.: The same? How?

PATRICIA: Like when I went to triage with that dry doctor. When I arrived he said, "And what's wrong with you?" Just like that. He said that I was already an adult person, that I was this, that I was that. I know I am an adult.

R.M.: The doctor in triage?

PATRICIA: Yes. He said, "What's wrong with you, my girl [*mi niña*], why are you here? I'm not going to do anything bad to you." But I came in very nervous and pressured because I didn't know what they were going to say to me.

R.M.: You say he spoke to you badly?

PATRICIA: Yes, he spoke to me badly. "What's wrong with you, my girl?" He should have asked it to me in another way, and I should have told him . . . I don't know, that I felt nervous. But he said to me, "What's wrong with you, my girl? Why are you that way? You are already an adult person."

R.M.: And how did you respond when he talked to you that way?

PATRICIA: I told him that I was afraid. I said, "Look, doctor, it's that I am afraid."

R.M.: And what did he say?

PATRICIA: I don't remember what he said, but don't tell the doctor because he will kill me.

R.M.: Oh no. Don't worry. As I said before, everything you tell me is confidential.

PATRICIA: If not, the doctor will kill me. The next time he sees me he will inject me with something.

R.M.: No. I keep everything confidential. Like I said, I don't even use your real name, and I assign you a number on the interview. You don't have to worry about that.

Patricia brought up a number of points about her hospital experience. She was wary of seeing a male doctor and had the expectation that male doctors would treat patients more brusquely than female doctors. She had heard stories to this effect from acquaintances and friends. This perception can also, at least partly, be traced to the fact that she has a very good relationship with her female doctor back home. A doctor who, as Patricia mentioned, had cried with her. I suspect that she attributes this emotional connection to her doctor with the fact that the doctor is female.

Her experience with the male doctor in the hospital's triage department, where first-time patients are given evaluative physical exams, served to confirm her concerns about the treatment she expected to receive from a male doctor. She felt that he treated her in a physically brusque manner during her physical examination and in a verbally demeaning manner. For example, the doctor's reminder to Patricia that she is an "adult person," served as an infantalizing reprimand for her nervous behavior. In addition, she did not think that his reference to her as *mi niña* was an appropriate form of address. Even after this interaction, Patricia remained worried about the actions of this doctor if he became aware of her critical comments about him. Only half-jokingly did she say that if he found out he would kill her by injecting something into her. I reassured her that all information would remain confidential. She reinforced the gender issue in relationship to treatment by stating that the doctor she had seen in the gynecology department had been good to her despite the fact that he was a man.

Interestingly, while the majority of women (62%) said that the gender of the doctor (that would examine them gynecologically) did not matter to them (see table 5.4), 36 percent said they would prefer to be examined by a female doctor and only 2 percent said they preferred a male doctor. Of those women who said they preferred a female doctor, the most often cited reasons were embarrassment and the belief that women can better understand women's bodies. In comparison, 41 percent of the doctors said they believe women prefer to be examined gynecologically by a male doctor. The general explanation for this response was that women tend to put more trust in male doctors than female doctors in a *machista* society. This, however, as we have seen, does not correspond to what the women said about who they want examining them. For most it doesn't matter, but only one woman said a male doctor was preferred.

One of the physicians who responded that female patients prefer female physicians explained that this is due to the patient's social status. He stated that lower-class women prefer female doctors because their lack of education

TABLE 5.4 Patient Responses to Questions: Would You Prefer to Be Examined Gynecologically by a Female or Male Doctor? and Doctor Responses to Question: Do You Think Women Prefer to Be Examined Gynecologically By a Female or Male Doctor?

Responses	Patients Frequency (N=45) %	Doctors Frequency (N=17) %
Prefer male doctor	1 2%	7 41%
Prefer female doctor	16 36%	5 29%
No preference	28 62%	5 29%

NOTE: The differences between patient and doctor responses are significant: $X^2(2) = 16.5$, $p < .05$. The chi-square value was partitioned and the interaction between prefer female doctor and prefer male doctor was also significant: $X^2(1) = 14.5$, $p < .05$. These statistical tests should be viewed as exploratory because the cell frequencies are quite low, calling into question the validity of the asymptotic assumptions in the chi-squared test.

makes them more likely to get embarrassed in front of a male doctor. Interestingly, social class once again seeps into explanations of patients' beliefs and behaviors; for him, gender difference is not as salient as class difference in his belief that female patients prefer female doctors. The assumption is that women from the upper classes would feel comfortable with male doctors because they are educated and by implication not backward, ignorant, and irrational like lower-class women.

Thus far, I have presented several issues that the women mentioned in terms of how they would like to be treated in the medical setting, including the desire for simple and nontechnical explanations, being able to approach and ask questions of the doctor, and their preference for the gender of the physician. However, despite the fact that many of the women had many unanswered questions after the examination, and some like Doña Estela and Rocío mentioned specific problems during their examinations, such as having many doctors in the exam room and being reprimanded by doctors, almost all of the women responded positively when asked how they felt the doctor(s) had treated them (see table 5.5). One hundred percent of the women at Padre Machado and 80 percent of the women at Razetti responded that the doctor(s) who had examined them had treated them either good or very good. None of the women stated that they were treated badly.

TABLE 5.5 Percentage of Responses to Question: How Do You Feel The Doctor Treated You?

Response	Padre Machado Response % (N=20)	Razetti Response % (N=25)
Good	75%	72%
Very good	25%	8%
Normal	0%	8%
Not badly	0%	4%
Professionally	0%	4%
Missing	0%	4%

Although this may appear to be a contradiction given the women's concerns, these views are not in fact contradictory. They were critical of certain aspects of the treatment that they received, but at the same time, they were thankful for the medical care, particularly given that they relied on the either low-cost or free services. The doctors also represented hope for them in a situation that for most creates uncertainty and is quite frightening. Despite issues of embarrassment, lack of privacy, and confusion over the meaning of a diagnosis or treatment procedure, ultimately the main desire remained getting medical treatment. This, however, does not mean that the concerns of the women should be ignored. Of course, the structural problems at both hospitals and the lack of resources available to doctors and hospital staff, coupled with the large number of patients who are seen, made it difficult to spend time explaining medical procedures and treatments to each individual patient. Even so, this needs to be an integral part of the examination and treatment process. For many of the women, having little explained to them and generally not knowing what was going on made them even more anxious and frustrated, leaving them to assume the worst.

In addition, some patients expressed that they appreciated the friendly and warm bedside manner of some of their doctors, and I imagine that those who felt rushed or mistreated would have enjoyed that same type of connection with their doctors. Recall, for example, the comment of Doña Estela in the previous chapter, who said she appreciated the touch of my hand on hers while she was being examined. Perhaps the feelings of Elena, age thirty-six, best exemplify the way in which women would like to be treated by their doctor(s):

    R.M.: How do you feel the doctor treated you?

    ELENA: Well, at one point he gave me a smile, when I went to touch his hand.

A smile is very important. When I grabbed his hand to get up, he gave me his hand in return. It is very important that they tell you, "Here I am, don't worry." It's those little details that make a big impression.

R.M.: That made you feel good?

ELENA: Yes, of course.

We must listen to women's narratives and to be able to understand, uncover, and be attuned to the ways in which marginalized women do act given the constraints that they face. In doing so, it is possible to highlight agency—to see, as I have pointed out, the ways in which women did seek to know in the face of a dearth of information being shared with them. To do otherwise would be to risk seeing working-class women as they have been constructed by public health officials and physicians in Venezuela—as *sin vocabulario* (without vocabulary), *conformistas* (conformists), uninterested in their health, and lacking the ability to receive and understand information. In one of the earlier works in medical anthropological discussions of agency in the doctor-patient interaction, Gregory Pappas (1990) took a critical look at two of the major theoretical perspectives on doctor-patient interactions at the time. Centering the work of Howard Waitzkin and Arthur Kleinman, Pappas argues that the former has tended to focus on structural explanations, subordinating the role of agency, while the latter draws on agency missing important integrations on structural or social causality. Using the work primarily of Anthony Giddens (1984), clarifying the structure-agency dichotomy in social science, Pappas centers power to disrupt this dichotomy and to understand the way it operates structurally and agentically in doctor-patient interactions. Although this is something we now take for granted in medical anthropology frameworks, it's important to revisit when reflecting on the patients' struggles to assert their health needs in microencounters within a macro-level public health system that wasn't meeting their needs. What happens in the patient-doctor interaction is not a reflection of structure or agency; it's a matter of both.

The women, in articulating the way they wanted to be treated in the medical setting, were making claims to citizenship: rights of dignity, respect, inclusion, and medical attention (in the sense of resources and in interpersonal interactions with doctors). They were claiming the right to be healthy citizens—to be visible and not marginalized. However, they were also appropriating the idea of being "sanitary citizens" so as to show that they were not "unsanitary subjects." And in this respect they were policing themselves by being disciplined bodies in their medical counters (e.g., not asking too many questions, being quiet), and yet they were also trying to regain agency by letting me know that they did have something to say about how they wanted to be treated and employing other ways of trying to figure out what was going on with their health.

What they did resist—in this context—was being only acted upon and not interacted with. Resistance was not overt and visible and didn't challenge the hegemonic construct of sanitary citizenship. In fact, their resistance took place within the construct of sanitary citizenship (Briggs and Mantini-Briggs 2004) itself. Resistance, as James Scott (1985) notes in *Weapons of the Weak*, can occur within micro-level interactions that may not directly challenge authority and may have little to do with disrupting dominant narratives. Moreover, Hollander and Einwohne (2004, n.p.) point out that "even while resisting power, individuals or groups may simultaneously support the structures of domination that necessitate resistance in the first place."

We should remember that, in this case, the women whom I interviewed were in a vulnerable space. They wanted or needed treatment and were glad and thankful for the medical attention that they received. They may have felt that confronting doctors directly from this space could jeopardize their health care. But this does not mean that their silence was due to a lack of interest. Even though in their conversations with me they expressed resistance to being uninformed, they didn't express those feelings to the doctors. Their critiques around doctors not providing them with adequate information did not necessarily translate into information obtainment in a direct and immediate sense (except in the cases of the women I would accompany back to see the doctor who had examined them). Their vulnerability in the medical encounter should not be understood as surrendering their agency. In the context of the micro-level examination, the power of overt action rests largely in the hands of medical professionals (Ehrenreich and England 1978; Lindenbaum and Lock 1993; Lupton 1995). So, what does it mean, then, that women patients enacted strategies for eliciting the information they needed? It means we must also view these covert strategies as agentic. Again, circling back to Amartya Sen (1985), "well-being" does not necessarily result from agency. What is important is that many women patients did strategize to receive answers to the questions that they formulated and voiced internally, if not externally. The work of Javier Auyero (2012, 115) in deconstructing the waiting that people must do in Argentina to access social services is helpful here. He points out:

> They don't publicly "voice" much of their discontent . . . because their sense of agency is infused by a perceived ineffectiveness. They simply don't think that protest can make much of a difference. We could then hypothesize, drawing upon the insights of social cognitive theory, that the very uncertain and arbitrary operation of the welfare office produces what, to borrow from Bandura, is an "outcome-based (perceived) futility." (Auyero 1982, 140)

We can understand the agency of the cervical cancer patients similarly. With the busyness of the doctors, the large numbers of patients to be seen, the need to make appointments at other clinics within the hospital before they closed, the duties of work, the obligations of childcare—what was the likelihood that they would get their questions answered in the context of these constraints? Their agency was also infused with a "perceived ineffectiveness." For a number of the women, "other ways of knowing" supplanted direct questioning.

Epilogue
From Neoliberalism to Chávez

MORE THAN A DECADE after first arriving in Venezuela, I returned to Caracas to survey the situation of cervical cancer under a social, economic, and political climate that had undergone much change. Gazing outside the airplane window, the dazzling lights surrounding the city that I described at the beginning of this book blinked brightly below as I had remembered; they were also still at the center of a geographical politics. The lights emanating from the poverty-stricken ranchos that cling to the hillsides, however, were now part of the political landscape that elected Hugo Chávez president in 1998. As I have noted throughout, the *ranchos* and the poor who reside in the *barrios* they form, had been characterized as a geography of shame, particularly during the neoliberal 1990s, when I conducted my first fieldwork. At that time, rather than being viewed as symptom of the economic crisis of the 1980s and 1990s, the ranchos dominating the hillsides in greater numbers were viewed as contributors to the economic crisis and a symbol of stalling modernization. As I looked down on those lights this time around, they took on a new meaning. The margin had moved in many respects to the center. Although the rise of Chávez as president has a long and much more complex history, he gained support from those who had been socially, politically, and economically marginalized in Venezuelan society.[1] This is the Venezuela I was returning to—one where the plight of the poor had gained voice through Chávez. I was returning to a very different Venezuela from the one I had left. By the time I returned to Venezuela in 2008, the country, under Chávez, had changed dramatically; his government rejected the neoliberalism of the previous governments and emphasized participatory democracy, a deepening of democratic participation in government.

Revisiting Home: Santa Eduvigis

Upon my return I learned that Henriqueta's concern about the apartment in her neighborhood being too costly for them to continue living there (mentioned in Chapter 1) was well founded. They no longer lived in the solidly middle-class neighborhood of Santa Eduvigis that I, too, had called home. They had moved to the outskirts of Caracas, where they found a cheaper apartment, but I didn't learn this until I made my way up Primera Avenida, which runs through the neighborhood of Altamira and to my old building in the adjoining neighborhood of Santa Eduvigis. It looked a bit more weathered, but pretty much the same. The yellow-green color that I had thought made it a bit of an eyesore among the more tempered creams and beiges of the other apartments surrounding it still stuck out for its dreary, mucous-like coloring. Throughout the 1990s, I had kept in touch with Henriqueta, who I had come to consider a mother figure during my year of fieldwork, and José (one of her sons who became like a brother to me) via letters. After a while, however, we slowly lost touch. I was hoping to find them at their apartment upon my return.

The neighborhood hadn't changed too much. The church down the street—Iglesia de la Preciosísima Sangre (the Church of Precious Blood, which sounds less macabre in Spanish)—known for its architecture, looked the same, with its picturesque twin bell towers. There was a new modern-looking hotel at the entrance to the neighborhood closest to Altamira, a business area with a mix of corporate buildings, shops, restaurants, and apartments. In Santa Eduvigis, a residential area that borders Altamira, apartment buildings interspersed with single-family homes were still the norm. I recognized the building immediately and pressed the buzzer for apartment 2A. The woman who answered said the family didn't live there anymore. I explained who I was, and she was cryptic when I asked if she knew how I could contact them. She told me to leave my number in case she heard from them, so I did, but given the curt conversation I wasn't too hopeful I'd be able to reconnect with them. To my surprise a few hours later I got a call at my hotel, and it was Henriqueta. She invited me to stay with them and told me she would be by with

José to pick me up. I checked out of the hotel and waited for them in the lobby. I saw Henriqueta first and rushed toward her to give her a warm embrace. She hugged me back tightly, as we both smiled and tearfully enjoyed our reunion after more than a decade. She started chatting right away in her usual gregarious way, and Jóse and I hugged as well. She was the same Henriqueta, talking a mile-a-minute, with her quick gesticulating hands matching the tempo of her speech. On our drive to their apartment I learned that *la abuela* (grandmother) Amalia had passed, Félix was married and had moved to another area of Caracas, and José, who had also married, had brought his wife to live with him in Henriqueta's apartment. I mentioned that I was surprised that she was able to contact me so quickly, since I had left a message at the old apartment only that morning. Henriqueta told me that she and the women who took over her apartment are related; she is the daughter of a cousin. But the woman was cautious with me because, as Henriqueta put it: "She was protecting us. You never know about people these days."

Civil Society and the Revolutionaries

I provide this account of my return because Henriqueta's comment ("you never know about people these days") is representative of the tensions middle- and upper-class Venezuelans were feeling during the Chávez administration. When I asked her to explain what she meant, she said that, although she voted for him the first time, she hadn't in the next election cycle, and non-Chavistas—*la sociedad civil* (civil society)—were worried about backlash from the Chávez government. She didn't elaborate, but I suspect her comment had to do with the narratives of middle- and upper-class angst that continue to circulate in Venezuela's more conservative newspapers, and largely in Western nations.[2] Divisions between the "revolutionaries" and "civil society" were pronounced,[3] even leading to an attempted coup against Chávez on April 11, 2002. Leftist media outlets in Latin America reported that the United States was involved and supporting the opposition.[4] Successive U.S. administrations have painted the leftist governments in Latin America as threats to U.S. political, economic, and social interests. Chávez had defined himself in opposition to what he saw as the neoliberalism and imperialism of the United States, and he famously called former president George W. Bush a "devil" in a speech to the United Nations in 2006.[5] Scholar of Venezuela Yolanda Salas (2005, 326) helps us to understand Henriqueta's comment in the context of the political polarization that has bred the type of social mistrust she expressed:

> What is certain . . . is that the popular social movements that have been developing have gained a great deal of power. For example, the indigenous movements, the popular anti-globalization movements, have gained power and are conquering a large space of visibility and agency in these new modes of political leadership. I am referring to what some prefer to call the Third Sector. Whilst in Venezuela in particular conservative society or rather those who traditionally held power have become a little left behind, now is the moment that its social movements, grouped together under the heading "civil society," are coming to the fore.
>
> We might say that what is under discussion is the concept of citizenship, which is also polarized because—in Venezuela—you're either a revolutionary or you belong to so-called civil society. But, undoubtedly, we are involved in a search for new subjectivities. And I for one think that it's important to fight for subjectivities of citizenship and of the spaces of civil power. Obviously I am thinking of a citizenship without discrimination, an inclusive citizenship, which is for everyone. (326)

Thus, Henriqueta's societal uneasiness reflected in her comment about "people these days" comes out of this struggle over citizenship. Henriqueta contrasted herself from the "other" people who were untrustworthy, but not because of any personal experience she had had. Rather, her vague statement made in passing speaks to claims of citizenship. The unasked question that floats in the air among people is "Whose side are you on?" For those who don't support Chávez, like Henriqueta, the "revolutionaries" are not legitimate citizens. Salas's analysis of the polarization is captured in Henriqueta's insecurities and the "protection" her relative provided her in case I had been, in the words of Holston (2008), an "insurgent citizen" (see Chapter 3). The struggle for new subjectivities of inclusive citizenship in Venezuela will be required, as Salas states, to address the deep political polarization.

Chávez and Health-Care Reform

Chávez's election platform, which emphasized participatory democracy and relief for the economic problems that were faced by the poorest in society and by the shrinking middle class as well, was favorably received by voters. His government, which in its first two years was a participatory democracy, progressively transformed into twenty-first-century socialism (Smilde 2011). This change came about after the coup attempt against Chávez and intensified political polarization; he was forced out of office for a few days before regaining control of the government. Smilde (2011, 11), in his extensive work on Venezuela's Bolivarian democracy, describes the political shift as follows:

> While this is frequently thought of as a dramatic political shift, it is better thought of as a progressive working out of a leftist interpretation of the Romantic tradition of democracy embodied by Bolívar. Eighteenth-century Romantic ideas of the fusion of individual and collective interests in an emergent, democratic general will were influential in Bolivar's thought. . . . The acute conflict after 2002 was interpreted by the Chávez government as evidence that simply mobilizing the masses was not enough. Chávez supporters in turn sought to further empower him as the one who could interpret the sentiment of "el pueblo" as the general will; and they saw this as more important than institutions of representative democracy. This underlying consistency is the reason we use the term Bolivarian democracy.

In this political context, Chávez's reform of the Venezuelan health-care system was increasingly focused on institutional changes to public health based on principles of social medicine. Immediately after his election, a convocation was called to set in motion participation of the citizenry in government. A key feature was the suspension of the previous administration's laws privatizing social security and health. In December 1999, a popular referendum was approved for the new Constitution of the Bolivarian Republic of Venezuela, which established the right to health care and social security (Alvarado et al. 2008). Stipulations on the right to health care are as follows:

> The State shall create, exercise leadership over, and manage a public health care system . . . integrated into the social security system, governed by the principles of free access, universality, integrality, equity, social integration, and solidarity. . . . The benefits and public health services are property of the State and cannot be privatized. The organized community has the right and responsibility to participate in decision-making around the planification, execution, and control of the public health institution policies. (Article 84, as cited in Alvarado et al. 2008, 117).

One of the most dramatic changes to the public health-care system that Chávez's government introduced was Misión Barrio Adentro (MBA, or Inside the Neighborhood Mission). The program has been described as one of the most "striking examples of Latin American social medicine" (Briggs and Mantini-Briggs 2009, 549). As discussed in Chapter 1, Latin American social medicine (LASM) was first established in Chile in the early part of the twentieth century and subsequently spread throughout Latin America; it emphasizes the connections between the health of populations and social conditions.

However, the Venezuelan Medical Federation, which had been supportive of the previous top-down, neoliberal policies, was opposed to these new health reforms. As a result, successful broad health-care changes under LASM were stunted and, in particular, were missing the promised community-based integration (Briggs and Mantini-Briggs 2009). Chávez's government thereafter began to work more closely with local community organizations throughout Venezuela and established the seedling of Inside the Barrio, which was known as Plan Barrio Adentro. The idea of the program was to have doctors live and work in the communities they were serving. Not too surprisingly, the middle- and upper-class Venezuelan doctors were not eager to live in the barrios, and many under the Venezuelan Medical Federation were not supportive of Chávez in general. Those who worked in the public health-care system, like those at Padre Machado and Razetti, often made money by working in private practice during the afternoons and evenings. To them, Chávez's government represented a threat to their private practice because part of the Barrio Adentro plan also included clinics within the city limits. Even in the mid-1990s I can recall more than a couple of conversations about the barrios with doctors who described them as dangerous places that they would never venture into. One of the doctors I spoke with described servicing the barrios as a matter of fulfilling a dreaded rotation requirement in medical school. Coupled with my earlier discussions of barrios in Venezuelan popular media, the welfare of the barrios and their residents was not a middle- or upper-class priority. Their desire, rather, was to be rid of the barrios.

As a result of this lack of local Venezuelan medical support, the Plan Barrio Adentro was reformulated to include an agreement with the Cuban government to bring Cuban doctors to Venezuela to live and work in the barrios. In 2003, fifty-eight Cuban doctors were brought to Venezuela to work with community health organizations who had already been installed to help establish health-care infrastructures and foster preventative care practices (Briggs and Mantini-Briggs 2009). The program became so popular that eventually it was set up nationally as Misión Barrio Adentro. Many more Cuban doctors came to Venezuela under an agreement between the two countries that would send subsidized oil to Cuba. MBA has grown into a multitiered system across the nation. According to Briggs and Mantini-Briggs (2009), "A second phase, initiated in 2004, included 319 integrated diagnostic centers, 430 integrated rehabilitation centers, and 15 high technology centers as of 2007. Some facilities were located in higher income areas. A third phase was established that involved upgrading hospitals. The fourth phase focuses on building 15 new public hospitals" (550). In 2010, estimates placed thirty thousand Cuban health-care professionals in Venezuela, including primary-care doctors, nurses, and dentists (*El Universal*, February 4, 2010). As stated earlier, this shift to principles of social medicine required a complete reorganization of the Ministry of Health and Social Welfare. Chávez even changed the name of this entity to the Ministerio del Poder Popular para la Salud, or Ministry of Popular Power for Health (MPPH), to indicate his government's emphasis on the power of *el pueblo*. Spending on MBA has been a major investment of the state in the health of its people. For example, in 2014 the National Assembly approved 1.13 billion bolivares (approximately US$2.5 million) with the goal of providing the Health Ministry funds to supply the nations' hospitals with resources and to incorporate more doctors into the public health system (Misión Verdad 2017). The goals and premise of MBA as of 2017 remain the same, but with the country's increasing economic struggles—exacerbated by food and medicine blockades by nations unfriendly toward the Venezuelan state, including harsh U.S. sanctions against Venezuela in August 2017 by the Trump administration—the ability to provide adequate health care through MBA has been severely compromised (Misión Verdad 2017). MBA has been one of the primary state programs since its implementation by Hugo Chávez in 2003, but given the local and global financial context that Venezuela finds itself in, its future effectiveness remains unclear.

Cervical Cancer

During the late 1980s and 1990s, the austere policies that cut back on state-funded care coincided with an increase in cervical cancer rates in Venezuela (Rodriguez de Sanchez and Surga Ruiz 2000). Since then, however, there have been dramatic political changes in Venezuela with Hugo Chávez's administration and that of his successor, Nicolás Maduro. Given the change in political leadership since my field research and then-president Chávez's explicit rejection of neoliberal policies, it was particularly timely to return and to examine the changes, if any, with the cultural politics discourse on cervical cancer in the context of political attention given to issues of structural inequality and social medicine.

When I returned to Venezuela, it was for only two months, and so I was not able to formally interview many women (only nine). My goal, instead, due in part to time constraints, was to gauge what was transpiring in terms of public health and medical discourse around cervical cancer, particularly since two things had changed: a system of socialized medicine had been implemented alongside the private one and the epidemiology of cervical cancer was clearer about the role of certain HPVs in terms of risk. Therefore, I reinterviewed some key people I had talked with during my fieldwork: some of the doctors I had met previously who were still working at the hospitals, the director of the MPPH division of oncology, and some people at the Venezuelan Cancer Society. I also conducted a few open-ended interviews with women patients at the same oncology hospitals, this time asking about the new health-care system implemented by the Chávez administration. I wanted to get an idea of their thoughts on their access to health care under this system. Moreover, I continued to look at newspaper articles and government websites about cervical cancer to also get an idea of how information about cervical cancer was being disseminated and presented. I limited this to large-circulation papers that also have a website presence, such as *El Nacional* and *El Universal*; they are also considered opposition papers and have been critical of the Chávez and Maduro administrations. This allowed me to see what the administration was covering about cervical cancer and how cervical cancer was being covered in more conservative outlets. I was most interested in whether there was a focus on social medicine and structural aspects of risk or whether they were still using discourses of individualism.

I was eager to reinterview the director of the Oncology Division of the then Ministry of Health and Social Welfare, Dr. Luis Capote, to get his perspective on the changes. He was working under the auspices of the Ministry of Popular Power for Health. When I contacted him, he remembered me and said he would be glad to speak with me. His office was no longer in the quiet suburb of San Bernardino, where I had last spoken to him over a decade earlier. His office was now downtown in a multiple-story cement-block building in a bustling area of the city. When I reached his office floor, I was surprised to see that he shared a not-very-private multiple-cubicle space that had the hustle and bustle of a newsroom, at least as I had seen them on TV. It was a stark contrast to the spacious wood-paneled office in a picturesque building that had blended seamlessly with the surrounding houses in the San Bernardino neighborhood. After we exchanged salutations, he led me the cubicle area where he had his office. He pulled up a chair for me and shuffled around some papers on his desk so I could set down my bag and notebook. I asked him about cervical cancer rates, which he said had remained about the same. I also asked if I could have copies of any new educational materials, such as pamphlets, but he told me that he didn't know of anything new that had been produced. That seemed odd given the new public health educational programs being established across the state. I moved on to ask him about his perspective on the dramatic changes in the health system brought about by the Chávez administration.

Dr. Capote comes from the traditional medical system under the auspices of the Venezuelan Medical Federation (VMF), which is critical of Chávez's government. Given the lack of privacy in the office environment, I do not think he was eager to say anything that sounded critical of the administration. However, he was insistent that little had been done in terms of cervical cancer health education when I asked about any current programs that the MPPH had undertaken. In the end, he was tight lipped and didn't provide me with much information about the MPPH or the state of cervical cancer beyond remarking that things had not improved. But it would be untrue to say that I hadn't learned anything from the interview. His silence around the Misión Barrio Adentro program told me much about the divisions between the VMF and the Chávez government. Moreover, I already knew Dr. Capote's views on health and disease were based on the individualist model of medicine. When I had interviewed him in the 1990s about cervical cancer, his perspective was in line with many of the doctors who focused on individual behaviors within a medico-moral framework. I was not surprised that he did not articulate any positive changes brought about by the social medicine model of health. In fact, in a 2015 article on cervical cancer, Dr. Capote continued to reinforce a link between cervical cancer and hygiene:

> Demographic factors include illiteracy, poverty and poor hygiene practices, little access to health services or attention to investigatory programmes based

on periodical smear testing. These factors are consistently linked to higher incidences of, and mortality due to, cervical cancer, from which comes the connotation that it is a third world cancer, or the view that a high mortality rate from cervical cancer is an indicator of underdevelopment, but it is certain that the impacts of these factors are given in determining the influence of risky sexual habits and the lack of timely and appropriate access to prevent and control measures. (Capote Negrín 2015, 9)

Interestingly enough, there are no citations, which would allow me to trace the research he is drawing on connecting poor hygiene practices and cervical cancer. At the same time, the research also concludes that "the most decisive risk factor in mortality due to cervical cancer is the absence of appropriate cytological testing" (10). Dr. Capote had devoted his career to the problem of cervical cancer in Venezuela and in Latin America more broadly. Still, his individualist perspective on health views disease through a lens of behavioral risk and doesn't incorporate the model of social medicine that engages a critical epidemiology. Beliefs about behaviors are produced in a social, cultural, and political environment. This is why I speak of a cultural politics of cervical cancer that produces risk factors and the idea of risk itself in a nexus of social relations. The "intersecting patters of subordination" based on social identities such as class, gender, and race (Crenshaw 1991) produce the risk of "poor hygiene," while public health simultaneously locates its epistemology in the "god trick" (Haraway 1988) of an objective and socially neutral medicine that has no origins other than the natural laws of science in the hands of *man*.

The MPPH had, in fact, developed a specific program geared toward cancer prevention entitled Prevention Program for Cancer Control (PPCC). The program goals were to develop community-based palliative and prevention-based educational materials and early detection strategies that would allow for the timely treatment of cervical cancer (*La Regional*, March 26, 2012). The MPPH also established March 26 as National Day for the Prevention of Cervical Cancer. On this day, statewide programs offered ambulatory Pap smear clinics as a way of encouraging early detection, particularly for those populations with difficulty accessing care. MPPH documents and programs emphasize prevention of cancer through early detection and have established free Pap smear programs to that end. These programs are not managed uniformly across the state, however, and a lack of resources to maintain them seems to be a chronic problem. One of the general critiques of the Chávez government has been the inability to create systemic structural change that can be sustained from the community level to the highest levels of government.

Among the risk factors for cervical cancer described by the MPPH, infection with human papilloma virus (HPV) is highlighted as the most important one. Other factors mentioned in a 2007 MPPH paper from the International Congress on Cancer Control included the following (in order): lack of Pap smears, HPV, sex at an early age (younger than 18), sexual promiscuity of the woman or her partner, smoking, poverty, and illiteracy. While behavioral risk factors are mentioned, the emphasis remains on lack of access and encouragement to obtain a Pap smear. However, the value-laden term *promiscuity* unfortunately remains in the health literature. More is known now about cervical cancer than had been known in the early 1990s; although HPV was highly suspected, the specific strands of the virus that are now identified as causal agents had not yet been pinpointed. While this certainly explains why MPPH would focus on the risk of HPV, it doesn't explain why some physicians and nongovernmental health organizations continue to emphasize culture and hygiene as risk factors. The Venezuelan Cancer Society is one such organization. Even as Chávez was beginning his reforms to the health-care system, focusing on community integration and partnerships with marginalized communities, the president of the Venezuelan Cancer Society (VCS) was invoking class-based arguments and expressing class and gender bias against poor women, a large constituency of Chávez supporters. A statement by the VCS president at the time, Gustavo Ott, crystalized the intersections of class and gender, marking poor women as threats to the nation and outside of legitimate claims to citizenship. He said:

> The problem of cervical cancer isn't medical, but social. Fifteen hundred women die each year and each one has four or five children. We are talking about 7,500 orphans each year that have the potential of becoming delinquents. (*El Universal*, March 14, 1999)

This quote appeared in an article in a Venezuelan national newspaper under the headline "7,500 Orphans Due to Cervical Cancer." The framing of cervical cancer as a social problem in Venezuela reflects much about the political, sociocultural, and economic history over the past twenty-five years (and arguably decades earlier). The number itself (7,500) is quite powerful in creating an image of disease and danger in Venezuela. However, in this case, the threat is not of disease itself but of the imagined delinquent orphans produced through the dangerously reproductive, poor female bodies. The numbers stand out here in a few ways: first, the mortality statistic is combined with a fertility statistic, thus linking mortality and fertility as partners in a perilous equation of mortality plus fertility equals violence. The resulting delinquency is what is clearly at issue in this formulation. The public discourse engendered by this formulation was meant to situate Venezuelans in relation to cervical cancer as its victims. Curiously, the women who are afflicted with and dying of cervical cancer are rendered conspicuously absent and invisible as victims, only to make an appearance as potential perpetrators of violence through their progeny. Second, the number of children that is multiplied in the fertility equation to produce the potential number of delinquents is five, although "four or five children" is mentioned. This mathematical equation begs the question, where do these numbers come from? Why four or five, but particularly why is five used as an estimate? As Briggs and Mantini-Briggs (2004, 25) note, "Numbers that [are] explicitly imaginary" serve to provide a projection of a potent potential threat. The number 5, of course, yields a larger projection of dangerous youth than the number 4 in this formulation, but both are made up numbers that bring to mind excess: out-of-control reproduction and violence through the production of illegitimate citizens who threaten civil society.

The unspoken danger is to middle- and upper-class Venezuelans. In Gustavo Ott's account, the "problem of cervical cancer" isn't that women are dying, but that they are producing orphaned delinquents through their deaths because women who get cervical cancer are also imagined to be without partners. They are decidedly women who transgress the social imaginary of the civil society, bourgeois nuclear family. The power of what Ian Hacking (2007, 150) describes as "the statistics of deviance" is in "making up people" through the categorization they are assigned and the ability to count them for social regulation. So-called delinquents are produced through their very categorization as such, and the statistical projection of 7,500 also creates them as a hoard or mob. The mere articulation of a statistic by an influential public person speaking on disease and public health gives the number a legitimacy and life all its own to be imagined in a myriad of threatening scenarios: robbery, rape, murder, assault—anything that a mind primed for fright can conjure up.

Four years into the Chávez presidency the new president of the Venezuelan Cancer Society voiced similar concerns about the problem of cervical cancer in a somewhat more tepid framing:

Fernando Guzman, president of Venezuela reminds us that among the principle causes of cervical cancer is infection with the Human Papilloma Virus (HPV) that is transmitted by unprotected sexual relations. "This is a health problem, but it is also a social problem," says Guzman, who points out that it's a consequence of "promiscuity, the initiation of sex at an early age, irresponsible pregnancy and nonexistent hygiene." (*El Universal*, November 27, 2003)

Although he did not refer specifically to statistics of delinquents, it is not difficult to discern the kind of social "problem" that he is imagining, as he is anything but subtle in using evaluative phrases like "irresponsible pregnancy" and "nonexistent hygiene." Once again, marginalized women are constructed as "unsanitary subjects" (Briggs and Mantini-Briggs 2004) and the root of societal ills through their perceived immoral behavior. It should not be surprising that both quotes by VCS presidents appeared in *El Universal*, a widely circulating paper that also became a source of opposition to the Chávez administration. While Chávez was fashioning *el pueblo bolivariano* (the Bolivarian community) from those who didn't have a place in formal organized society, the opposition was identifying the various ways in which the public sector was a threat. The arena of public health provided another vehicle for media opposition to construct Chávez supporters as dangers to civil society. Because cervical cancer in Venezuela has been identified with the "disorderly" bodily habits of poor women, it could be used as a stand-in for civil disorder. The concern over cervical cancer in both statements isn't about the health of poor women; it is about the threat to power of those who had long held it.

A current Venezuelan Cancer Society health education pamphlet on cervical cancer that was given to me when I went to the VCS office in Caracas still mentioned hygiene. Under the heading "How to Prevent Cervical Cancer," the following guidelines are listed in order: hygienic norms, practice safe and monogamous sex, barrier method (condoms), go to the doctor regularly (Pap smear), and treat cervical infections and abnormal lesions. While the pamphlet also describes HPV in some detail, the vague phrase "hygienic norms" is not only present but listed as the first course of action for prevention. The second guideline, "practice safe and monogamous sex," seems to be geared toward the woman reader, and her sexual practices—nothing is said about the sexual practices of partner, as in the MPPH risk factors. Given that more recent research on the sexual behavior of women and cervical cancer risk in Venezuela indicates that women do not tend to have high numbers of sexual partners, the emphasis on women's sexual behavior alone is squarely misplaced (Núñez-Troconis et al., 2009). For example Núñez-Troconis and colleagues (2009, 206–207, 210), in a study of asymptomatic sexually active women in Venezuela, found that "the average number of sexual partners was 1.57 for women younger than 30 years of age, 2.01 for women 30 to 39 years, 1.4 for women older than 40 years. . . . The present study did not find any correlation between civil status, number of partners, age of first intercourse, number of pregnancies and deliveries, and HPV infection." Although sexual behavior is correlated with HPV infection, the health strategy of ignoring the social medicine model by emphasizing Venezuelan women's sexual behavior and hygienic habits above routine Pap smears will not make the most effective prevention program. Obtaining regular Pap smears is the penultimate recommendation, even though they have been shown to be the most effective guideline in early detection, early treatment, and recovery. In this regard, the pamphlet looks very similar to the 1990s publications coming from both the old Ministry of Health and Social Welfare and the Venezuelan Cancer Society, except for the more detailed explanation of HPV. This contrasts to the current MPPH publications that, as I have stated, focus on structural barriers to health care and on encouraging women to obtain Pap smears. The MPPH website also often announces programs in various regions where women can obtain the exams free of charge.

Razetti

Although my follow-up research in Venezuela did not include systematic interviews with doctors, I did conduct informal interviews with a few of them to get their perspectives on the new health-care system and to see whether culture and hygiene were still being associated with cervical cancer risk. When I returned to the Instituto Oncológico Luis Razetti, I hoped that I would see some of the same doctors who I had worked with over a decade earlier. Recall that the hospital is located on the outskirts of the sector Cotiza in the northwestern part of the city. A barrio is located a few blocks to the south of the hospital and the area, including the hospital, is known colloquially as *la zona roja* (the red zone) because of the perceived danger of the area. As I got off of the familiar bus route this time, I was pleasantly surprised to see that a fresh coat of paint had been applied to the building, giving the former convent an even more picturesque image than before. Inside, it looked like a construction site: walkways were closed off as fresh cement was being poured, the sound of hammers and saws echoed in the corridors, and the smell of paint wafted from the newly painted walls. What remained the same were the full waiting chairs and patients, some with their children walking the floors and waiting, waiting, and waiting.[6] It appeared that the government was keeping its promise to reinsert capital into the public hospitals whose funding had been deeply cut do to the austerity measures of the 1980s and 1990s. I made my way to the gynecological oncology department; I knew the path almost instinctively I'd walked it so many times.

As I neared, I didn't know what to expect. What if none of the doctors who I'd worked with previously was there? But as I got close I recognized the distinctive gray and white hair and the nose with the pronounced bend. Then I heard his deep voice that always sounded like he had a cold. Dr. Cortez was standing in the waiting area just outside the department entrance. He was talking with a small group of doctors when I approached. I greeted him and asked if he remembered me. He took a moment to register my face, then smiled and greeted me with a hug and a "What are you doing here?" I explained that I was there to find out about the current state of cervical cancer and that I wanted to interview doctors and patients again. I had already spoken to Dr. Capote, who said I would have no problem returning to Razetti and Padre Machado to observe and do interviews. As soon as I saw Dr. Cortez I knew that would be the case. I wouldn't have to introduce myself to an entirely new set of people. Most of all it was good to see him again and to learn about all the others who had been there during my fieldwork in 1994.

After introducing me to the other doctors we went into the department and made our way past the examination rooms and into the conference space where I had spent so many days. I could tell there was new paint on the walls, but the setup was pretty much the same. The conference room now had paneled lights on the walls where X-rays could be hung to be read. As we sat down I asked about who was still around from when I was there last. He told me that Dr. Molina was still at the hospital, but Dr. Valdez had moved on to focus on private practice. Then he mentioned the name of the doctor who had sexually harassed me, and I felt my body tense up. He said that this man had died of a heart attack a few years earlier. I was taken aback and told Dr. Cortez I was sorry for his loss. I was honestly sad to hear of his death. He was a well-trained doctor, was an integral part of the department and had treated many women. At the same time, I had been worried and even angry about seeing him and a sense of relief flashed through me at the news—and I felt guilt for experiencing it.

These are some of the many feelings that we ethnographers experience and should acknowledge as part of our work (Davies and Spencer 2010). Davies and Spencer (2010), for example, argue, "Understanding fieldwork from only the traditional standpoint marginalizes, expels, or simply ignores the wider domains of experience, action, and interaction which fall outside its methodological competence" (26). Fieldwork involves human interaction and reaction with all parties involved. Applying reflexivity to our own and "to others' reactions and emotions evoked in the field" is a legitimate methodological concern: "The study of these, while often testing, we believe is intellectually and methodologically compelling to the degree that it will further realize the rich potential of fieldwork research. (26)."

To that end, I analyze my interaction, noting my ability to connect empathetically with Dr. Cortez on the loss of a friend and colleague while also validating the complex emotions I was experiencing. I am an anthropologist, and I am also a woman who faced harassment in the field. Acknowledging the stress, anxiety, and anger that it brought about during my fieldwork shouldn't be ignored; to do that is to participate in rendering invisible the global experiences of women. It is not a "personal problem." As I discussed in Chapter 4, women in the hospital were subjected to various intensities of sexism; whether doctors, nurses, patients, or anthropologist, we all navigated an environment that upheld patriarchal structures. If we speak of these issues in our fieldwork, we also challenge the charge of "nonprofessional" that women may be worried of having attached to us as ethnographers and scientists.[7] Giving voice to these experiences contests this charge and resists sexism's relegation to the "personal." The moment of relief that shuttered through my body—as I learned of the death of the doctor who had harassed me—and the immediate feeling of guilt accompanying it, were simply human emotions to be felt, analyzed, and dealt with. Had I buried the experience of sexual harassment—and the accompanying emotions then and upon my return—I wouldn't have been propelled to help reduce the silence around it both in my discipline and in the formal and informal pedagogy I do with my students. As Smith and Kleinman (2010) note, "The powerful emotions that arise in the processes of acknowledgment and advocacy—often negative and disabling emotions of guilt and powerlessness—can be productively transformed through this move to doing something concrete in the world" (185).

After chatting with some of the doctors and nurses, none of who was familiar to me, Dr. Molina entered the conference room. He appeared to have not aged a bit. I stood up, he had a look of surprise on his face, and we embraced in a warm greeting. After some conversation about the changes in our lives over the years, he was back in doctor mode with residents and patients. I sat toward the end of the big table where I wouldn't be in the way and continued to observe interactions among the doctors. Throughout the late morning, they continued coming in and out, discussing patient charts. One of the interactions that captured my attention was a conversation between Dr. Molina and a female resident. She had put up an X-ray; they were pointing to it and discussing what they saw in it. She asked him what she should tell the patient about the results of the X-ray. Dr. Molina turned his head slightly in my direction and told her, "A patient should always be spoken to clearly and maintained informed about what is going on with her condition." Given the lack of attention that had been given to information sharing with patients thirteen years before, the comment caught me by surprise. Because he looked my way, I wasn't sure if he was saying that for my benefit or not. However, it was at least clear that the discourse of patient's rights was being passed onto a resident, and she appeared to receive it as authentic.

Thereafter, another male Venezuelan doctor walked into the conference room. Dr. Molina introduced us. He appeared to be in his forties and was also an attending physician. I started to chat with him about my previous fieldwork research and eventually asked him what he believed to be the risk factors for cervical cancer. He remarked: "Those people live differently . . . they have economic obstacles and cultural ones. It's a question of education, of going to the doctor for prevention to have the Pap smear. This type of behavior [preventative exams] is seen in those people who have superior cultural ones. They use condoms, for example." His response was typical of what I found speaking informally with doctors at the hospitals, who were not supportive of Chávez's health-care reforms. They typically belonged to the middle or upper classes and still emphasized culture and hygiene, even when acknowledging economic barriers to care. For him and for doctors like him, the idea of prevention is only found among those who are culturally "superior," similar to what Bourdieu (1984) describes in terms of class rankings of cultural traits and dispositions. In this case, disease prevention and "good" hygiene are deemed to be positive cultural traits associated with the middle and upper classes, but not the poor. The generalization of poor women as unhygienic is class-based bias. What this demarcation of cultural hierarchy also does is mask social inequalities that were heightened under the previous decades of neoliberalism.

In my first visit, I had found that physicians and public health officials regarded promiscuity, lack of hygiene, and a lack of culture as risk factors. Even when I returned in 2008, some physicians, particularly those who were not supportive of the Chávez reforms, still mentioned these "risks." These terms were a part of the official medical profile of cervical cancer and made their appearance as morally neutral scientific epidemiological fact. Because these risks were enveloped in a discourse of scientific legitimacy—even though they are not epidemiologically supported and are morally laden terms—they carried much power to reference and to name not only the disease, but those who were afflicted with it as well. Consequently, the women themselves were not only characterized as engaging in unhygienic, uncultured, and promiscuous behaviors; they became embodiments of these behaviors. Ultimately then, women with cervical cancer were charged with bringing this disease upon themselves—structural inequality was not a central part of the equation. Classifications of bodily difference lead to definitions of at-risk populations and to recommendations of who should be regulated, how, and why. Such definitions are likely based more on perceptions of class difference than on epidemiological evidence. As pointed out in Chapter 3, cervical cancer public health messages, which focused on the nuclear family as a health strategy for women, were reflecting social ideologies about the role of women and less about health strategies that may be beneficial but not morally sanctioned (i.e., why not recommend the use of condoms for their partners?). The public health assumption that working-class women are sexually promiscuous orients health intervention messaging to focus on their role within the nuclear family as the appropriate way for women to maintain health. This message also aligns well with the neoliberal centering of individualism. In contrast, the health messages of a socialist Venezuela are very different. The emphasis on *pueblo* (or community) centers not on a cultural politics of uncivilized, immoral, unhygienic bodies, but rather on one that emphasizes social justice for marginalized bodies through a call for a united, constructed Bolivarian history.

Cuban Doctors

In this section I draw on two interviews with women who I spoke with at Hospital Oncológico Padre Machado to compare and contrast their views on the Cuban doctors who came to Venezuela under the Misión Barrio Adentro program: Did they have any experiences with Cuban doctors, and what did they think of them? When I arrived at Padre Machado, I found it had undergone many changes. I didn't recognize the oncology department, not only because it had been moved to another floor, but also because government money had been poured into the hospital and extensive renovations had been made (and were still ongoing when I was there). However, Dr. Cortez (from Razetti) had mentioned that Padre Machado was still "closed down since the state had taken it over." In November 2006 the hospital started using a provisional operating room, and the renovations still had not been completed as of my return in July 2008. In a newspaper interview, Dr. Patricia Núñez, head of oncology services at Padre Machado, stated that oncology is very specialized and surgery is "at the heart" of the practice. While radiation therapy and first-line chemotherapy were available, she explained that almost 80 percent of tumors are managed with surgery and, without an operating room, the hospital was "limping."[8] Even with the changes I was seeing, Padre Machado was still in a dire situation.

Although I didn't see any of the doctors I had worked with previously, Dr. Molina said I should go to the hospital and let them know he had sent me. He worked at both hospitals in addition to keeping hours at a private clinic. When I finally located the department of gynecological oncology, I introduced myself to the woman who was seated at the front desk. After a short time, one of the attending physicians came up to me, and I explained who I was. He invited me to the examination and office meeting area, where he introduced me to other doctors. They were closing the department for the day, and so I said I'd return another day the following week.

Because the hospital didn't have surgery services, the number of women patients there were few in number. However, as I was also interested in the question of what Venezuelans thought about the pubic health changes the Chávez administration had implemented, I was able to find some women who were there for radiation treatment, but few had yet to have experiences with the Misión Barrio Adentro clinics. As I wasn't able to interview the numbers of women I wanted that would enable me to see any emerging patterns regarding opinions about the medical system changes, I offer two different perspectives I encountered that exemplify the polarization of the "two bolivarianos" articulated by Yolanda Salas (2005) at the beginning of this epilogue.

I interviewed María, a twenty-eight-year-old from Los Teques, which is the capital city of the state of Miranda approximately forty-five minutes from Caracas. She said she doesn't have much confidence in Misión Barrio Adentro, explaining that "many people who can't pay [for health care] go, but I don't feel comfortable going." When I asked her why she said, "I have heard that they don't have training, that they haven't studied medicine for long and just aren't good doctors." When I asked her where she had heard this she replied, "You hear it around. People tell you and you see it in the news." I pressed her some for specifics, but she didn't elaborate. I suspect that the idea that Cuban doctors aren't properly educated as doctors may be something that had been circulating in the news, in conservative papers like *El Universal* and *El Nacional*. The Venezuelan Medical Federation is aligned with the conservative politics of the nation and has been explicit in its critique of Chavez and his reforms (Briggs and Mantini-Briggs 2009). As a result, critiques of Cuban doctors have circulated in the press since as long as they began working in Venezuela.

The middle-class physicians at Razetti and Padre Machado echoed these critiques when I asked them about their impressions of Misión Barrio Adentro. For example, a male doctor in his thirties at Razetti told me, "The idea isn't bad, but it's politicized." He went on to explain about both Cuban doctors and the MBA model: "They don't have a good plan or idea of preventative care. Preventative care isn't simply about giving someone an aspirin. It's about education, diet, nutrition, Pap exams, and it's expensive if you want to do it right because you need to provide specialists and services. You can't just give some an aspirin and call it preventative medicine." Another male doctor at the same hospital echoed a similar belief: "The Misión was based on a model of 1950s medicine because they didn't use specialists or technologies, but more like just general medicine. But people don't go see general doctors when they are sick, they see specialists for the particular problem that they have." As doctors trained in the specialty of gynecological oncology, their perspectives were steeped in their own experiences of providing specialized, technology-based care. They were also in line with the negative views of MBA that Chávez opposition doctors had expressed because they saw the program as competition for private health clinics and Ministry of Health hospitals (Briggs and Mantini-Briggs 2009).

Dr. Molina also offered a critique of the Cuban doctors but focused on their role as outsiders engendering distrust among patients. At the same time, he argued that their incorporation also spelled doom for MBA: "The doctors come from Cuba and so many Venezuelans do not trust them because they are outsiders. At first the doctors were in the barrio clinics but they started to integrate in Venezuela and Venezuelan ways and abandoned them. Some took advantage and left for Miami. I don't think they are having a lot of success." Dr. Molina acknowledged that Cuban doctors—unlike Venezuelan doctors—lived in the barrio communities, an important component of MBA's egalitarian principles of horizontal (not top-down) development, planning, and execution of the program. As I discussed in Chapter 3, Venezuelan doctors were sometimes required to do *pasantías* (internships) in the barrios, but they regarded this as a negative part of the training that they had to get through. The idea that doctors would live in poor communities was not only strange to Venezuelan physicians, but it was strange to those living in the barrios as well. As Briggs and Mantini-Briggs (2009) note in their study of MBA, "When the first 58 Cuban physicians arrived, many residents reported that they were astonished that these doctors would live in poor neighborhoods and share the daily lives of residents" (550). Ironically, Dr. Molina argued that when Cuban doctors started to be "Venezuelan" in their "ways," they also began to abandon the barrios. This statement is quite revelatory regardless of whether it is true. In his assessment, to be or become Venezuelan means to distance oneself from the barrios. Defining Venezuelanness in opposition to the barrios is also about denying residents of peripheral neighborhoods a claim to citizenship.

In contrast to these critiques, I interviewed a patient at Padre Machado named Catia, who said she had gone to a Barrio Adentro clinic in the city, where a Cuban doctor treated her very well. She offered a contrast to Venezuelan doctors based on the attention paid to her and the idea of respect: "The Cuban doctors treat you in a way that is different from the doctors here. The way they talk to you is respectful. They listen to you and ask you if you understand everything. If it was clear. They aren't short with you or curt like the doctors here can be. They pay attention to you and treat you with affection and respect." For Catia, the outsider status of Cuban doctors didn't diminish her trust. In fact, their outsider status marked them as refreshingly different compared to Venezuelan doctors who she had experienced as curt and disrespectful. Catia was articulating her needs as a patient in a holistic way that included not just attention to her body, but regard for her feelings and human dignity. In her study of MBA patient-doctor interactions at a state run clinic in Santa Teresa, a hybrid working-class and middle-class neighborhood in central Caracas, Amy Cooper (2015a) found that Cuban doctors were distinguished from Venezuelan doctors for the same behaviors Catia had expressed to me: the respect, time, and attention they gave to their patients. She notes, "Communicative practices, including eye contact, listening without interrupting, the amount of time doctors spent with patients, explanations of diagnoses and treatments, and even the use of pet names were commonly noted by patients as meaningful behaviors" (467). Moreover,

> Barrio Adentro patients could be highly critical of what some called the "older generation" of Venezuelan doctors, interpreting their unwillingness to travel to the barrios as showing contempt for their poorer fellow citizens and as betraying the Venezuelan idea of how a doctor should behave. In a sociopolitical context of marked spatial segregation along class lines, in which the vast majority of middle- and upper-class Venezuelans are unlikely to visit poor Caracas neighborhoods, the symbolic (not to mention pragmatic) significance of having a medical professional living and working inside a poor community is clear. Patients' insistence that doctors be willing to physically travel to and live in poor areas challenged long-standing spatial divisions between marginalized and privileged social groups in Caracas and reflected an important aspect of medical embodiment according to which doctors were evaluated. (465)

For working-class and poor patients like Catia and those who Cooper (2015) and Briggs and Mantini-Briggs (2009) interviewed, their demands that doctors treat them with respect are not only a commentary on desired health care but also a positioning of political subjectivity in a struggle over what it means to be Venezuelan. For them, a legitimate Bolivarian state embodies a spatial, psychic, economic, and social solidarity with *el pueblo popular* (the popular sector). They are making claims to a Bolivarian citizenship that represents the heart of a popularly imagined Venezuela envisioned through historical figures, particularly that of Simón Bolívar (Salas 2005; Fernandes 2010).

What's Next? From Neoliberalism to Socialism to Neoliberalism?

So, what's next? This is the question weighing on the global politics that the Bolivarian Revolution has brought to the fore. What will happen with Misión Barrio Adentro, public health, and the centering of social medicine as theory and praxis if the opposition to Venezuelan socialism is successful? Will the public health framing of cervical cancer and other diseases and illnesses that are shaped by moral-medical narratives of classism, sexism, and racism turn again to actively emphasize the individualism of blame? Will "the people" center their counterresponse to the opposition around health as the Bolivarian Revolution did with the development of MBA? Who are "the people" in the current era of opposition and the Bolivarian revolutionaries who demand accountability from Maduro's government and continue to push political change of inclusive citizenship forward? George Ciccariello-Maher argues that even those who supported Chávez were not a singular group:

> The process of political change currently underway in Venezuela exploded out of the tense overlap of multiple combative identities in movement—Bolivarian, revolutionary, Chavista, Afro-Venezuelan, Indigenous, feminist—each with their own dialectics. But no political identity has been more central than that which draws them together in a combative whole that is nevertheless far from a singularity: the people. (2017, locs. 2861–2863)

He refers to this diverse group as a "combative identity." Using this frame, we can understand that the response to the current opposition may invite others into the process while some decide that their interests are no longer served. How then to articulate common struggle to bring together the "combative identity," which "across much of Latin America, [is] in part due to the 'historical-structural heterogeneity' that colonialism imposed on the region, in which a complex constellation of class relations and other exclusions coexist" (Ciccariello-Maher 2017, 128)? Will a more radical sense of agency develop vis-à-vis the opposition? If it does, the women who have located themselves centrally in Venezuelan political transformation will likely continue to do so. As I pointed out in the previous chapter, these women are drawn from the same periphery as those who have been central to the Bolivarian Revolution:

> While there has been a feminization of poverty, there is also a feminization of resistance that is reconfiguring and reimagining the nature, meaning, and subjects of political resistance and social transformation. This is notably the case in Venezuela, where women are numerically a majority of the social support base of Chavismo and where the political conjuncture has created possibilities for the development of new forms of revolutionary subjectivity. (Motta 2013, 36)

I argue that the revolutionary subjective challenges will continue to come in the form of contestations over health care as a central organizing principal of resistance. Although not necessarily primary, narratives of health risks are also spaces where systemic inequities will likely continue to challenge behavioral constructions of risk. In doing so, the principles of social medicine—focusing on the social causes of disease and illness—are invoked, even if not directly referenced. Recall that in their own perceptions of risk, the women who I interviewed during my first fieldwork refused to accept characterizations of them that used largely sexist and classist framings and instead raised lack of access to care in relation to their own health.

As I argue in this book, discourse about disease risk for cervical cancer used by physicians and public health entities relied on a cultural politics to blame "backward" cultural practices of marginalized women for their own disease. I'm not speaking of a conspiracy; I'm speaking of the ways in which hegemonic discourses function so as to appear normal and unquestionable. The individualism in neoliberal politics squared well with an invention of risk that targeted women for lacking "control" over their sexuality, fertility, and medical care. Austerity programs can be felt in the language of public health—not only in terms of focusing on individuals rather than institutions but also in the cultural politics of risk itself. Drawing on the work of Lisa Duggan (2004, xii) on neoliberal and cultural politics in the United States:

> During every phase, the construction of neoliberal politics and policy in the U.S. has relied on identity and cultural politics. The politics of race both overt and covert, have been particularly central to the entire project. But the politics of gender and sexuality have intersected with race and class at each stage as well.

When national public health entities disseminate information about risk factors for cervical cancer, they are not only relaying health information to the population; they are providing information about "sanitary citizenship," the regulation of sexuality and reproduction, and demonstrating the priorities and agendas of the health system whatever those may be. Throughout this book I have underscored the ways in which intersections of gender, race, and class in political agendas can have profound implications for not only macro questions of health-care access for those deemed nondeserving but also for micro-level interactions between patients and their doctors. The consequences can be negative for patients if they are seen as "backward" and "unsanitary subjects" who do not deserve to be treated as capable individuals worthy of information sharing in respectful communication (see Briggs and Mantini-Briggs 2004).

Under the political transformations of the Chávez era, public health messages about cervical cancer have not focused so much on questions of individualism but rather on problems of structural violence and access to care. This doesn't mean that individual moral behaviors of women are not still scrutinized, as occurs broadly within hegemonic patriarchy. As intersectional theory shows us, the racism and classism that are also interwoven have not been erased in the current era. Briggs and Mantini-Briggs (2016)—with their heartbreaking ethnography of rabies deaths among the Warao Indians of Venezuela—remind us that blame continues to be present in the revolution. This latest work is all too reminiscent of their previous ethnography documenting cholera deaths among the Warao, as the public health institution in 1991 insisted on blaming them, with racist narratives of their so-called cultural backwardness, for their own deaths. Instead, what Chávez health reforms have ushered in is a discourse that centers the role of the state along with the power of community in a horizontal—not top-down—approach to maintaining the health of the population. At the time of my initial fieldwork, concepts of shared power and patient-centeredness had not been integrated into the Venezuelan medical system. The idea that health care should be horizontal and not vertical—with the hegemonic power relationships between doctors and patients called into question—would not take root until the health-care reforms initiated by the Chávez administration. At the same time, even before this profound shift, women patients did not unquestioningly accept this set of circumstances (as I spell out in Chapters 4 and 5). They used various techniques of resistance to enact their agency in attempts to access the information they were denied by doctors who either didn't think to or were unwilling to share it. Now, in the post-neoliberal era, we see the popular sector more overtly making demands for inclusivity from the public health sector. Through community-based activism, they are asserting their citizenship and redefining what it means to be Venezuelan. The implications for community-based horizontal egalitarianism go well beyond Venezuela and even Latin America. Wherever neoliberal health-care policies are enacted, we must consider the effects on intimate patient-doctor interactions, as well as the broader structural outcomes. Whose interests are at center when States articulate their goals and policies for a healthy population? That is a question we must always insist on asking.

Appendix

APPENDIX 1 Occupations of Patients at Razetti (Public Hospital)

Occupation	Frequency (N=25)	
Homemaker	11	44%
Sells clothes out of home	3	12%
Management (supervisor in factory, personnel analyst and personnel head)	3	12%
Student	2	8%
Secretary	1	4%
Seamstress	1	4%
Nurse	1	4%
Elementary school teacher	1	4%
Raises animals on ranch	1	4%
Waitress	1	4%

APPENDIX 2 Occupations of Patients at Padre Machado (Private Hospital)

Occupation	Frequency (N=20)	
Homemaker	13	65%
Housekeeper	5	25%
Sells clothes out of home	1	5%
Receptionist	1	5%

APPENDIX 3 Mean Age, Income, and Education for Patients at Both Hospitals

	Patients at Razetti (Public)	Patients at Padre Machado (Private)
Mean age	40	38
Mean monthly income	US$172 (29,174 bs.)	US$255 (43,316 bs.)
Mean years of formal education	6.70	7.05

APPENDIX 4 Demographics for Doctors at Razetti (Public Hospital)

ID No.	Sex	Age	Marriage status	Monthly income	Education
202r	Male	46	Divorced	400,000 bs. ($2,353)	23 yrs.
203r	Male	40	Divorced	150,000 bs. ($882)	24 yrs.
205r	Male	30	Married	240,000 bs. ($1,412)	19 yrs.
207r	Female	35	Married	220,000 bs. ($1,294)	21 yrs.
210r	Male	49	Married	400,000 bs. ($2,353)	23 yrs.
211r	Male	29	Single	120,000 bs. ($706)	18 yrs.
215r	Male	44	Single	700,000 bs. ($4,118)	27 yrs.

APPENDIX 5 Demographics for Doctors at Padre Machado (Private Hospital)

ID No.	Sex	Age	Marriage status	Monthly income	Education
200m	Male	43	Married	130,000 bs. ($765)	27 yrs.
201m	Male	47	Married	400,000 bs. ($2,353)	26 yrs.
204m	Male	38	Married	500,000 bs. ($2,941)	23 yrs.
206m	Male	38	Single	130,000 bs. ($765)	19 yrs.
208m	Male	32	Single	160,000 bs. ($941)	20 yrs.
209m	Female	34	Married	200,000 bs. ($1,176)	23 yrs.
212m	Male	34	Married	200,000 bs. ($1,176)	24 yrs.
213m	Male	33	Divorced	500,000 bs. ($2,941)	22 yrs.
214m	Male	34	Married	500,000 bs. ($2,941)	22 yrs.
216m	Female	33	Married	55,000 bs. ($324)	21 yrs.

APPENDIX 6 Doctors' Mean Age, Income, and Years of Formal Education

	Doctors at public hospital	*Doctors at private hospital*
Mean age	39.0	32.8
Mean monthly income	US$1,874 (318,580 bs.)	US$1,632 (277,500 bs.)
Mean years Formal education	22.1	22.7

APPENDIX 7 Medical Background for Doctors at Padre Machado (Private)

ID No. (N=10)	Medical specialization(s)	Years in practice
200m	General surgery, gynecology, and oncology	12
201m	General surgery and surgical oncology	19
204m	General surgery and surgical oncology	12
206m	Currently specializing in OB/GYN	5
208m	Currently specializing in OB/GYN	7
209m	Currently specializing in OB/GYN	7
212m	General surgery and currently specializing in gynecologic surgery	8
213m	OB/GYN	8
214m	General surgery and currently specializing in surgical oncology	11
216m	General Surgery and currently specializing in surgical oncology	5.5

APPENDIX 8 Medical Background for Doctors at Razetti (Public)

ID No. (N=7)	Medical specialization(s)	Years in practice
202r	General surgery, gynecology, and surgical oncology	23
203r	General surgery and surgical oncology	15
205r	Currently specializing in OB/GYN	4
207r	General surgery and currently specializing in surgical oncology	8.5
210r	General surgery and surgical oncology	25
211r	Currently specializing in OB/GYN	4
215r	General surgery and surgical oncology	18

APPENDIX 9 Workweek Hours for Doctors at Razetti

ID No.	Hrs. per week in Razetti	Hrs. per week in private practice	Hrs. per week at other hospitals	Total hrs. per week
202r	20	20	~20[a]	~60
203r	24	12 (3 per wk.)	n/a	36
205r	25	n/a	17 (1 per wk.)	42
207r	40	n/a	36[b]	76
210r	20	12	n/a	32
211r	25	n/a	20 (1 per wk.)	45
215r	30	14	21[c]	65

[a] This doctor also worked a number of hours at Padre Machado and was a médico adjunto at both hospitals. His total workweek hours thus were actually closer to sixty than forty. Although I did not ask him exactly how many hours he worked per week at Padre Machado, I estimate that he put in about 20 hours there as well.
[b] This doctor also works in a Naval hospital during the week.
[c] This doctor also works at a public clinic 20 hours per week. He estimates that he works fifteen hours a day as a physician, although according to his responses his total workweek comes to 65 hours per week.

APPENDIX 10 Workweek Hours for Doctors at Padre Machado

ID No.	Hrs. per week in Padre Machado	Hrs. per week in private practice	Hrs. per week at other hospitals	Total hrs. per week
200m	20	4	30[a]	54
201m	14	11	24[b]	49
204m	17	15	n/a	32
206m	30	n/a	24[c]	54
208m	35	n/a	48[d]	83
209m	46	n/a	24[e]	70
212m	45	4	n/a	49
213m	40	n/a[f]	n/a	40
214m	70	13	n/a	83
216m	60	n/a	n/a	60

[a] This doctor also works at a public hospital where he is the hospital director.
[b] He works a 24-hour shift on Mondays at a public hospital.
[c] He works a 24-hour shift on the weekend at the Maternidad Santa Ana where he is specializing in obstetrics and gynecology.
[d] He works as a resident at a private clinic 24 hours a week as well as doing a 24-hour shift on the weekend at the Maternidad Santa Ana where he is specializing in obstetrics and gynecology.
[e] She works a 24-hour shift on the weekend at the Maternidad Santa Ana where she is specializing in obstetrics and gynecology.
[f] He has a private practice but it is suspended while he is working at Padre Machado.

Notes

Chapter 1

1. Information obtained from national Venezuelan newspaper, *El Universal* (April 3, 1997).
2. This was told to me by Dr. Linares, a *médico adjunto* and surgical oncologist who at the time of this research had been working at the hospital for twelve years.
3. See *El Universal*, June 10, 1997.
4. These and subsequent dollar amounts are calculated at the exchange rate during the time of fieldwork (1994–1995). The rate was 170 bolivares to US$1.

Chapter 2

1. This call for a critical conceptualization of processes of categorization comes from Valverde's (1992) approach to understanding social welfare as an historical and political taxonomy.
2. The program *A puerta cerrada* (Behind Closed Doors) at the time of this research was broadcast on weekday mornings. It had a talk-show format with a panel of guest speakers and experts who varied according to topic. Some of the women whom I interviewed mentioned this program as a source of their information about cervical cancer.
3. See McMullin et al. (1994) for an informative discussion about the role of experience in physicians' perceptions regarding cancer.

Chapter 3

1. This idea of an "annual control" was also extended to cancer (various forms, not solely cervical cancer) patients who were to come in yearly (or whenever was deemed necessary) for follow-up exams after treatments.

2. "From The Rural Choza To the Urban Hut," *El Universal*, April 1, 1997.

3. See Chávez (1991) for a discussion of the outsider status of Mexican and Central American immigrants in the United States. Parallels can be drawn between these immigrants and the barrio residents of Caracas, who are also imagined as outside of the community (the city).

4. George Ciccariello-Maher (2013) notes that some prefer El Sacudón, because Caracazo is "misleading, concealing as it does the generalized and national nature of the rebellion . . . whereby popular upheaval is translated a sort of geological 'tremor'" (93).

5. Others, like George Ciccariello-Maher (2013), go back further to trace the rise of Hugo Chávez: "After all, where did 1989 come from? Here are regression is not infinite, and the clash between the 'from below' and 'from above' that occurred on the streets in February 1989 finds both sides constituted in the years after 1958: in the guerrilla struggle and its collapse and the period of autonomous movement-building that followed in its wake" (15).

6. From Caswell (2014:2): "The communal councils are public community governance venues that were implemented in April, 2006through the Law of Communal Councils (Ley de los Consejos Comunales). Today, there are approximately thirty thousand nationwide. . . . In a communal council there are 'different thematic working groups—energy, telecommunications, land tenure, health, recreation, water, garbage, etc.—based on the articulated needs of the population'" (p. 15).

7. See, for example, various newspaper articles printed in *El Universal*: "Cultural Roots," December 9, 1996; "About Culture and Identity," January 2, 1998; and "The Country Needs a Cultural Revolution," 1997.

8. The popular icon of Madonna and the Christ child is an obvious example of the coupling of women (as nurturers) and children (as nurtured).

9. Interestingly, multiparity is considered to be a risk factor for cervical cancer in Venezuela, and when this subject would come up in the hospitals, much discussion revolved around the problem of poor women having too many children.

10. An association between prior sexually transmitted diseases (particularly herpes simplex 2 and a couple of virulent strains of human papilloma virus) and risk for cervical cancer has been reported in the biomedical literature.

11. For a critical examination of the safe sex concept for women, see Singer (1993).

Chapter 4

1. This figure includes an outlier of sixteen minutes. If this mean is recalculated without this outlier, the amount of time spent decreases to 1.9 minutes.

2. Doctors would sometimes refer to cervixes that were free from disease as "clean."

3. In a telling analysis of the film *Dead Ringers*, a film about a childhood fascination for science, Kapsalis (1997, 139) points out a passage that draws out the links between women and the proper passive scientific object: "In the opening of Dead Ringers . . . boys discuss the difference between fish reproduction and human reproduction. . . . They then ask a girl classmate of theirs if she will join them in an experiment and have sex with them. She tells them to 'fuck off.' The next scene shows the twins operating on a toy: a plastic, see-through woman with removable organs they carefully extract with tweezers. The message here is that resistant women (those who tell little boys to 'fuck off') must be avoided in lieu of more compliant patient objects (doll-like, passive, plastic models), a preference and pattern that can be located, as we have seen, throughout the history of gynecological practice and pedagogy."

4. When Francia, a patient at Padre Machado whom I had interviewed, was asked about the type of birth control she was using, she responded that her husband had had a vasectomy. The doctor said that was surprising since in Venezuela it is rare for a man to have a vasectomy.

5. For example, when patients would arrive late to their appointments, they were often told that they would have to reschedule or, if lucky, wait until every other patient was seen. Some pleaded to be seen and those who did often were seen that day.

6. Interestingly, the opposite argument, that women are more dexterous than men, has been used to explain the preference for women factory workers in the electronics industry. The idea is that women have smaller and more nimble fingers than men and are thus able to better work with the extremely small components (Fernandez Kelley 1983). In both cases, women's biology is defined in particular ways so as to legitimize social and economic phenomena.

Epilogue

1. It should be noted that Chávez also gained support from the Venezuelan middle class, although these categorizations do not capture the varied interests of diverse groups considered middle class and the tenuous nature of the category itself.

2. A 2006 story in *The Telegraph*, for example, focuses on middle-class Venezuelans leaving the country. See http://www.telegraph.co.uk/news/worldnews/south america/venezuela/1512168/Venezuelan-middle-class-flees-Chávez-rule-of-hate.html (Arie, March 5, 2006).

3. I'm using the descriptions of the dichotomy between Chávez supporters and anti-Chavistas provided by Yolanda Salas: "On Chavismo: An Interview with Yolanda Salas (Caracas, 7 September, 2004)," available at http://tandfonline.com/doi/abs/10.10 80/13569320500382641?journalCode=cjla20.

4. See, for example, the website http://www.telesurtv.net/english/analysis/The -US-Role-in-the-Failed-Attempt-to-Overthrow-Hugo-Chávez-20151118-0014.html (Telesur, November, 18, 2015).

5. See: http://www.nytimes.com/2006/09/20/world/americas/20cnd-Chávez.html (Stout, September 20, 2006).

6. See Javier Auyero's (2012) book *Patients of the State: The Politics of Waiting in Argentina*, for a thorough account of waiting, the state, and control.

7. Women scientists' experiences of sexual harassment in fieldwork are finally beginning to be addressed. See http://www.nature.com/news/many-women-scientists-sexually-harassed-during-fieldwork-1.15571 (Simmonds, July, 16, 2014).

8. See *El Universal* online article: http://www.eluniversal.com/2008/03/06/imp_ccs_art_quince-meses-sin-qui_744198.shtml (Brassesco, March 6, 2008).

Bibliography

Adentro, P. M. B. (2006). *The right to health and social inclusion in Venezuela*. Caracas: PAHO.

Alvarado, C. H., Martínez, M. E., Vivas-Martínez, S., Gutiérrez, N. J., & Metzger, W. (2008). Social change and health policy in Venezuela. *Social Medicine, 3*(2), 95–109. Retrieved from http://socialmedicine.info/index.php/medicinasocial/article/view/202

Alvarez, S. L. (1998). Aspectos socio-culturales de la sexualidad como factores obstaculizantes de la prevención secundaria del cáncer cérvico uterino. *Cadernos de saúde pública, 14*, S33–S40.

Andersen, B. (1991). *Imagined communities: Reflections on the origin and spread of nationalism*. Retrieved from http://sites.middlebury.edu/utopias/files/2013/02/imaginedcommunities.pdf.

Anderson, W. (1992). "Where every prospect pleases and only man is vile": Laboratory medicine as colonial discourse. *Critical Inquiry, 18*(3), 506–529. https://doi.org/10.1086/448643

Anton-Culver, H., Bloss, J. D., Bringman, D., Lee-Feldstein, A., DiSaia, P., & Manetta, A. (1992). Comparison of adenocarcinoma and squamous cell carcinoma of the uterine cervix: A population-based epidemiologic study. *American Journal of Obstetrics and Gynecology, 166*(5), 1507–1514.

Appelbaum, N. P., Macpherson, A. S., & Rosemblatt, K. A. (2003). *Race and nation in modern Latin America*. Chapel Hill, NC: University of North Carolina Press.

Arellano, O. L., Escudero, J. C., & Carmona, L. D. (2008). Los determinantes sociales de la salud: Una perspectiva desde el Taller Latinoamericano de Determinantes Sociales de la Salud, ALAMES. *Medicina social, 3*(4), 323–335.

Arie, S. (2006, March 5). Venezuelan middle class flees Chávez rule of hate. *Telegraph.*

Retrieved from http://www.telegraph.co.uk/news/worldnews/southamerica/venezuela/1512168/Venezuelan-middle-class-flees-Chavez-rule-of-hate.html

Armada, F., Muntaner, C., Chung, H., Williams-Brennan, L., & Benach, J. (2009). Barrio Adentro and the reduction of health inequalities in Venezuela: An appraisal of the first years. *International Journal of Health Services*, *39*(1), 161–187.

Armada, F., Muntaner, C., & Navarro, V. (2001). Health and social security reforms in Latin America: The convergence of the World Health Organization, the World Bank, and transnational corporations. *International Journal of Health Services*, *31*(4), 729–768.

Arnold, D. (1993). *Colonizing the body: State medicine and epidemic disease in nineteenth-century India*. Berkeley, CA: University of California Press.

Auyero, J. (2012). *Patients of the state: The politics of waiting in Argentina*. Durham, NC: Duke University Press.

Azocar, J., Abad, S. M. J., Acosta, H., Hernandez, R., Gallegos, M., Pifano, E., . . . Kramar, A. (1990). Prevalence of cervical dysplasia and HPV infection according to sexual behavior. *International Journal of Cancer*, *45*(4), 622–625.

Babaria, P., Abedin, S., Berg, D., & Nunez-Smith, M. (2012). "I'm too used to it": A longitudinal qualitative study of third year female medical students' experiences of gendered encounters in medical education. *Social Science & Medicine*, *74*(7), 1013–1020.

Balibar, E., & Wallerstein, I. M. (1991). *Race, nation, class: Ambiguous identities*. New York, NY: Verso.

Balshem, M. (1991). cancer, control, and causality: Talking about cancer in a working-class community. *American Ethnologist*, *18*(1), 152–172.

Balshem, M., Oxman, G., Van Rooyen, D., & Girod, K. (1992). Syphilis, sex and crack cocaine: Images of risk and morality. *Social Science & Medicine*, *35*(2), 147–160.

Bandura, A. (1982). Self-efficacy mechanism in human agency. *American Psychologist*, *37*(2), 122.

Barthes, R. (1978). *A lover's discourse: Fragments*. New York, NY: Macmillan.

Bartky, S. L., Diamond, I., & Quinby, L. (1988). Feminism and Foucault: Reflections on resistance.

Bernard, H. R. (1988). *Research methods in cultural anthropology*. Newbury Park, CA: Sage.

Blanco, C. (1993). *Venezuela, del siglo 20 al siglo 21: Un proyecto para construirla*. Copre.

Bolivar, A., Chollett, M. B., Bisbe, L., Briceño-León, R., Ishibashi, J., Kaplan, N., . . . Velasquez, R. (2009). A "café con leche" country. *Racism and Discourse in Latin America*, 291.

Bonnett, A. (2002). The metropolis and white modernity. *Ethnicities*, *2*(3), 349–366.

Bordo, S. (1990a). " Material girl": The effacements of postmodern culture. *Michigan Quarterly Review*, *29*(4), 653–677.

Bordo, S. (1990b). Feminism, postmodernism, and gender-scepticism. *Feminism/Postmodernism*, *145*, 144.

Bordo, S. (1997). *The body and the reproduction of femininity*. Retrieved from https://philpapers.org/rec/BORTBA

Bourdieu, P. (1984). *Distinction: A social critique of the judgement of taste*. Cambridge, MA: Harvard University Press.

Bourdieu, P. (1990). *The logic of practice*. Stanford, CA: Stanford University Press.

Brandt, A. M., & Rozin, P. (2013). *Morality and health*. New York, NY: Routledge.

Brassesco, J. (2008, March 6). Quince meses sin quirófano tiene oncológico Padre Machado. *El Universal*. Retrieved from http://www.eluniversal.com/2008/03/06/imp_ccs_art_quince-meses-sin-qui_744198.shtml

Breilh, J. (2010a). *Hacia un nuevo paradigma de los derechos humanos y la salud*. Retrieved from http://repositorionew.uasb.edu.ec/handle/10644/3401

Breilh, J. (2010b). La epidemiología crítica: Una nueva forma de mirar la salud en el espacio urbano. *Salud Colectiva*, 6(1), 83–101.

Briceño-León, R. (1992). *Venezuela: Clases sociales e individuos: Un enfoque pluriparadigmático*. Fondo Editorial Acta Científica Venezolana.

Briceño-León, R., García, B., Rodríguez, V., & Tovar, L. (2003). Las ciencias sociales y la salud en la modernización de Venezuela. *Cien Saude Colet*, 8(1), 63–77.

Briggs, C. L. (2004). Theorizing modernity conspiratorially: Science, scale, and the political economy of public discourse in explanations of a cholera epidemic. *American Ethnologist*, 31(2), 164–187.

Briggs, C. L., & Mantini-Briggs, C. (2004). *Stories in the time of cholera: Racial profiling during a medical nightmare*. Berkeley, CA: University of California Press.

Briggs, C. L., & Mantini-Briggs, C. (2007). "Misión Barrio Adentro": Medicina social, movimientos sociales de los pobres y nuevas coaliciones en Venezuela. *Salud colectiva*, 3(2), 159–176.

Briggs, C. L., & Mantini-Briggs, C. (2009). Confronting health disparities: Latin American social medicine in Venezuela. *American Journal of Public Health*, 99(3), 549–555.

Browner, C. H., & Sargent, C. F. (2011). *Reproduction, globalization, and the state: New theoretical and ethnographic perspectives*. Durham, NC: Duke University Press.

Bruni, L., Barrionuevo-Rosas, L., Albero, G., Aldea, M., Serrano, B., Valencia, S., ... (2015). *Human papillomavirus and related diseases in India: Summary report*, 12–23. ICO Information Centre on HPV and Cancer (HPV Information Centre).

Burggraaff, W. J., & Millett, R. L. (1995). More than failed coups: The crisis in Venezuelan civil-military relations. *Lessons of the Venezuelan Experience*, 54–78.

Burke, T. (1996). *Lifebuoy Men, Lux Women: Commodification, consumption, and cleanliness in modern Zimbabwe*Durham, NC: Duke University Press.

Butler, J. (1990). *Gender Trouble: Feminism and the subversion of identity*. London: Routledge.

Butler, J. (1993). *Bodies that matter: On the limits of "sex."* London: Routledge.

Caldeira, T. P. (2000). *City of walls: Crime, segregation, and citizenship in São Paulo*. Berkeley, CA: University of California Press.

Caldeira, T. P., & Holston, J. (1999). Democracy and violence in Brazil. *Comparative Studies in Society and History, 41*(4), 691–729.

Capote Negrin, Luis G. (2006). Aspectos epidemiológicos del cáncer en Venezuela. *Revista venezolana de oncología, 18*(4), 269–281.

Capote Negrín, Luis G. (2015). Epidemiology of cervical cancer in Latin America. *Ecancermedicalscience, 9*. Retrieved from http://pubmedcentralcanada.ca/pmcc/articles/PMC4631571/

Casper, M. J., & Moore, L. J. (2009). *Missing bodies: The politics of visibility.* New York, NY: NYU Press.

Cassell, J. (1996). The woman in the surgeon's body: Understanding difference. *American Anthropologist, 98*(1), 41–53.

Castaño, L. S. Á., & Stella, L. (2009). Los determinantes sociales de la salud: Más allá de los factores de riesgo. *Revista gerencia,* 69–79.

Caswell, C. M. (2014). *Mothers of the Revolution: Barrio Women's Social Activism and Agency in the Bolivarian Process.* Ottawa: Université d'Ottawa/University of Ottawa. Retrieved from https://137.122.14.44/handle/10393/31775

Center for History and New Media. (n.d.). *Zotero quick start guide.* Retrieved from http://zotero.org/support/quick_start_guide

Chavez, L. R. (1986). Mexican immigration and health care: A political economy perspective. *Human Organization, 45*(4), 344–352.

Chavez, L. R. (1991). Outside the imagined community: Undocumented settlers and experiences of incorporation. *American Ethnologist, 18*(2), 257–278.

Chavez, L. R. (2001). *Covering immigration: Popular images and the politics of the nation.* Berkeley, CA: University of California Press.

Chavez, L. R., Hubbell, F. A., McMullin, J. M., Martinez, R. G., & Mishra, S. (1995). Structure and meaning in models of breast and cervical cancer risk factors: A comparison of perceptions among Latinas, Anglo women, and physicians. *Medical Anthropology Quarterly, 9*(1), 40–74.

Chibber, V. (2013). How does the subaltern speak? *Jacobin.* Retrieved from https://www.jacobinmag.com/2013/04/how-does-the-subaltern-speak

Ciccariello-Maher, G. (2013). *We created Chávez: A people's history of the Venezuelan revolution.* Durham, NC: Duke University Press.

Ciccariello-Maher, G. (2017). *Decolonizing dialectics.* Durham, NC: Duke University Press.

Comaroff, J., & Comaroff, J. (1991). *Of Revelation and Revolution: Vol. 1. Christianity, colonialism, and consciousness in South Africa.* Chicago, IL: University of Chicago Press.

Comaroff, J. L., & Comaroff, J. (1992). *Ethnography and the historical imagination.* Boulder, CO: Westview Press.

Cooper, A. (2015a). The doctor's political body: Doctor–patient interactions and sociopolitical belonging in Venezuelan state clinics. *American Ethnologist, 42*(3), 459–474.

Cooper, A. (2015b). What does health activism mean in Venezuela's Barrio Adentro program? Understanding community health work in political and cultural context. *Annals of Anthropological Practice, 39*(1), 58–72.

Coronil, F. (1997). *The magical state: Nature, money, and modernity in Venezuela.* Chicago, IL: University of Chicago Press.

Coronil, F. (2013). Beyond Occidentalism: Toward nonimperial geohistorical categories. *Cultural Anthropology, 11*(1), 51–87.

Coronil, F., & Skurski, J. (1991). Dismembering and remembering the nation: The semantics of political violence in Venezuela. *Comparative Studies in Society and History, 33*(02), 288–337.

Cortés, J. V. (2017). *Obstetricia y ginecología: Relación médico-paciente.* Retrieved from http://www.revistaobgin.cl/files/pdf/041.pdf

Craske, N. (2005). Ambiguities and ambivalences in making the nation: Women and politics in 20th-century Mexico. *Feminist Review, 79*(1), 116–133.

Crenshaw, K. (1991). Mapping the margins: Intersectionality, identity politics, and violence against women of color. *Stanford Law Review*, 1241–1299.

Cruz, E. R. B., & Perea, R. S. S. (2008). Programa Nacional de Formación en Medicina Integral Comunitaria, Venezuela. *Medicina Social, 3*(4), 285–298.

Csordas, T. J. (1994). *Embodiment and experience: The existential ground of culture and self* (Vol. 2). Cambridge: Cambridge University Press.

Davies, J., & Spencer, D. (2010). *Emotions in the field: The psychology and anthropology of fieldwork experience.* Stanford, CA: Stanford University Press.

Davis-Floyd, R. E., & Sargent, C. (1997). *Childbirth and authoritative knowledge: Cross-cultural perspectives.* Berkeley, CA: University of California Press.

De Los Monteros, K. E., & Gallo, L. C. (2011). The relevance of fatalism in the study of Latinas' cancer screening behavior: A systematic review of the literature. *International Journal of Behavioral Medicine, 18*(4), 310–318.

De Vos, P., Ceukelaire, W. D., & Stuyft, P. V. der. (2006). Colombia and Cuba, contrasting models in Latin America's health sector reform. *Tropical Medicine & International Health, 11*(10), 1604–1612.

Deeds, S. M. (2008). Gender, ethnicity, and agency in Latin American history. *Journal of Women's History, 20*(4), 195–202.

DeVault, M. L. (1994). *Feeding the family: The social organization of caring as gendered work.* Chicago, IL: University of Chicago Press.

D'Gregorio, R. P. (2010). *Obstetric violence: A new legal term introduced in Venezuela.* Elsevier.

Di Leonardo, M. (1991). Habits of the cumbered heart: Ethnic community and women's culture as American invented traditions. In J. O'Brien & W. Roseberry (Eds.), *Golden ages, dark ages: Imagining the past in anthropology and history* (pp. 234–252). Berkeley, CA: University of California Press.

Di Leonardo, M., & Lancaster, R. N. (1997). Introduction: Embodied meanings, carnal practices. In R. N. Lancaster & M. Di Leonardo (Eds.), *The Gender/Sexuality Reader.* New York, NY: Routledge.

Diamond, I., & Quinby, L. (1988). *Foucault and feminism: Reflections on resistance.* Boston, MA: Northeastern University Press.

DiGiacomo, S. M. (1992). Metaphor as illness: Postmodern dilemmas in the representation of body, mind and disorder. *Medical Anthropology, 14*(1), 109–137.

Diprose, R. (2005). *The bodies of women: Ethics, embodiment and sexual differences.* New York, NY: Routledge.

Dominguez, V. R. (1992). Invoking culture: The messy side of cultural politics. *South Atlantic Quarterly, 91*(1), 19–42.

Donzelot, J. (1979). *The policing of Families, with a foreword by Gilles Deleuze, translated from the French by Robert Hurley.* New York, NY: Pantheon Books.

Douglas, M. (1966). *Purity and danger: An analysis of the concepts of pollution and taboo.* London: Routledge.

Douglas, M. (1970). *Natural symbols.* New York, NY: Vintage.

Douglas, M. (1992). *Risk and blame: Essays in cultural theory*New York, NY: Routledge.

Douglas, M., & Wildavsky, A. (1983). *Risk and culture: An essay on the selection of technological and environmental dangers.* Univ of California Press.

Dubos, R. (1984). *Women: A feminist perspective.* In J. Freeman (Ed.).

Duggan, L. (2004). *The twilight of equality? Neoliberalism, cultural politics, and the attack on democracy.* Boston, MA: Beacon Press.

Durán, M. (2012). *Medicalización, higienismo y desarrollo social en Chile y Argentina, 1860–1918* (Thesis). Universidad de Santiago de Chile.

Ehrenreich, B., & English, D. (1978). *For her own good: Two centuries of the experts' advice to women.* New York, NY: Anchor.

Ehrlich, P. R. (1968). *The population bomb.* New York, NY: Sierra Club/Ballantine.

Eldredge, J. D., Waitzkin, H., Buchanan, H. S., Teal, J., Iriart, C., Wiley, K., & Tregear, J. (2004). The Latin American social medicine database. *BMC Public Health, 4*(1), 69.

Ellner, S. (1993). The deepening of democracy in a crisis setting: Political reform and the electoral process in Venezuela. *Journal of Interamerican Studies and World Affairs, 35*(4), 1–42.

Ellner, S. (1994). A tolerance worn thin corruption in the age of austerity. *NACLA Report on the Americas, 27*(3), 13–16.

Ellner, S. (2008). *Rethinking Venezuelan politics: Class, conflict, and the Chávez phenomenon.* Boulder, CO: Rienner.

Espinoza, E. (2014). En el camino hacia un nuevo modelo de desarrollo, Estado y sociedad/Toward a new model of development, the state, and society. *Medicina social, 9*(1), 1–12.

Faneite, J., Feo, A., & Toro Merlo, J. (2012). Grado de conocimiento de violencia obstétrica por el personal de salud. *Rev obstet ginecol venez 72*(1), 4–12.

Farmer, P. (1993). *AIDS and accusation: Haiti and the geography of blame.* Berkeley, CA: University of California Press.

Farmer, P. (2001). *Infections and inequalities.* Berkeley, CA: University of California Press.

Featherstone, M., Hepworth, M., & Turner, B. S. (1991). *The body: Social process and cultural theory* (Vol. 7). Thousand Oaks, CA: Sage.

Fee, E. (1989). Venereal disease: The wages of sin? In K. L. Peiss & C. Simmons (Eds.), *Passion and power: Sexuality in history*. Philadelphia: Temple University Press, 1989.

Felitti, K. (2008). La "explosión demográfica" y la planificación familiar a debate: Instituciones, discusiones y propuestas del centro y la periferia. *Revista escuela de historia, 7*(2).

Feo, O. (2003). Reflexiones sobre la globalización y su impacto sobre la salud de los trabajadores y el ambiente. *Ciência & saúde coletiva, 8*(4).

Feo, Ó. (2004). La salud pública en los procesos de reforma y las funciones esenciales de salud pública. *Revista Facultad Nacional de Salud Pública, 22*(99), 61–71.

Feo, Ó. (2008). Las políticas neoliberales y su impacto sobre la formación en salud pública. *Medicina social, 3*(4), 275–284.

Feo, O., & Curcio, P. (2004). La salud en el proceso constituyente venezolano. *Revista Cubana de Salud Pública, 30*(2).

Fernandes, S. (2007). Barrio women and popular politics in Chávez's Venezuela. *Latin American Politics and Society, 49*(3), 97–127.

Fernandes, S. (2010). *Who can stop the drums? Urban social movements in Chávez's Venezuela*. Durham, NC: Duke University Press.

Fernández-Kelly, M. P. (1983). *For we are sold, I and my people: Women and industry in Mexico's frontier*. Albany, NY: SUNY Press.

Finkler, K. (1991). *Physicians at work, patients in pain: biomedical practice and patient response in Mexico*. Boulder, CO: Westview Press.

Finkler, K. (1994). *Women in pain: Gender and morbidity in Mexico*. Philadelphia: University of Pennsylvania Press.

Fisher, S. (1986). *In the patient's best interest: Women and the politics of medical decisions*. Retrieved from https://repository.library.georgetown.edu/handle/10822/811286

Fisher, S., & Todd, A. D. (1983). *The social organization of doctor-patient communication*. Washington, DC: Center for Applied Linguistics.

Foucault, M. (1970). *The order of things: An archaeology of the human sciences*. New York, NY: Vintage.

Foucault, M. (1975). *The birth of the clinic: An archaeology of medical perception*. New York, NY: Vintage.

Foucault, M. (1978). *The history of sexuality: An introduction* (Vol. 1). New York, NY: Vintage.

Foucault, M. (1979). *Discipline and punish: The birth of the prison* (A. Sheridan, Trans.). London: Penguin.

Franco, E. L. (1991). The sexually transmitted disease model for cervical cancer: Incoherent epidemiologic findings and the role of misclassification of Human papillomavirus infection. *Epidemiology*, 98–106.

Frankenberg, R. (1993). Risk: Anthropological and epidemiological narratives of

prevention. *Knowledge, Power, and Practice: The Anthropology of Medicine and Everyday Life*, 219–242.
Franklin, S. (1995). Science as culture, cultures of science. *Annual Review of Anthropology*, 24(1), 163–184.
Fraser, N., & Nicholson, L. (1988). Social criticism without philosophy: An encounter between feminism and postmodernism. *Theory, Culture & Society*, 5(2), 373–394.
Fraser, N., & Nicholson, L. J. (1990). Social criticism without philosophy: An encounter between feminism and postmodernism. In L. J. Nicholson (Ed.), *Feminism/postmodernism* (pp. 19–38). New York, NY: Routledge.
Freeman, J. E. (1979). *Women: A feminist perspective*. Palo Alto, CA: Mayfield.
Freitez, A. (2017, April 11). *Family planning in Venezuela*. Retrieved from http://www.alapop.org/alap/SerieInvestigaciones/InvestigacionesSI1aSi9/DemogTransformations_ParteIII-12.pdf
French, W. E., & Bliss, K. E. (2006). *Gender, sexuality, and power in Latin America since independence*. Lanham, MD: Rowman & Littlefield.
Gaitan, E., Garcia, B. M., & Rawls, W. E. (1990). Sexual behavior, venereal diseases, hygiene practices, and invasive cervical cancer in a high-risk population. *Cancer*, 65380, 386.
Gal, S. (1989). Between speech and silence: The problematics of research on language and gender. *Papers in Pragmatics*, 3(1), 1–38.
Garro, L. C. (1988). Explaining high blood pressure: Variation in knowledge about illness. *American Ethnologist*, 15(1), 98–119.
Gastaldo, D. (1997). Is health education good for you? Re-thinking health education through the. *Foucault, Health and Medicine*, 113.
Giddens, A. (1984). *The constitution of society: Outline of the theory of structuration*. Berkeley, CA: University of California Press.
Gifford, S. M. (1986). The meaning of lumps: A case study of the ambiguities of risk. In *Anthropology and epidemiology* (pp. 213–246). New York, NY: Springer.
Gilman, S. L. (1988). *Disease and representation: Images of illness from madness to AIDS*. Ithaca, NY: Cornell University Press.
Gilman, S. L. (1992). Plague in Germany, 1939/1989: Cultural images of race, space, and disease. In A. Parker, M. Russo, D. Sommer, & P. Yaeger (Eds.), *Nationalisms and sexualities* (pp. 175–200). New York, NY: Routledge.
Ginsburg, F. D., & Tsing, A. L. (1990). *Uncertain terms: Negotiating gender in American culture*. Boston, MA: Beacon Press.
Ginzberg, E. (1991). Access to health care for Hispanics. *JAMA*, 265(2), 238–241.
Giovanella, L., Feo, O., Faria, M., Tobar, S., & others. (2012). *Sistemas de salud en Suramérica: Desafíos para la universalidad la integralidad y la equidad*. ISAGS.
Goffman, E. (1963). *Stigma: Notes on a spoiled identity*.
González, R., & Marino, J. (2001). *Reformas del sistema de salud en Venezuela (1987–1999): Balance y perspectivas*. Santiago de Chile: Naciones Unidas.
Goodman, L. W. (1995). *Lessons of the Venezuelan experience*. Washington, DC: Woodrow Wilson Center Press.

Goodyear-Smith, F., & Buetow, S. (2001). Power issues in the doctor-patient relationship. *Health Care Analysis, 9*(4), 449–462.

Gordon, A., & Ryan, M. (1994). *Body politics: Disease, desire, and the family.* Boulder, CO: Westview Press.

Gordon, D. R. (1988). Tenacious assumptions in Western medicine. In *Biomedicine examined* (pp. 19–56). New York, NY: Springer.

Gordon, D. R., & Lock, M. M. (1988). *Biomedicine examined.* New York, NY: Kluwer Academic.

Gramsci, A. (1971). *Selections from the prison notebooks of Antonio Gramsci* (Q. Hoare & G. Nowell Smith, Eds. and Trans.) International.

Greenhalgh, S. (2008). *Just one child: Science and policy in Deng's China.* Berkeley, CA: University of California Press.

Gregg, J. L. (2003). *Virtually virgins: Sexual strategies and cervical cancer in Recife, Brazil.* Stanford, CA: Stanford University Press.

Grosz, E. A. (1994). *Volatile bodies: Toward a corporeal feminism.* Bloomington, IN: Indiana University Press.

Guy, D. J. (1990). Public health, gender, and private morality: Paid labor and the formation of the body politic in Buenos Aires. *Gender & History, 2*(3), 297–318.

Guy, D. J. (2000). *White slavery and mothers alive and dead: The troubled meeting of sex, gender, public health, and progress in Latin America* (Vol. 5). Lincoln, NE: University of Nebraska Press.

Haggerty, R. A., & Blutstein, H. I. (1993). *Venezuela, a country study.* Headquarters, Dept. of the Army.

Hanmer, L., & Klugman, J. (2016). Exploring women's agency and empowerment in developing countries: Where do we stand? *Feminist Economics, 22*(1), 237–263.

Haraway, D. (1999). The biopolitics of postmodern bodies: Determinations of self in immune system discourse. *Feminist Theory and the Body: A Reader, 1*(1), 203.

Haraway, D. (2013). *Simians, cyborgs, and women: The reinvention of nature.* New York, NY: Routledge.

Haraway, D. (n.d.). Fractured identities. In P. Joyce (Ed.), *Class* (pp. 95–99). New York, NY: Oxford University Press.

Haraway, D. J. (1997). The persistence of vision. In K. Conboy, N. Medina, & S. Stanbury (Eds.), *Writing on the body: Female embodiment and feminist theory* (pp. 283–297). New York, NY: Columbia University Press.

Hardeman, R. R., Medina, E. M., & Kozhimannil, K. B. (2016). Structural racism and supporting black lives—The role of health professionals. *New England Journal of Medicine, 375*(22), 2113–2115.

Harding, S. G. (1991). *Whose science? Whose knowledge? Thinking from women's lives.* Ithaca, NY: Cornell University Press.

Hartmann, C. (2016). Postneoliberal public health care reforms: Neoliberalism, social medicine, and persistent health inequalities in Latin America. *American Journal of Public Health, 106*(12), 2145–2151.

Hawkins, K. A., Rosas, G., & Johnson, M. E. (2011). The *misiones* of the Chávez government. *Venezuela's Bolivarian Democracy*, 186–218.

Hedican, E. J. (2006). Understanding emotional experience in fieldwork: Responding to grief in a northern Aboriginal village. *International Journal of Qualitative Methods*, 5(1), 17–24.

Henslin, J. M., & Biggs, M. A. (1971). Dramaturgical desexualization: The sociology of vaginal examination. In J. M. Henslin (Ed.), *Studies in the sociology of sex*. New York, NY: Appleton-Century-Crofts.

Hernández-Torres, I., Fernández-Ortega, M. A., Irigoyen-Coria, A., & Hernández-Hernández, M. A. (2006). Importancia de la comunicación médico-paciente en medicina familiar. *Archivos en medicina familiar*, 8(2), 137–143.

Herrera Salas, J. M. (2004). Racismo y discurso político en Venezuela. *Revista venezolana de economía y ciencias sociales*, 10(2).

Herrera Salas, J. M. (2005). *Economía política del racismo en Venezuela*.

Herrero, R., Brinton, L. A., Reeves, W. C., Brenes, M. M., Tenorio, F., de Britton, R. C., ... Rawls, W. E. (1990). Sexual behavior, venereal diseases, hygiene practices, and invasive cervical cancer in a high-risk population. *Cancer*, 65(2), 380.

Hill Collins, P. (2002). *Black feminist thought: Knowledge, consciousness, and the politics of empowerment*. New York, NY: Routledge.

Hollander, J. A., & Einwohner, R. L. (2004). Conceptualizing resistance. In *Sociological forum* (Vol. 19, pp. 533–554). New York, NY: Springer.

Holloway, K. F. (2011). *Private bodies, public texts: Race, gender, and a cultural bioethics*. Durham, NC: Duke University Press.

Holston, J. (1999). *Cities and citizenship*. Durham, NC: Duke University Press.

Holston, J. (2008). *Insurgent citizenship: Disjunctions of democracy and modernity in Brazil*. Princeton, NJ: Princeton University Press.

Homedes, N., & Ugalde, A. (2005). Las reformas de salud neoliberales en América Latina: Una visión crítica a través de dos estudios de caso. *Rev panam salud pública*, 17(3), 211.

Homedes, N., & Ugalde, A. (2005). Why neoliberal health reforms have failed in Latin America. *Health Policy*, 71(1), 83–96.

Hsiung, P.-C. (1996). Between bosses and workers: The dilemma of a keen observer and a vocal feminist. In D. L. Wolf (Ed.), *Feminist dilemmas in fieldwork* (pp. 122–137). Boulder, CO: Westview Press.

Htun, M. (2003). *Sex and the state: Abortion, divorce, and the family under Latin American dictatorships and democracies*. Cambridge: Cambridge University Press.

Hunt, L. M. (1994). Practicing oncology in provincial Mexico: A narrative analysis. *Social Science & Medicine*, 38(6), 843–853.

Hunt, L. M., Browner, C. H., & Jordan, B. (1990). Hypoglycemia: Portrait of an illness construct in everyday use. *Medical Anthropology Quarterly*, 191–210.

Inhorn, M. C., & Wentzell, E. A. (2012). *Medical anthropology at the intersections: Histories, activisms, and futures*. Durham, NC: Duke University Press.

Irwin, S., & Jordan, B. (1987). Knowledge, practice, and power: Court-ordered Cesarean sections. *Medical Anthropology Quarterly, 1*(3), 319–334.

Jacobus, M., Keller, E. F., & Shuttleworth, S. (2013). *Body/politics: Women and the discourses of science.* New York, NY: Routledge.

Jayant, K., Notani, P. N., Gadre, V. V., Gulati, S. S., & Shah, P. R. (1987). Personal hygiene in groups with varied cervical cancer rates: A study in Bombay. *Indian Journal of Cancer, 24*(1), 47.

Jolly, M. (2004). Embodied states: Familial and national geneologies in Asia and the Pacific. In *Borders of being: Citizenship, fertility, and sexuality in Asia and the Pacific.* Ann Arbor, MI: University of Michigan Press.

Jolly, M., & Ram, K. (2004). *Borders of being: Citizenship, fertility, and sexuality in Asia and the Pacific.* Ann Arbor, MI: University of Michigan Press.

Jordan, B. (1989). Cosmopolitical obstetrics: Some insights from the training of traditional midwives. *Social Science & Medicine, 28*(9), 925–937.

Jordan, B. (1997). Authoritative knowledge and its construction. *Childbirth and Authoritative Knowledge: Cross-Cultural Perspectives,* 55–79.

Jorgensen, D. L. (n.d.). *Participant observation: A methodology for human studies.* Newbury Park, CA: Sage.

Kabeer, N. (2008). *Paid work, women's empowerment and gender justice: Critical pathways of social change.* Retrieved from https://www.mysciencework.com/publication/show/ed3d171779a989f6225624f6d1c0ff38

Kapsalis, T. (1997). *Performing gynecology from both ends of the speculum: Public privates.* Durham, NC: Duke University Press.

Kaufert, P., & O'Neil, J. (1993). Analysis of a dialogue on risks in childbirth: Clinicians, epidemiologists, and Inuit women. *Knowledge, Power and Practice: The Anthropology of Medicine in Everyday Life,* 32–54.

Keller, E. F. (1982). Feminism and science. *Signs: Journal of Women in Culture and Society, 7*(3), 589–602.

Kingsbury, D. V. (2016). From populism to protagonism (and back?) in Bolivarian Venezuela: Rethinking Ernesto Laclau on populist reason. *Journal of Latin American Cultural Studies, 25*(4), 495–514.

Kingstone, P. (2011). *The political economy of Latin America: Reflections on neoliberalism and development.* New York, NY: Routledge.

Kleinman, A. (1980). *Patients and healers in the context of culture: An exploration of the borderland between anthropology, medicine, and psychiatry* (Vol. 3). Berkeley, CA: University of California Press.

Kleinman, A. (1988). *The illness narratives: Suffering, healing, and the human condition.* New York, NY: Basic Books.

Krieger, N. (2003). *Latin American social medicine: The quest for social justice and public health.* American Public Health Association.

Kuipers, J. C. (1989). "Medical discourse" in anthropological context: Views of language and power. *Medical Anthropology Quarterly, 3*(2), 99–123.

Lancaster, R. N., & Di Leonardo, M. (1997). *The gender/sexuality reader: Culture, history, political economy.* New York, NY: Routledge.

Laurell, A. C. (1982). La salud-enfermedad como proceso social. *Revista latinoamericana de salud, 2*(1), 7–25.

Laurell, A. C. (2007). Interview with Dr. Asa Cristina Laurell. *Social Medicine, 2*(1), 46–55.

Laurell, A. C., Merchan-Hamann, E., & Tajer, D. (2000). Globalización y reforma del Estado. In *Saúde, equidade e gênero: Um desafio para as políticas públicas* (pp. 35–59). UnB. Retrieved from http://bases.bireme.br/cgi-bin/wxislind.exe/iah/online/?IsisScript=iah/iah.xis&src=google&base=LILACS&lang=p&nextAction=lnk&exprSearch=274964&indexSearch=ID

Lazarus, E. S. (1988). Theoretical considerations for the study of the doctor-patient relationship: Implications of a perinatal study. *Medical Anthropology Quarterly, 2*(1), 34–58.

Leeds, A. (1994). *Cities, classes, and the social order.* Ithaca, NY: Cornell University Press.

Levine, D., & Crisp, B. (1995). Legitimacy, governability, and reform in Venezuela. In *Lessons of the Venezuelan experience* (pp. 223–251). Baltimore, MD: Johns Hopkins University Press.

Levine, D. H. (1993). *Constructing culture and power in Latin America.* Ann Arbor, MI: University of Michigan Press.

Levine-Rasky, C. (2012). *Working through whiteness: International perspectives.* Albany, NY: SUNY Press.

Lewis, O. (1971). The culture of poverty. *Poor Americans: How the White Poor Live,* 20–26.

Lieberman, M. D. (2013). *Social: Why our brains are wired to connect.* New York, NY: Oxford University Press.

Linde-Laursen, A. (1993). The nationalization of trivialities: How cleaning becomes an identity marker in the encounter of Swedes and Danes. *Ethnos, 58*(3–4), 275–293.

Lindenbaum, S., & Lock, M. (1993). *Knowledge, power and practice: The anthropology of medicine and everyday life.* Berkeley, CA: University of California Press.

Lingis, A. (2014). *Foreign bodies.* New York, NY: Routledge.

Lock, M. (1993). Cultivating the body: Anthropology and epistemologies of bodily practice and knowledge. *Annual Review of Anthropology, 22*(1), 133–155.

Lock, M., & Gordon, D. (2012). *Biomedicine examined* (Vol. 13). Boston, MA: Kluwer Academic.

López, R. N. (2014). *A history of family planning in twentieth-century Peru.* Chapel Hill, NC: University of North Carolina Press.

Lupton, D. (1994). *Medicine as culture: Illness, disease and the body in Western societies.* London: Sage.

Lupton, D. (1995). *The imperative of health: Public health and the regulated body* (Vol. 90). London: Sage.

Lutz, C., & Collins, J. (1997). The color of sex: Postwar photographic histories of race and gender in *National Geographic* magazine. *The Gender Sexuality Reader: Culture, History, Political Economy*, 291–308.

MacGregor, F. E., Correa, M. R., & Walter, S. (1993). Regional synthesis on violence and pacification. In *Violence in the Andean region*. Assen, The Netherlands: Van Gorcum.

MacKinnon, C. A. (1982). Feminism, Marxism, method, and the state: An agenda for theory. *Signs: Journal of Women in Culture and Society*, 7(3), 515–544.

MacKinnon, C. A. (1983). Feminism, Marxism, method, and the state: Toward feminist jurisprudence. *Signs: Journal of Women in Culture and Society*, 8(4), 635–658.

Mahmood, Q., & Muntaner, C. (2013). Politics, class actors, and health sector reform in Brazil and Venezuela. *Global Health Promotion*, 20(1), 59–67.

Mahmood, Q., Muntaner, C., del Valle Mata León, R., & Perdomo, R. E. (2012). Popular participation in Venezuela's Barrio Adentro health reform. *Globalizations*, 9(6), 815–833.

Malkki, L. H. (1995). Refugees and exile: From "refugee studies" to the national order of things. *Annual Review of Anthropology*, 24(1), 495–523.

Mani, L. (1987). Contentious traditions: The debate on sati in colonial India. *Cultural Critique*, (7), 119–156.

Mani, L. (1990). Contentious traditions: The debate on sati in colonial India, 1780–1833.

Martin, E. (1987). *The woman in the body: A cultural analysis of reproduction*. Boston, MA: Beacon Press.

Martin, E. (1990). Science and women's bodies: Forms of anthropological knowledge. *Body/Politics: Women and the Discourses of Science*, 69–82.

Martínez, I. L. (2002). *Danzas nacionalistas*: The representation of history through folkloric dance in Venezuela. *Critique of Anthropology*, 22(3), 257–282.

Martinez, R. C., Chavez, L. R., & Hubbell, F. A. (1997). Purity and passion: Risk and morality in Latina immigrants' and physicians' beliefs about cervical cancer. *Medical Anthropology*, 17(4), 337–362.

Martínez, R. G. (2005). "What's wrong with me?": Cervical cancer in Venezuela—living in the borderlands of health, disease, and illness. *Social Science & Medicine*, 61(4), 797–808.

McKinstry, B. (1992). Paternalism and the doctor-patient relationship in general practice. *Br J Gen Pract* 42(361), 340–342.

McMullin, J. M., Chavez, L. R., & Hubbell, F. A. (1994). Knowledge, power and experience: Variation in physicians' perceptions of breast cancer risk factors. *Medical Anthropology*, 16(1–4), 295–317.

Mead, N., & Bower, P. (2000). Patient-centeredness: A conceptual framework and review of the empirical literature. *Social Science & Medicine*, 51(7), 1087–1110.

Menéndez, E. (1988). Modelo médico hegemónico y atención primaria. *Segundas Jornadas de Atención Primaria de la Salud*, 30, 451–464.

Menéndez, E. L. (1981). *Poder, estratificación y salud: Análisis de las condiciones sociales y económicas de la enfermedad en Yucatán* (Vol. 13). CIESAS. Retrieved from https://books.google.com/books?hl=en&lr=&id=3fXzqhEFY-IC&oi=fnd&pg=PA11&dq=Poder+estratificion+y+salud&ots=taVi-xj5tE&sig=fkicym5iSoxkngWgIkdD3OpXXGs

Menéndez, E. L. (1997). Antropología médica: Espacios propios, campos de nadie. *Nueva Antropología, 51*, 83–103.

Menendez, E. L. (2005). El modelo médico y la salud de los trabajadores. *Salud colectiva, 1*(1), 9–32.

Menéndez, E. L. (1983). *Hacia una práctica médica alternativa: Hegemonía y autoatención (gestión) en salud* (Vol. 86). Secretaria de Educacion Publica. Retrieved from http://bases.bireme.br/cgi-bin/wxislind.exe/iah/online/?IsisScript=iah/iah.xis&src=google&base=REPIDISCA&lang=p&nextAction=lnk&exprSearch=134020&indexSearch=ID

Menéndez, E. (1990). *Morir de alcohol: Saber y hegemonía médica*. Retrieved from http://www.sidalc.net/cgi-bin/wxis.exe/?IsisScript=AGRIUAN.xis&method=post&formato=2&cantidad=1&expresion=mfn=029970

Ministerio de Sanidad y Asistencia Social, Dirección de Oncología (MSAS). (1987a). *Programa de Control del Cancer Cervicouterino: Manual de normas y procedimientos*. Ministerio de Sanidad y Asistencia Social.

Ministerio de Sanidad y Asistencia Social, Dirección de Oncología (MSAS). (1987b). *Taller Nacional de evaluación e integración del Programa Control de Cancer Cervico-Uterino*. Schering AG.

Ministerio de Sanidad y Asistencia Social, Dirección de Oncología (MSAS). (1991). *Estrategias de comunicación, educación y participación de la mujer para la prevención del cancer de cuello uterino*. LITROBRIT.

Misión Verdad. (2017, December 4). *Four effects of the blockade against Venezuela*. Retrieved from https://venezuelanalysis.com/analysis/13529

Mohideen, R. (2005). Challenges to economic fundamentalism: Venezuelan Women and the "Bolivarian Revolution." *Women in Action—Rome then Manila, 2*, 66.

Montañez, L. (1993). *El racismo oculto de una sociedad no racista*. Fondo Editorial Tropykos.

Montañez, L., Sánchez, L. M., & Salinas, J. (2002). Proyecto imagen del negro en la Venezuela de hoy: Una reflexión metodológica. *Revista interamericana de psicología, 37*(1), 31–49.

Montenegro, R. A., & Stephens, C. (2006). Indigenous health in Latin America and the Caribbean. *Lancet, 367*(9525), 1859–1869.

Moore, P., Gomez, G., Kurtz, S., & Vargas, A. (2010). La comunicación médico paciente: ¿Cuáles son las habilidades efectivas? *Revista médica de Chile, 138*(8), 1047–1054.

Moreno, M. (2016). *El país posible: La marginalidad y los barrios marginales en Venezuela, la necesidad y posibilidad de erradicarlos* (Kindle ed.). Retrieved from https://www.amazon.com/pa%C3%ADs-posible-marginalidad-posibilidad-erradicarlos-ebook/dp/B01MRMV2X0/ref=sr_1_1?ie=UTF8&qid=1513901128&sr=8-1&keywords=Miguel+moreno+El+pais+posible

Morgan, L. M., & Roberts, E. F. (2012). Reproductive governance in Latin America. *Anthropology & Medicine*, *19*(2), 241–254.

Morris, D. L., Lusero, G. T., Joyce, E. V., Hannigan, E. V., & Tucker, E. R. (1989). Cervical cancer, a major killer of Hispanic women: Implications for health education. *Health Education*, *20*(5), 23–28.

Motta, S. C. (2013). "We are the ones we have been waiting for": The feminization of resistance in Venezuela. *Latin American Perspectives*, *40*(4), 35–54.

Munn, N. D. (1992). The cultural anthropology of time: A critical essay. *Annual Review of Anthropology*, *21*(1), 93–123.

Muntaner, C., Armada, F., Chung, H., Mata, R., Williams-Brennan, L., & Benach, J. (2008). Barrio Adentro en Venezuela: Democracia participativa, cooperación sur-sur y salud para todos. *Med Social*, *3*, 306–322.

Muntaner, C., Salazar, R. M. G., Benach, J., & Armada, F. (2006). Venezuela's Barrio Adentro: An alternative to neoliberalism in health care. *International Journal of Health Services*, *36*(4), 803–811.

Muntaner, C., Salazar, R. M. G., Rueda, S., & Armada, F. (2006). Challenging the neoliberal trend: The Venezuelan health care reform alternative. *Canadian Journal of Public Health*, *97*(6), 119.

Murillo, R., Herrero, R., Sierra, M. S., & Forman, D. (2016). Cervical cancer in Central and South America: Burden of disease and status of disease control. *Cancer Epidemiology*, *44*, S121–S130.

Murray, P. S. (Ed.). (2014). *Women and gender in modern Latin America: Historical sources and interpretations*. New York, NY: Routledge.

Núñez-Troconis, J., Delgado, M., González, J., Mindiola, R., Velásquez, J., Conde, B., ... Munroe, D. J. (2009). Prevalence and risk factors of human papillomavirus infection in asymptomatic women in a Venezuelan urban area. *Investigacion clínica*, *50*(2). Retrieved from http://200.74.222.178/index.php/investigacion/article/view/10927

Núñez-Troconis, J., Velásquez, J., Mindiola, R., & Munroe, D. (2008). Educational level and cervical cancer screening programs in a Venezuelan urban area. *Investigación clínica*, *49*(3). Retrieved from http://www.produccioncientificaluz.org/index.php/investigacion/article/view/10857

Paluzzi, J. E., & Arribas-García, F. (2008). Salud para todos: Alma Ata está sana ya salvo en Venezuela. *Medicina Social*, *3*(4), 270–274.

Pappas, G. (1990). Some implications for the study of the doctor-patient interaction: Power, structure, and agency in the works of Howard Waitzkin and Arthur Kleinman. *Social Science & Medicine*, *30*(2), 199–204.

Parker, D. (2005). Chávez and the search for an alternative to neoliberalism. *Latin American Perspectives*, *32*(2), 39–50.

Patton, C. (1992). From nation to family: Containing African AIDS. In A. Parker, M. Russo, D. Sommer, & P. Yaeger (Eds.), *Nationalisms and sexualities* (pp. 218–234). New York, NY: Routledge.

Peiss, K. L., & Simmons, C. (1989). *Passion and power: Sexuality in history.* Philadelphia, PA: Temple University Press.

Pérez D'Gregorio, R. (2010). Obstetric violence: A new legal term introduced in Venezuela. *International Journal of Gynaecology and Obstetrics, 111*(3), 201.

Pérez, O. J. (2013). The basis of support for Hugo Chavez: Measuring the determinants of presidential job approval in Venezuela. *Latin Americanist, 57*(2), 59–84.

Perlman, J. E. (2005). The myth of marginality revisited: 9. The case of favelas in Rio de Janeiro, 1969–2003. In M. Hanley, B. A. Ruble, & J. S. Tulchin (Eds.), *Becoming global and the new poverty of cities.* Washington, DC: Woodrow Wilson International Center for Scholars. Retrieved from https://www.wilsoncenter.org/sites/default/files/BecomingGlobal.pdf#page=15

Piotrow, P. T. (1973). *Population and family planning in Latin America* (Report No. 17). Retrieved from http://eric.ed.gov/?id=ED103208

Piper Mooney, J. P. (2014). The new gospel of family planning: Case of Chile, 1960s. In P. S. Murray, *Women and gender in modern Latin America: Historical sources and interpretations* (pp. 300–303). New York, NY: Routledge.

Polanco, J. D. (1993). La investigación sobre salud en Venezuela: El papel de las ciencias sociales. *Cuadernos del CENDES,* (24), 71–96.

Posner, T. (1991). What's in a smear? Cervical screening, medical signs and metaphors. *Science as Culture, 2*(2), 167–187.

Posner, T., & Vessey, M. P. (1988). *Prevention of cervical cancer: The patient's view.* London: King's Fund.

Povinelli, Elizabeth A. (n.d.). Sex acts and sovereignty: Race and sexuality in the construction of the Australian nation. In R. N. Lancaster & M. Di Leonardo (Eds.), *The gender sexuality reader: Culture, history, political economy.*

Quinby, L., & Diamond, I. (1988). *Feminism and Foucault: Reflections on resistance.* Boston, MA: Northeastern University Press.

Ramazanoglu, C. (1993). *Up against Foucault: Explorations of some tensions between Foucault and feminism.* New York, NY: Routledge.

Reeves, W. C., Brinton, L. A., García, M., Brenes, M. M., Herrero, R., Gaitán, E., ... Rawls, W. E. (1989). Human papillomavirus infection and cervical cancer in Latin America. *New England Journal of Medicine, 320*(22), 1437–1441.

Rial y Costas, G. (2011). Spaces of insecurity? The "favelas" of Rio de Janeiro between stigmatization and glorification. *Iberoamericana, 11*(41), 115–128.

Rivkin-Fish, M., Pigg, S. L., & Adams, V. (2005). *Sex in development: Science, sexuality, and morality in global perspective.* Durham, NC: Duke University Press.

Roberts, E. F. (2012). *God's laboratory: Assisted reproduction in the Andes.* Berkeley, CA: University of California Press.

Rodríguez de Sánchez, H., & Surga Ruiz, B. (2000). Cáncer de cuello uterino en el Registro Regional de Tumores del Estado Sucre en el período 1979–1993. *Rev. obstet. ginecol. Venezuela, 60*(1), 31–4.

Rodriguez García, M., Heerma van Voss, A. F., & van Nederveen Meerkerk, E. (2017).

Selling sex in the city: A global history of prostitution, 1600s–2000s. *Studies in Global Social History, 31.*

Rodriguez, J. (2006). *Civilizing Argentina: Science, medicine, and the modern state.* Chapel Hill, NC: University of North Carolina Press.

Rosaldo, R. (1989). *Culture & truth: The remaking of social analysis: with a new introduction.* Boston, MA: Beacon Press.

Roseberry, W. (1989). *Anthropologies and histories: Essays in culture, history, and political economy.* New Brunswick, NJ: Rutgers University Press.

Rosner, D. (1989). Losing patients: Culture, consumption and popular ideas about science and medicine. *Reviews in American History,* (6), 241.

Rotkin, I. D. (1967). Adolescent coitus and cervical cancer: Associations of related events with increased risk. *Cancer Research, 27*(4), 603–617.

Rubel, A. J., & Garro, L. C. (1992). Social and cultural factors in the successful control of tuberculosis. *Public Health Reports, 107*(6), 626.

Rupesinghe, K., & Correa, M. R. (1994). *The culture of violence* (Vol. 81). Tokyo: United Nations University Press.

Sahasrabuddhe, V. V., Parham, G. P., Mwanahamuntu, M. H., & Vermund, S. H. (2012). Cervical cancer prevention in low-and middle-income countries: feasible, affordable, essential. *Cancer Prevention Research, 5*(1), 11–17.

Salas, M. T. (2009). *The enduring legacy: Oil, culture, and society in Venezuela.* Durham, NC: Duke University Press.

Salas, Y. (2005). La dramatización social y política del imaginario popular: El fenómeno del bolivarismo en Venezuela. In *Cultura, política y sociedad: Perspectivas latinoamericanas.* CLACSO, Consejo Latinoamericano de Ciencias Sociales. Retrieved from http://bibliotecavirtual.clacso.org.ar/clacso/gt/20100912062306/12Salas.pdf

Scarry, E. (1985). *The body in pain: The making and unmaking of the world.* New York, NY: Oxford University Press.

Schein, L. (1994). The consumption of color and the politics of white skin in post-Mao China. *Social Text,* (41), 141–164.

Scheper-Hughes, N. (1993). *Death without weeping: The violence of everyday life in Brazil.* Berkeley, CA: University of California Press.

Scheper-Hughes, N., & Lock, M. M. (1987). The mindful body: A prolegomenon to future work in medical anthropology. *Medical Anthropology Quarterly, 1*(1), 6–41.

Scott, J. C. (1985). *Weapons of the weak: Everyday forms of resistance.* New Haven, CT: Yale University Press.

Scott, J. W. (1995). Language, gender, and working-class history. In P. Joyce (Ed.), *Class* (pp. 154–161). New York, NY: Oxford University Press.

Seltzer, J., & Gomez, F. (1998). Family planning and population programs in Colombia 1965 to 1997. *Population Technical Assistance Project (POPTECH) Report,* (97–114), 062.

Sen, A. (1985). Well-being, agency and freedom: The Dewey lectures 1984. *Journal of Philosophy, 82*(4), 169–221.

Sheehan, E. (1997). Victorian clitoridectomy: Isaac Baker Brown and his harmless operative procedure. In R. N. Lancaster & M. Di Leonardo (Eds.), *The gender sexuality reader* (pp. 325–334). New York, NY: Routledge.

Shilling, C. (1993). *The body and social theory.* Newbury Park, CA: Sage.

Simmonds, A. (2014, July 16). Many women scientists sexually harassed during fieldwork. *Nature*. Retrieved from http://www.nature.com/news/many-women-scientists-sexually-harassed-during-fieldwork-1.15571

Singer, L. (1993). *Erotic welfare: Sexual theory and politics in the age of epidemic.* New York, NY: Routledge, Chapman, and Hall.

Smart, C. (1992). *Regulating womanhood: Historical essays on marriage, motherhood and sexuality.* New York, NY: Routledge.

Smedley, B. D., Stith, A. Y., & Nelson, A. R. (2003). *Patient-provider communication: The effect of race and ethnicity on process and outcomes of healthcare.* Washington, DC: National Academies Press. Retrieved from https://www.ncbi.nlm.nih.gov/books/NBK220354/

Smilde, D., & Hellinger, D. (2011). *Venezuela's Bolivarian democracy: Participation, politics, and culture under Chávez.* Durham, NC: Duke University Press.

Smith, L., & Kleinman, A. (2010). Emotional engagements: Acknowledgement, advocacy, and direct action. In *Emotions in the field: The psychology and anthropology of fieldwork experience* (pp. 171–90). Stanford, CA: Stanford University Press.

Socorro, M. (2010, May 17). Entrevista con Michaelle Ascensio. Retrieved from http://milagrossocorro.com/2010/05/entrevista-con-michaelle-ascensio/

Somerville, S. (1997). Scientific racism and the emergence of the homosexual body. In *The gender sexuality reader* (pp. 325–334). New York, NY: Routledge.

Spivak, G. C. (1990). *The post-colonial critic: Interviews, strategies, dialogues.* New York, NY: Routledge.

Stacey, J. (1988). Can there be a feminist ethnography? In *Women's Studies International Forum* (Vol. 11, pp. 21–27). Elsevier. Retrieved from http://www.sciencedirect.com/science/article/pii/0277539588900040

Stallybrass, P., & White, A. (1986). *The politics and poetics of transgression.* Ithaca, NY: Cornell University Press.

Stocking, G. W. (1968). *Race, culture, and evolution: Essays in the history of anthropology.* Chicago, IL: University of Chicago Press.

Stoler, A. L. (1996). Carnal knowledge and imperial power: Gender, race, and morality in colonial Asia. *Feminism and History*, 209–266.

Stoler, A. L. (1997). Making empire respectable: The politics of race and sexual morality in twentieth-century colonial cultures. *Cultural Politics*, *11*, 344–373.

Stout, D. (2006, September 20). Chávez calls Bush "the devil" in UN speech. *New York Times*. Retrieved from http://www.nytimes.com/2006/09/20/world/americas/20cnd-chavez.html

Strathern, M. (1987). An awkward relationship: The case of feminism and anthropology. *Signs: Journal of Women in Culture and Society*, *12*(2), 276–292.

Sturma, M. (1988). Public health and sexual morality: Venereal disease in World War II Australia. *Signs: Journal of Women in Culture and Society, 13*(4), 725–740.

Sylvia, C., & Nikki, C. (2003). *Gender in Latin America.* New Brunswick, NJ: Rutgers University Press.

Tablante, L. (2006). La pobreza como tema político y mediático en Venezuela. *Cahiers des Amériques Latines,* (53), 117–146.

Telesur. (2015, November 18). The US role in the failed attempt to overthrow Hugo Chavez. *Telesur.* Retrieved from https://www.telesurtv.net/english/analysis/The-US-Role-in-the-Failed-Attempt-to-Overthrow-Hugo-Chávez-20151118-0014.html

Tesh, S. N. (1988). *Hidden arguments: Political ideology and disease prevention policy.* New Brunswick, NJ: Rutgers University Press.

Todd, A. D. (1989). *Intimate adversaries: Cultural conflict between doctors and women patients.* Retrieved from https://repository.library.georgetown.edu/handle/10822/828188

Treichler, P. (1992). AIDS and HIV infection in the third world: a first world chronicle. *AIDS: The Making of a Chronic Disease,* 376–412.

Turner, B. S. (1984). *The body and society: Explorations in social theory.* New York, NY: Blackwell.

Turner, B. S. (1987). *Medical power and social knowledge.* Beverly Hills, CA: Sage.

Turner, B. S. (1992). *Regulating bodies: Essays in medical sociology.* New York, NY: Routledge.

Urbaneja, M. (1991). *Privatizacion en el sector salud en Venezuela.* Caracas: CENDES.

Valdivieso, Elisa Alejandra. (2017). *Patriarcado y salud sexual y/o reproductiva en Venezuela.* Retrieved from http://actacientifica.servicioit.cl/biblioteca/pn/PN47/P_EValdiviesoIde.pdf

Valverde, M. (1992). Representing childhood: The multiple fathers of the Dionne quintuplets. In C. Smart (Ed.), *Regulating womanhood* (pp. 119–147). New York, NY: Routledge.

Vaughan, M. (1991). *Curing their ills: Colonial power and African illness.* Stanford, CA: Stanford University Press.

Velasco, A. (2011). "We are still rebels": The challenge of popular history in Bolivarian Venezuela. In D. Smilde & D. Hellinger (Eds.), *Venezuela's Bolivarian democracy: Participation, politics, and culture under Chavez* (pp. 157–85). Durham, NC: Duke University Press.

Velasco, A. (2015). *Barrio rising: Urban popular politics and the making of modern Venezuela.* Berkeley, CA: University of California Press.

Wailoo, K. (2006). Stigma, race, and disease in 20th century America. *Lancet, 367*(9509), 531–533.

Wailoo, K., Livingston, J., Epstein, S., & Aronowitz, R. (2010). *Three shots at prevention: The HPV Vaccine and the Politics of Medicine's Simple Solutions.* Baltimore, MD: Johns Hopkins University Press.

Wailoo, K., Nelson, A., & Lee, C. (2012). *Genetics and the unsettled past: The collision of DNA, race, and history*. New Brunswick, NJ: Rutgers University Press.

Waitzkin, H. (1991). *The politics of medical encounters: How patients and doctors deal with social problems*. New Haven, CT: Yale University Press.

Waitzkin, H., Iriart, C., Estrada, A., & Lamadrid, S. (2001a). Social medicine in Latin America: Productivity and dangers facing the major national groups. *Lancet, 358*(9278), 315–323.

Waitzkin, H., Iriart, C., Estrada, A., & Lamadrid, S. (2001b). Social medicine then and now: lessons from Latin America. *American Journal of Public Health, 91*(10), 1592–1601.

Waitzkin, H., & Jasso-Aguilar, R. (2015). Empire, health, and health care: Perspectives at the end of empire as we have known it. *Annual Review of Sociology, 41*, 271–290.

Weyland, K., Madrid, R. L., & Hunter, W. (2010). *Leftist governments in Latin America: Successes and shortcomings*. Cambridge: Cambridge University Press.

Whitehead, J. (1995). Bodies clean and unclean: Prostitution, sanitary legislation, and respectable femininity in colonial North India. *Gender & History, 7*(1), 41–63.

Wiesenfeld, E. (1997a). Construction of the meaning of a barrio house: The case of a Caracas barrio. *Environment and Behavior, 29*(1), 34–63.

Wiesenfeld, E. (1997b). From individual need to community consciousness: The dialectics between land appropriation and eviction threat (a case study of a Venezuelan "barrio"). *Environment and Behavior, 29*(2), 198–212.

Wolf, D. L. (1996). *Feminist dilemmas in fieldwork*. Boulder, CO: Westview Press. Retrieved from https://philpapers.org/rec/WOLFDI

Wood, K., Jewkes, R., & Abrahams, N. (1997). Cleaning the womb: Constructions of cervical screening and womb cancer among rural black women in South Africa. *Social Science & Medicine, 45*(2), 283–294.

World Health Organization. (1978). *Declaration of Alma-Ata: Internal Conference on Primary Health care*, Alma Ata, Soviet Union, 6–12. Retrieved from http://www.who.int/publications/almaata_declaration_en.pdf

World Health Organization. (2013). *Cancer in the Americas, country profiles 2013*. Washington, DC: Pan-American Health Organization.

Wright, P., & Treacher, A. (1982). *The problem of medical knowledge: Examining the social construction of medicine*. Edinburgh: Edinburgh University Press.

Wright, W. R. (1993). *Café con leche: Race, class, and national image in Venezuela*. Austin, TX: University of Texas Press.

Young, K. (1989). Disembodiment: The phenomenology of the body in medical examinations. *Semiotica, 73*(1–2), 43–66.

Zavella, P. (1996). Feminist insider dilemmas: Constructing ethnic identity with "Chicana" informants. In D. L. Wolf (Ed.), *Feminist dilemmas in fieldwork* (pp. 138–159). Boulder, CO: Westview Press.

Zola, I. K. (1972). Medicine as an institution of social control. *Sociological Review, 20*(4), 487–504.

Zola, I. K. (1985). Structural constraints in the doctor-patient relationship: The case of non-compliance. In L. Eisenber & A. Kleinman (Eds.), *The relevance of social science for medicine* (pp. 241–252). Dordrecht: Reidel. Retrieved from http://link.springer.com/chapter/10.1007/978-94-009-8379-3_11

Zúquete, J. P. (2008). The missionary politics of Hugo Chávez. *Latin American Politics and Society, 50*(1), 91–121.

Index

Page locators in italics refer to figures and tables

"7,500 Orphans Due to Cervical Cancer" (Ott), 222
23 de Enero (January 23) barrio, 102

aboriginal, as term, 75
abortion, 89, 90, 122, 167–68
The Abortion (film), 88–89
activism: agency and, 185–86; in barrios and favelas, 92–93, 102–3, 185–86; Bolivarian Revolution, 5, 9, 10, 11, 102, 185
Africa: AIDS discourse, 121–22
agency, 168, 185–211, 236; in barrios, 102–3, 185–86; defined, 186; listening in on conversations, 189, 198–200; patient feelings about treatment by doctor, 200–211; questions, concerns, and other ways of knowing, 187–200; reading bodies, 196–200; subtle actions, 186–87; theoretical perspectives, 209; well-being and, 186, 210
AIDS/HIV, discourse of, 12, 13, 57, 121–22
Allende, Salvador, 30

Anderson, Benedict, 62, 107, 117
Anderson, Warwick, 64
anthropology, body as project of, 63–65
anxiety, 47, 163, 167, 174–75, 180; lack of diagnostic clarity, 47, 189–94; middle- and upper-class, 1–2, 214–15; "nervousness," 159–61
appointments, 133–34, 159, 174–75, 243n5
Argentina, 86–87, 211
Ascencio, Michaelle, 27–28
Association for the Protection of the Family (APROFA), Chile, 88
"at risk" populations, 10, 21, 63, 96, 118, 123, 125
austerity, neoliberal, 2–3, 9, 32, 100–101, 235; increase in cervical cancer and, 218–19
Australian "aboriginals," 95
authoritative knowledge, 162
Auyero, Javier, 40, 158, 211

"backwardness," 4, 48, 60–62, 97, 99, 109, 235
bank collapse, 7

barrios, 2, 9, 90, 92–93, 212; 23 de Enero (January 23) barrio ("El 23"), 102; agency in, 102–3; community in, 103–7; disease and violence attributed to, 2, 21, 99, 100–101; lack of addresses, 39; locating lawlessness and disorder, 100–101; otherness attributed to, 95, 97, 98, 101; political mobilization, 102–3; psychosocial profile by physician, 94–96; rural-urban hybridity, 96–98; as self-contained, 98–99; as "unhealthy," 91, 95–96, 104, 107

"Barrio Women and Popular Politics in Chávez's Venezuela" (Fernandes), 103

Barthes, Roland, 178

Biggs, M. A., 155

biology, control through, 63–64

biomedicine, 13–14, 75; materiality, 156; mind/body distinction, 154, 164; taken-for-granted assumptions, 145

biopsies, 147, 150, 151, 162–63; cone, 136, 191, 195

birth control, 82–83, 88–89

The Birth of the Clinic (Foucault), 143

body, 13–14; as anthropological project, 63–65; classification of, 184, 229; colonial discourse, 63–64, 68; disciplining of patient, 132–34, 174; on display during examination, 143–46; "docile," 132, 143; machine metaphor, 154; marginalization of women professionals, 183–84; mind/body distinction, 154, 164; reading body language, 196–200; as symbolic form, 63

Bolivar, A., 26

Bolívar, Símon, 216

Bolivarian democracy, 216, 230–31, 233, 234

Bolivarian Revolution, 5, 9, 10, 11, 102, 185

Bolivia, 32

Bonnet, Alastair, 114

Bordo, Susan, 132, 169–70

Bourdieu, P., 132, 183, 184, 227

Brandt, A. M., 57

Brazil, 92, 98, 126, 133

Breilh, Jaime, 32

Briggs, Charles, 29, 30–31, 107–8, 217, 218, 223, 232–33, 236

Buenos Aires, Argentina, 86–87

Burke, T., 58

Bush, George W., 214

Butler, J., 119, 156

café con leche ideology, 26–28, 114, *115*

Caldera, Rafael, 7, 103, 111

caloric intake, 8–9

Campíns, Luis Herrera, 8

capitalist order, 88

Capote, Luis, 219–21

Capriles, Henrique, 10–11

Caracas, 1–2, 21, 93; anthropomorphization of, 98; El Caracazo (1989), 6, 7, 100, 102, 242n4; Cotiza sector, 33; nostalgia for imagined, 98

Cartesian dualism, 154, 164

"cases," patients as, 155–56

Cassell, J., 170, 183, 184

Caswell, C. M., 242n6

cells, orderly and disorderly, 96

cervical cancer: advanced stages, 43; biomedical model, 83; control and class, 91–92; cultural politics of, 3–4, 75–76; diagnosis, lack of clarity, 47; epidemiological profiles, 20, 57, 65–66, 84; hygiene not significant factor, 60–61; moral connotations, 75–76; patient beliefs, 76–83, *77*; public health pamphlets, 90; rates, 3, 14–15; social construction of, 14, 48–49; as social problem, 222–24; as

stand-in for civil disorder, 224; stigmatization, 4
cervix: examination of, 154–56; hygiene and, 22, 36–38, 58, 71; imagery of, 36–37, 155. *See also* biopsies
Chávez, Hugo, 5, 9, 10, 93, 185, 212–13; Bolivarian Revolution, 5, 9, 10, 11, 102, 185; cervical cancer programs under, 218–24; middle- and upper-class angst about, 214–15; participatory democracy, 213, 215–16; political mobilization and, 102–3; racism, discussions of, 28; social medicine perspective and health-care reform, 18, 22, 215–29
Chavez, L. R., 58
childbirth pain, 159–61
child metaphor, 112–13
Chile, 30, 88–89, 217
China, 109
cholera, 29, 30, 87
Ciccariello-Maher, George, 102, 234, 242n4, 242n5
círculos femeninos, 103
citizenship, 232; agency and, 209–10; gendered, 107–8, 116–17; healthy, 4; insurgent, 92–93, 215; "sanitary," 107–9, 209–10, 224; as white, 114
civilizing mission, 109–13, 124
civil society, 87, 92, 214–15, 223, 224
class difference, 23, 86, 214, 227; control and cancer, 91–92; as cultural distinction, 96; "culture," lack of, 73–75; disease, relation to, 48; gender preference for physicians, 206–7, *207*; hygiene, beliefs about, 70–73, 83–84; middle- and upper-class anxiety, 1–2, 101, 214–15, 223; race and, 26, 28–29; Venezuelan society, 6–11
classification, 58, 59, 62, 241n1; of body, 184, 229; statistics of deviance, 223

clitoridectomy, 12
colonial discourse, 12, 58, 59–60, 68, 234; of "aboriginals," 95; of body, 63–64, 68; whiteness, 114–16, *115*
colonial legacy, 26, 28
Comaroff, J., 63–64
Comaroff, J. L., 63–64
combative identity, 234
committees, 111
Committees Against Displacement, 103
commonsense way of thinking, 145–46
community: in barrios, 103–7; imagined, 107, 117
community clinics, 9
community organizing, 102–3, 236
competency, perceptions of, 73–74
condom use, lack of information about, 122
conformistas, 2
connections, personal, 33–34
Constitution of the Bolivarian Republic of Venezuela, 216
contacts, 23
contagion, 57
Contagious Diseases Act (India), 88
control: of cells, 96; class and cancer, 91–92; education as regulation, 124–25; as medical term, 75, 76, 86, 91, 110, 242n1; through biology, 63–64
Cooper, Amy, 232–33
Coronil, F., 8, 62, 100–101, 169
Cotiza sector, Caracas, 33
Craske, Nikki, 116
Crenshaw, K., 221
Critically Modern (Knauft), 99–100
crowded conditions, 76, 91–92
crying, 157–58
Cuban physicians, 217–18, 229–33
cultural context of risk, 3–4, 20, 56–57
"cultural feminism," 172–73
cultural practice, medicine as, 13–14

culture: divisions, 3–4, 10, 96–97; interwoven with class and nationality, 74; mediated by class, 75; popular, 109–13; power relationships and, 48–49; risk and, 3–4, 20, 56–57; urban civilizing mission, 109–13
"culture," lack of, 73–75
"culture of poverty," 96

danger: areas of city as, 1, 33, 43; poor as threat, 2, 6, 21; "uncleanliness" as, 45; women's bodies as, 12
Davies, J., 16, 227
Declaration of Alma-Ata, 9
delinquency, fears of, 222–23
Delta Amacuro, Venezuela, 29
determinism, 60
deviance, statistics of, 223
diagnosis: class differences, 87; lack of clarity, 47, 189–94
difference, erasing of, 170–71
disciplining, 18, 21–22, 74, 76, 121, 202; education as, 124–25; gendered, 169; negotiation and compliance, 22; of patient, 132–34, 174; of poor women, 86–87; in public health pamphlets, 113–14; regulation of hospital women, 169–78, 227; regulation of poor women, 6, 86–87; regulation of reproduction, 167–68; reprimands, 157–58, 197, 204–6; of reproduction, 167–68; self-disciplining, 169–70, 209–10; waiting as, 40, 132–34
disease: embodiment and, 13–14, 73; hospital encounter and, 163–68; social construction of, 3, 19, 22, 30; as social threat, 222–24
Division of Culture, 112
Division of Social Development, 112
"docile body," 132, 143, 156–57, 196
doctoras (women doctors), 169, 183–84
Dominguez, V. R., 3, 110
Donzelot, J., 122
douching, beliefs about, 70, 71, 81, 82

Douglas, Mary, 56, 59, 63
Duggan, Lisa, 235
Duran Sandoval, Manuel Alejandro, 87

Ecuador, 32
education: lack of, as risk factor, 71, 74, 110, 124–25; level of physicians, 52; level of women, 50–51; participatory model, 126–28; as regulation, 124–25
Ehrenreich, Barbara, 11
Ehrlich, Paul, 89
Einwohne, R. L., 210
El Cementerio (The Cemetery), 43
Eldredge, J. D., 30
electrofulguration, 144
El Paquete, 7
embarrassment, 151–53, 190, 191, 203
emotion, 15–17
Emotions in Fieldwork (Davies and Spencer), 16
empowerment, 186
English, Deirdre, 11
epidemiological profiles of cervical cancer, 20, 57, 65–66, 84, 119, 229
equality, narrative of, 11
equity, narrative of, 11
essentialization, 60, 62, 130, 169–71, 173
ethics, professional, 80–81
ethnography: emotions and, 15–17, 135–36, 150–51, 179–80, 226–27; ethnographer's support of informant, 151–54, 173; location of ethnographer, 170–78; sexual harassment in the field, 17, 69, 178, 180–84, 244n7
examinations, 22; body on display, 143–46; history of, 156; interactions during, 134, 141–43; joking during, 144–45; pain during, 147, 149–50

family: policing of, 122; violence against women in, 121, 165–67
family planning campaigns, 88–90, 117

Farmer, Paul, 10
fatalism, attributed to women, 185–86
favelas, 92–93, 98–99
feminist theory, 64–65, 108, 169; self-reflection, 171, 178
Feo, Oscar, 31, 32,
Fernandes, Sujatha, 103
fertility, as threat, 222–23
First National Congress of Culture, 111
Foucault, Michel, 62, 96, 132, 143, 156, 168, 169
"From the Rural *Choza* [Hut] to the Urban *Rancho*" article, 97–98
Fundación Bigott, 111
fund-raising, 42, 43

Gastaldo, D., 133
gender, 3, 19; citizenship and, 107–8, 116–17; colonial discourse, 68; male doctors, 202–6; preference for in physicians, 206–7, *207*; regulating hospital women, 169–78, 227; sexual harassment in the field, 17, 69, 178, 180–84, 244n7; socialization, characterization of, 94–96. *See also* women
Giddens, Anthony, 209
Gifford, S. M., 56
Gordon, D. R., 13
Gramsci, Antonio, 145
Guy, Donna, 86–87
Guzman, Fernando, 223–24
"gynecological infections," 119
gynecology, 12

habitus, 184
Hacking, Ian, 223
Haraway, Donna, 64–65, 181, 221
Hartmann, C., 7
health care access, 15, 20–21, 159, 164, 235
health-care system, 2–3; under Chávez, 215–29; national health policy, 125–31

Hedican, E. J., 16
hegemonic politics, 29, 109, 119, 159, 173, 210, 235–36; in medicine, 63–64, 145
Hellinger, Daniel, 5
Henslin, J. M., 155
herpes simplex virus (HSV), 65
Herrera Salas, Jesús María, 27, 28
higienistas (hygienists), 86–88
A History of Family Planning in Twentieth-Century Peru (Necochea López), 117
Hollander, J. A., 210
Holston, James, 92–93, 102, 215
hospital encounter, 132–84; as disciplinary practice, 132–34; disease and, 163–68; examination and body on display, 143–46; examination interactions, 134, 141–43; explanations to patient, lack of, 135, 140–41, 148–51, 158, 167–68, 200–202, 208; introductions and greetings, 135, 139–40; observers, 143–45; office interactions, 135–41; pain, experience of, 146–63; public vs. private, 192–93; regulating non-patient hospital women, 169–78, 227; rushed, 190–94; seeing the doctor, 134–43; teaching hospitals, 38, 141, 155–56, 200–201
Hospital Oncológico Padre Machado, 20, 23, 33–34, 42–46; disciplining of patients, 133; office interactions, 139–40; physical plant, 43–44; as private hospital, 42–43; questions and concerns of patients, 187–89, *188*; renovations, 230; routine, 46
hospital politics, 177–78
hospitals: lack of resources, 32–33; racial dynamics in, 24–26; religious artifacts in, 44–45; sexism in, 24; structural inequities in, 22. *See also* Hospital Oncológico Padre Machado; Instituto Oncológico Luis Razetti

housing struggles, 103
"How to Prevent Cervical Cancer" pamphlet, 224
Hsuing, P.-C., 173
Hubbell, F. A., 58
human papillomaviruses (HPVs), 15, 65, 67, 68, 122, 222, 242n10
hygiene: class distinctions, 70–73, 83–84; patient views of, 80–82; in public health literature, 119, 220–21; risk and, 58–62, 66; vague definitions, 66, 119, 224

identity, 181–82
imagined community, 107, 117
immigrants, undocumented, 2, 21, 104–6
immigration, Chile, 88–89
incest, 91
incommunicability, 57
India, 59, 60, 88
indigenous women, 74–75
individualist model, 3, 10, 31, 32, 73, 220–21, 235; blame of doctors for structural problems, 41; medical definitions of risk and, 57; rejected by LASM, 32; women as responsible for cancer, 75, 122–25, 129–30, 229; women's views, 78–79
infection, rhetoric of, 45
insider and outside status, 171–77, 181–82
Inside the Neighborhood Mission (Misión Barrio Adentro, MBA) program, 9, 130, 217; Cuban physicians, 217–18, 229–33; phases, 218; Plan Barrio Adentro, 217
Instituto Oncológico Luis Razetti, 20, 23, 225–29; background, 33–42; cafeteria, 25; disciplinary processes, 133; gatekeeping, 40; gynecology department, 34–35; MSAS evaluation, 40–42, 49; office interactions, 135–39; routine, 35, 37–38; social services department, 39–40; workweek, 53–54
insurgent citizenship, 92–93
Insurgent Citizenship: Disjunctions of Democracy and Modernity in Brazil (Holston), 92–93
International Conference on Primary Health Care (1978), 9
International Congress on Cancer Control, 222
International Monetary Fund (IMF), 7, 32
International Planned Parenthood Federation, 89
intersections of class, race, and gender, 3, 19, 170–71, 222; racism, 26–27
interviews and observations, 46–49

Jiménez, Marcos Pérez, 6
Jolly, Margaret, 108
Jordan, B., 162
Justice First, 11

Kabeer, Naila, 186
Kapsalis, T., 157
Kleinman, Arthur, 164, 209, 227
Knauft, Bruce, 99–100
knowledge: alternative discourses, 64–65, 155–56, 161–62; authoritative, 162; "official," 64; situated, 65
Kultur, 110

labels, 62
Latin America: cervical cancer research, 59; debt crisis, 7; public health campaigns, 86–90
Latin American Association of Social Medicine, 32
Latin American Social Medicine (LASM), 30–33, 130, 217; scholars, 31–32

laundry women, 87
Laurell, Asa Cristina, 31–32
Leeds, A., 98–99
Lewis, Oscar, 96
linguistics, 132
Lock, M., 63
López Ortega, Antonio, 111
A Lover's Discourse: Fragments (Barthes), 178
lower class patients: cancer, control, and class, 91–92; discourse about, 83–84, 91–92, 168; regulation of reproduction, 167–68
lower-class women, nineteenth century regulation of, 86–87

Machado, Padre, 44
"made body," 132
Maduro, Nicolás, 10–11, 220
Mahmood, Q., 6–7
malignancy, as term, 188
Mani, L., 64
Mantini-Briggs, Clara, 29, 30–31, 217, 218, 223, 232, 233, 236
Maracaibo, 2
marginalization of professionals, 183–84
marking of women, 73, 123–24, 156
Martin, Emily, 11–12
Martínez, I. L., 110
Martínez, R. G., 58, 79–80
materiality, 156
Maternidad Santa Ana, 35, 46, 54
Mayhew, Henry, 95
media discourse, 21, 219
medical attention, lack of, 76–79, 77, 83
medical discourse, 5, 9; native populations controlled through, 63–64; social construction of, 12, 14
medical interactions, 3–4, 18
medical practice, as cultural practice, 13–14
médico cirujano (surgical doctor), 53

médicos adjuntos (attending physicians), 34, 36, 45, 52–54
men, role in cervical cancer, 21, 60, 68, 71, 72, 79, 80, 82, 117–18, 131
middle and upper classes: class anxieties, 1–2, 101, 214–15, 223; women as moral, 72–73, 87, 96, 123, 124, 228
mind/body distinction, 154, 164
Ministry of Health and Social Assistance (MSAS), 33, 40–42, 113, 122; changes under Chávez, 218; literature about cervical cancer, 65–66; Program of Cervical Cancer Control, 1987, 125–26
Ministry of Popular Power for Health (MPPH), 218–22, 225. *See also* Ministry of Health and Social Assistance (MSAS)
Misión Barrio Adentro. *See* Inside the Neighborhood Mission (Misión Barrio Adentro, MBA) program
modernity, 3, 99–100; urban civilizing mission, 109–13; whiteness of, 114
modernization, 58; family planning campaigns, 88–90, 117; legitimization of, 5
Mohideen, Reihana, 103
"Mom I need you for a long time" pamphlet, 117–18, *118*
Montañez, Ligia, 26, 28
Mooney, Jadwiga Pieper, 88–89
moral discourses, 12–14, 18, 20–21, 84–85; class differences, 86–87; crowded conditions, 91–92; language of risk, 57; middle- and upper-class women as moral, 72–73, 87, 96, 123, 228; poor women as immoral, 123–24, 228–29; women's relationships with men, 21
mortality, as social threat, 222–23
motherhood, 117–18, *118*

multiparity, 65–66, *67*, 69, *77*, 119, 123, 156, 168, 242n9
"multiple husbands," as phrase, 69, 86, 91
multiple sexual partners, 65, 66–67, 121; misplaced emphasis on, 224–25; vs. "promiscuity," 58–59; urban vs. indigenous, 74
Munn, N. D., 63
Muntaner, C., 6–7

National Day for the Prevention of Cervical Cancer (March 26), 221
nationalism, 3; nurturing, discourses of, 113–22; public health and, 87, 90; urban civilizing mission, 109–13
natural, concept of, 12, 59–60, 62–63, 119
Necochea López, Raúl, 117
negotiation, 22, 130–31
neighborhoods, peripheral, 92–93
neoliberalism, 185, 212; austerity, 2–3, 9, 32; cancer, relation to, 3, 218–19; effect on marginalized populations, 32; future in Venezuela, 233–36; structural adjustment programs, 7; "woman's disease," 75–76
nervousness, 159–61
nineteenth century public health policy, 86–88
North Orange County, California study, 79–80
Núñez, Patricia, 230
Núñez-Troconis, J., 225
nurses, 149–50
nurturing, nationalist discourses of, 113–22

office interactions, 135–41
order, 96–98; barrios as location of disorder, 100–101
"order of things," 96
Orinoco Delta region, 29

otherness, 12, 101
Ott, Gustavo, 222

pacientes de cortesia (courtesy patients), 34
Padre Machado hospital. *See* Hospital Oncológico Padre Machado
pain, 137, 143, 146–63, *147*; bypassing of, 154–55; during examination, 147, 149–50; measured against sexual and childbirth experiences, 159–63; narratives of, 146–47; reprimands for expressing, 157–58, 197, 206; "talking back," 156–59; virginity, ideas of, 162–63
pamphlets, public health, 113–22, 220; "How to Prevent Cervical Cancer," 224; "Mom I need you for a long time," 117–18, *118*; public health literature, 3–4, 5, 21; "Woman, A Health Message for You," 114, *115*; "Woman! Your Health Depends on You," 122–25, 127–28. *See also* public health campaigns
panfemale identity, 172–73
Pap exams, 17, 33, 35, 47; as "annual control," 91; education of patients and doctors, 125–26; frequency of, 117–18; not emphasized, 224, 225; pain during, 147; public health pamphlets, 113–22, *128*, 128–29
Pappas, Gregory, 209
partial positioning, 176, 178
participant observation, 48
participatory democracy, 213, 215–16
participatory model of education, 126–28
partriarchal social order, 87–88
pasantes (doctors doing rotation), 35, 45, 46, 52, 54, 141, 232
pathology of excess, 92
patient-doctor interactions, 48–49;

class differences, 38; differences between hospital settings, 55; fear of physician, 78, 129, 152, 157–58, 196–97, 205; lack of information given to patient, 38; micro level, 4, 5, 10, 18–19, 49, 127, 134; patient approval of physicians, 207–9, *208*; patterns of, 39; theoretical perspectives, 209. *See also* hospital encounter; patients; physicians

"patient performance," 157

patients: beliefs about cervical cancer, 76–83; as cases, 141, 155–56; demographics, *237–38*; embarrassment, 151–53, 190, 191, 203; interviews with, 49–52; lack of medical attention, 76–79, *77*, 83; as "lower class," 91–92; objectification of, 22, 123, 127, 145, 153–54; people converted into, 132–33; talking back, 156–59

Patients of the State: The Politics of Waiting in Argentina (Auyero), 40, 158, 211

Patton, C., 121

peasant, configurations of, 97

Pérez, Carlos Andrés, 2, 7–8, 10, 41, 100–101

Pérez Jiménez, Marcos, 111–12

Philippines, 64

physicians: beliefs about cervical cancer, 65–76, *67*, 83–85, 119; Chávez administration and, 220–24, 228–29, 231; Cuban, 217–18, 229, 233; demographics, 52–53, *238–40*; fear of, 78, 129, 152, 157–58, 196–97, 205; health activism, 93–94; internal struggle, 164–65; interviews with, 48, 52–55; moral judgments, 58–59; oncology training, 34–35; patient approval of, 207–9, *208*; personal histories, 31; women,

183–84, 243n6. *See also* questions for doctor

Piaroa aboriginal culture, 74–75

Piotrow, Phyllis, 89

policing of families, 122

political economy approach, 29–33

The Political Economy of Racism in Venezuela (Herrera Salas), 29

political mobilization, 102–3

poor: hygiene, focus on, 70–73; morality used against, 86–87; as promiscuous, 68, 222; regulation of, 6, 86–87; as threat, 2, 6, 21, 87, 92, 222

Population and Family Planning in Latin America (Piotrow), 89

The Population Bomb (Ehrlich), 89

population "explosion" discourse, 89–90

positivist model, 154

Posner, T., 47, 58

poverty, 9; "culture of," 96; feminization of, 185, 234; physician beliefs, *67*, 68

Povinelli, Elizabeth A., 92, 95

power relations, 109, 127; colonial discourse, 64; creditor/debtor relationship, 180; cultural images, 48–49; in medical examinations, 22, 156, 161–62; mixed effects, 130; panfemale identity, 172–73; between researcher and subject, 180; symbols of, 173–75

pregnancy, 159–60; multiparity as risk, 65–66, *67*, 69, *77*, 119, 123, 156, 168, 242n9

Prevention Program for Cancer Control (PPCC), 221

privacy and confidentiality, 37–38, 48, 137, 139; observers during examinations, 143–45

private practices, 33–34, 53–54

privatization, 3, 7, 9, 11, 31–32

Program of Cervical Cancer Control, 1987, 125–26

progress, narratives of, 74
promiscuity: physician beliefs, 66–73, 67, 83; as term, 12–13, 58–59, 222. *See also* multiple sexual partners
prostitutes, 87, 88, 95–96
protectionism, 100–101
psychological disorders, women associated with, 12
public health: as disciplinary form, 90
public health administrators, interviews with, 5, 48–49
public health campaigns: "culture" addressed, 112; modernization and, 88–90; nineteenth century, 86–88; pamphlets, 113–29, *118, 120, 123, 128*; risk factors pamphlet, 119–21, *120,* 123; understanding of in barrios, 94; whiteness, images of, 114–16, *115*; women as targets of, 86–90. *See also* pamphlets, public health
public health intervention programs, 5, 17–19, 21, 35, 48
public health sector, 2–3, 9–11; Latin American Social Medicine (LASM), 30–33; racism in, 24, 29–30
pueblo, 10
A puerta cerrada show, 79, 241n2
Punto Fijo, 6–7, 8

questions for doctor, 38–39, 81, 134–42, 145, 151, 186, *187, 188*; explanations to patient, lack of, 135, 140–41, 148–51, 158, 167–68, 200–202, 208; ignored by doctor, 142, 162, 168; initiated by doctor, 137, 138, 140, 156–57, 161, 167–68, 189, 197–98, 202

rabies deaths, blame for, 236
racism, 105; Chavez-era discussions, 27–28; evolutionary, 64; hidden, 26–29; in hospital settings, 24–26; structural, 29
ranchos, 1–2, 5, 94, 212; order and, 96–98; targeted for removal, 103, 107
rape, rhetoric of, 152
Rapp, Rayna, 130
Razetti hospital. *See* Instituto Oncológico Luis Razetti
Razetti Medical Society, 49
referrals, 34
religious artifacts, in hospitals, 44–45
reproduction, regulation of, 167–68
resilience. *See* agency
resistance, 109, 127, 130–31
respectability, discourse of, 90
reuniones de médicos, 35, 39, 45
"revolutionaries," 214
risk: cultural context, 3–4, 20, 56–57; hygiene and, 58–62, 66, 70; lack of medical attention, 76–79, *77,* 83; language of, 56; morality and, 57; multiparity as, 65–66, *67,* 69, *77,* 119, 123, 156, 168, 242n9; multiple sexual partners, 58–59, 65; neoliberal discourse, 3–4, 10, 14; overview of doctors' and patients' beliefs, 83–85; patient beliefs about, 76; physician beliefs about, 65–67, *67,* 119; promiscuity as term for, 12–13, 58–59; public health pamphlet, 119–21, *120,* 123; sex at early age, 20, 57, 65, 66, *67,* 70; social construction of, 20, 76; as structural problem, 10; "underdeveloped" regions, studies of, 59–62; women's perceived hypersexuality, 12–13
Risk and Blame (Douglas), 56
Roseberry, W., 97, 112
Rosner, D., 14
Rozin, P., 57
ruralization of urban, 2, 96–97
rural-urban hybridity, 96–98

Salas, Yolanda, 214–15, 230
"sanitary citizens," 107–9, 209–10, 224
Santa Eduvigis neighborhood, 213–14
Scarry, Elaine, 146–47, 154–55
Schein, L., 109
scientific discourses, 5
Scott, James, 172, 210
Sen, Amartya, 186, 210
sexual harassment in the field, 17, 24, 69, 178, 180–84, 226–27, 244n7
sexuality: misplaced emphasis on, 224–25; moral discourse of, 12; promiscuity, beliefs about, 12–13, 58–59, 66–73, 67, 83, 222
sexually transmitted diseases (STDs), 18, 57, 122; human papillomaviruses (HPVs), 15, 65, 67, 68, 122, 222, 242n10; patient views, 77, 79, 83; physician views, 65–67, 67, 70, 72
Sheehan, Elizabeth, 12
Singer, L., 116, 121
situated knowledge, 65
Skurski, J., 101
Smart, C., 95–96, 130
Smilde, David, 5, 216
Smith, L., 227
social context of disease, 30
social democracy, 9
social hegemony, 145
socialization, as gendered, 94–96
social justice, 5, 30, 108, 229
social medicine, 9, 18, 216–23, 225
social security hospitals, 80
social workers, hospital, 34, 39–40, 46
socioeconomic factors, 164
Socorro, Milagros, 27–28
Spencer, D., 16
Stacey, J., 172
statistics, 222–24; of deviance, 223
stigmatization, 4
Stories in the Time of Cholera: Racial Profiling During a Medical Nightmare (Briggs and Mantini-Briggs), 29, 30

Strategies of Communication, Education, and Participation of the Woman for the Prevention of Cervical Cancer (1991), 126
structural adjustment policies, 3, 7
structural inequities, 10, 22, 31, 73, 227–29, 234–35; doctors blamed for, 41; as group pathologies, 124; within hospital, 22; ignored in characterization of cities, 98–99
structural violence, 10, 236
subalternity, 84, 96, 123, 168–69

teaching hospitals, 38, 141, 155–56, 200–201
Tesh, S. N., 56
Third Sector, 215
"third world," 60–62; fertility and family planning, 89–90
tradition, 62, 98, 109, 111
transference, 178
Turner, B. S., 57

uncleanliness, rhetoric of, 21, 45, 59–60, 70, 73, 80–85, 86–87, 90–91
"underdeveloped" regions, studies of, 59–62
United States, 214, 218, 235; cervical cancer literature, 122
El Universal, 49, 98, 224, 231
Universidad Central de Venezuela (UCV) hospital, 33, 38
"unsanitary subjects," 108, 209, 224, 235
urban civilizing mission, 109–13
urban growth, 1–2, 92–93

Vaughn, M., 75
Velasco, Alejandro, 102
Venezuela: anthropomorphization of, 98, 113; as *café con leche* society, 26–28; child metaphor, 112–13; colonial legacy, 26, 28; coups, attempted, 7, 102, 214,

Venezuela (*continued*)
  216; economic demise, 7, 20; embargoes, 218; historical context, 6–11, 20; neoliberalism, future of, 233–36; petroleum boom, 6; political instability, 2–3, 6–7, 21; protectionism, 100–101; racism, hidden, 26–27
Venezuelan Cancer Society (Sociedad Anti-Cancerosa), 15, 33–34, 42, 43, 113, 117, 119, 139, 222; articles, 222–24
Venezuelan Medical Federation (VMF), 217, 220, 231
Virchow, Rudolph, 30
virginity, 162–63
vocabulary, lack of, 94

waiting, 44, 211, 226; for appointments, 133–34, 159, 174–75; regulatory, 40, 158–59; transference, 178
Waitzkin, Howard, 31, 48, 164, 209
Walter, Carlos, 41
Warao Indians, 236
"weapon of the weak," 172, 210
Weapons of the Weak (Scott), 210

well-being, 186, 210
"Western influence," 74–75
Whitehead, J., 88
whiteness, 114–16, *115*
Wiesenfeld, E., 106
woman, as category, 170–71
"Woman, A Health Message for You" pamphlet, 114, *115*
"Woman! Your Health Depends on You" pamphlet and slogan, 122–25, 127–28
women: community organizing, 102–3; dichotomous construction of, 4–5; fatalism attributed to, 185–86; physicians, 183–84, 243n6; role limited to sexuality and reproduction, 87–88; subjectivity, 90; as targets of public health campaigns, 86–90; as threat, 12. *See also* gender
"women's diseases," 11–13
World Bank, 7, 32
World Health Organization, 126
Wright, Winthrop, 26

Zavella, P., 171–73